AF505077

# Along the Bolivian Highway

CONTEMPORARY ETHNOGRAPHY

Kirin Narayan and Alma Gottlieb, Series Editors

A complete list of books in the series is available from the publisher.

# Along the Bolivian Highway

*Social Mobility and Political Culture in a New Middle Class*

Miriam Shakow

**PENN**

UNIVERSITY OF PENNSYLVANIA PRESS

PHILADELPHIA

Published by
University of Pennsylvania Press
Philadelphia, Pennsylvania 19104-4112
www.upenn.edu/pennpress

Printed in the United States of America
on acid-free paper

10 9 8 7 6 5 4 3 2 1

*Library of Congress Cataloging-in-Publication Data*
Shakow, Miriam.
    Along the Bolivian highway: social mobility and political culture in a new middle class / Miriam Shakow.—1st ed.
        p. cm.— (Contemporary ethnography)
    Includes bibliographical references and index.
    ISBN 978-0-8122-4614-8 (hardcover : alk. paper)
    1. Sacaba (Bolivia)—Politics and government. 2. Political culture—Bolivia—Sacaba.
3. Middle class—Political activity—Bolivia—Sacaba. 4. Group identity—Bolivia—
Sacaba. I. Title. II. Series: Contemporary ethnography.
    F3351.S215S53 2014
    320.0984—dc 3
                                                                                        2013047829

*To Don Shakow and to Theo Don McGreevey*

Contents

*Note on Language*

Central Bolivia is a bilingual region in which many people speak a mixture of Spanish and Quechua, Latin America's most widely spoken indigenous language. Throughout the book, Spanish and Quechua words are italicized to illustrate the multilingual character of conversation in this region and the practice of creative code-switching.

# Introduction

This book traces the experience of a new Bolivian middle class. Though seldom acknowledged, middle classes have deeply influenced politics and social life in Bolivia, as in much of Latin America and the Third World.[1] Over the past twenty years, with the rise of powerful new leftist parties, Bolivians have faced surprising dilemmas in their everyday lives. Those who aspire to become middle class—first-generation teachers, agronomists, lawyers, and prosperous merchants—have encountered daily conflicts over the question of whether to promote racial and class superiority or equality. Their personal struggles to assert themselves as morally upright, sometimes through ideals of equality and sometimes through ideals of superiority achieved by raising their economic and social status, deeply shaped their political participation. Focusing on upwardly mobile residents of Sacaba, a booming provincial municipality in central Bolivia, I examine the ways in which new middle classes shaped political culture in a moment of intense change.

Recent, local political conflicts in Sacaba have been exacerbated by a pervasive climate of mutual suspicion, fueled in part by the lack of fit between class and race identities and the binaries of wealthy or poor, and white or indigenous, in Bolivian political discourse. The very ambiguity of middling identities created a political context ripe for conflict. This was especially true given that most Bolivians professed the hope for an end to political patronage (*clientelismo*)—the exchange of favors, government jobs, and resources for political support between well-placed political leaders and their supporters—even as such patronage was one of few avenues for economic advancement in Bolivia's provincial towns. Upwardly mobile people often faced accusations that they were "selfish" for not sharing their new-found wealth with neighbors or family members, or not letting others "take a turn" at a local government job.

Bolivia's middle classes have not figured prominently in accounts of the country's dramatic political transformations during the past two decades. In December 2005, Evo Morales, Bolivia's first self-identified indigenous *campesino* (peasant) president, was elected in a landslide victory on the ticket of the MAS (Movimiento al Socialismo, Movement Toward Social-ism) party. Social movements had mobilized over the previous two decades to assert the rights of an indigenous and poor majority. Most studies of the region have framed Bolivian society in similar ways, providing an extraordi-nary example to the world of a long-marginalized and oppressed group working to rid the country of deep inequality and virulent racism against indigenous people. In response to Bolivia's long-held status as one of the Western Hemisphere's poorest and most unequal countries with one of the largest indigenous populations, scholars, Bolivian activists, and sympathetic foreigners have greeted the rise of leftist and indigenous political parties in Bolivia and in many Latin American countries over the past decade with hope and excitement (e.g., Lazar 2008, Postero 2007; Gustafson 2009; Goo-dale 2009; Canessa 2012).

And yet middle-class groups comprise a significant segment of the popu-lation.[2] The characterization of Bolivia as split between a tiny, white, super-elite minority and an indigenous, impoverished majority is true on a national level, but breaks down in some local contexts. In Sacaba, people could not live these categories in practice. In this book, I highlight the experiences of those Bolivians whose incomes and aspirations gave them the option of choosing to ally themselves either with elites or with the indigenous and poor. Middle classes are privileged relative to the poor majority, including the 37 percent of Bolivians classified as very poor who struggle to feed, clothe, and house themselves and their families (Interamerican Development Bank 2008). Yet, though members of the new middle class have high hopes to leave behind their campesino parents and neighbors, they often have limited means to achieve this goal of economic and social upward mobility. Within the rigid binary opposition of elite and subaltern categories of identity in Bolivia, there is little room for them to identify themselves as being in the middle (see also Albro 2010).[3] Despite the lack of acknowledgment of these middling groups, Bolivian politics and social life have been deeply shaped by the emergence of middle classes. The many Bolivians who aspired to join the middle class often brought to light the contradictions inherent in the goal of radically transforming Bolivian politics away from corruption and clientelism and toward redistribution of wealth and publicly minded governance.

Many Sacabans hoped to become middle class. They responded with a mixture of skepticism, disgust, and pride to the rise of a new left-wing indigenous movement and party. In the chapters that follow, I examine how this new middle class's concerns and hopes responded to a dynamic political and economic environment: draconian free-market reforms, a government decentralization that gave increased power and funding to local governments but created new political conflicts, the rise of MAS with Morales at its head, and an unstable economy that had been sustained during the 1980s and 1990s largely through production of coca leaves—an ancient, sacred crop in the Andes and a key ingredient in the modern cocaine industry.[4] In response to these multiple pressures and opportunities, rising middle classes often wavered between asserting ideals of their own social superiority and ideals of social equality in relation to Bolivia's poor majority—including neighbors, friends, and family members. I focus on how middle-class identities shaped, and were shaped by, new models of citizenship and political mobilization. Angelique Haugerud and Tom Young have called our attention to the "no-man's-land" between anthropology and political science: the gap between ethnographic attention to individuals' and groups' intimate experiences and large-scale studies of political institutions and their transformations (Haugerud 1995:15; Young 1993:307). In this book I show the mutual effects of everyday efforts to forge both new middle-class identities and political transformations of the Bolivian nation.

Middle-class concerns are all the more important to explore given that the Morales administration, now in its eighth year, has to date been unable to reduce unemployment significantly, and most Bolivians are disappointed at the seeming failure of Morales's promises to enact a total transformation of political life. Indeed, four years into Morales's second term, the buoyant public sentiment of triumph has ebbed considerably in Bolivia. For the past year, the Morales administration has been besieged by daily strikes, protests, and tumultuous marches, much as his elite predecessors were. The government and its allies stand accused of corruption, nepotism, continuing to pursue free-market economic policies in contravention of its political platform, and selling out the indigenous poor in favor of the old-time elites.[5] This hard fall is not particularly surprising, considering the mismatch between the high expectations at the time of Morales's election and the realities of Bolivia: the country's precarious position in the global economy, elite opposition to change, the Morales government's inexperience in governing, and the competing goals in Morales's diverse left-indigenous social movement coalition. The actual practice of governing, as so often happens following the coming to power of groups promising radical change, has shown the difficulty of harmonizing competing groups' interests. I contend in this book that some of these challenges can be understood as the outcome of the conflicted ideals, ambiguous identities, and moral dilemmas experienced by Bolivia's new middle classes.

## The Sacaba Highway: Metaphor and Conduit of Bolivia's Moving Middle

To understand the connection between individual experience and these broad shifts in political practices—and to make research most useful to social movements with whose political aims we sympathize—we must look beyond core movement activists to the rank and file and those disaffected by movements (Hess 2007:465; Edelman 2001:309; Burdick 1998). In order to engage diverse experiences in Bolivia's political life, I focused on people residing at least part-time within the municipality of Sacaba rather than focusing my work squarely on MAS activists. Between 1995 and 2009, I conducted research along the frenetically busy highway that serves as a vital artery for Sacaba Municipality and for the country as a whole.[6] I interviewed Sacaba residents who were both enchanted and disgusted with electoral politics, as well as elected and appointed municipal officials in Sacaba, MAS and other political party leaders, Sacaba political activists, and agrarian union leaders. I watched municipal city council sessions, residents' meetings with Sacaba mayors, and street protests. I attended meetings of local agrarian unions, women's groups, youth groups, potable water associations, irrigation associations, church masses, and planning sessions inspired by the Popular Participation Law. These conversations in this highly bilingual region took place in the rich local mix of Spanish and the indigenous language, Quechua.

A central aspect of my work also involved accompanying people who resided and worked in Sacaba Municipality on their short and long commutes throughout the municipality, to the city of Cochabamba, and to the tropical Chapare coca-growing region to the east. Sacaba municipality hugs the eastern edge of the large central Bolivian city of Cochabamba. Most

Sacabans spent considerable time traveling along the Cochabamba–Santa Cruz highway, Bolivia's busiest, which runs through the municipality and leads to the Chapare and to agribusiness regions beyond. Bolivia's eleventh largest municipality in 2006 and in 2005 and containing 150,000 registered residents, Sacaba Municipality was made up of a zone of explosive suburban sprawl bordering Cochabamba, a booming provincial town famous for its potato market, and rural districts that officially contained 30 percent of the municipal population but most of its territory. Sacaba has also been infamous as a "red zone" of cocaine production. As in many Bolivian and Latin American provincial towns (*provincias*), Sacaba town dwellers since the Spanish conquest have vigorously distinguished their social status from that of campesinos. Yet maintaining these racial and class distinctions remains a more difficult task than in cities because campesinos are so close geographically; share town dwellers' physical appearance and often, indigenous language; and sometimes possessed comparable levels of wealth.

Racial and class identities were deeply connected to ideas about geography in Bolivia; people were often imagined to be tied rigidly to either rural or urban spaces. The active movement of people along the highway provides a strikingly immediate contradiction to that polarized social geography by which people are imagined to be stuck in place. A brief tour by bus of the travels made daily by Sacabans provides a sense of the constant movement of people in this region, their alternation between elite and subaltern identities, and the blurring in practice of spaces classified officially and in the popular imagination as urban and rural. The highway also serves as a metaphor for the anxieties and aspirations of the upwardly mobile in Sacaba, their fears of remaining trapped in a rural identity while also valuing the ideal of peasant community as a refuge from the hectic pace of urban life.

When Amanda, a lawyer from the rural Sacaba locality of Choro, took me with her to attend a monthly meeting of her parents' coca growers' union in the Chapare in August 2009, we began the trip from downtown Cochabamba City (see maps in Figures 1 and 2).[7] Hopping on a minibus in the Cancha, Cochabamba's enormous open-air market, in the early morning, commuters and long-distance travelers could take refuge from the smell of diesel fuel and the sounds of thousands of vendors hawking plastic bags, calla lilies, and bicycle tires. After inching through the market crowds, the minibus sped past the public university district, hospitals, a military base, and a botanical garden whose high walls were covered with competing graffiti from the early 2000s condemning or supporting road blockades pressuring for nationalization of natural gas.

The border between Cochabamba City and Sacaba Municipality was unmarked and unnoticeable amid the sprawl as the minibus passed a strip of triple-story hardware stores and rotisserie chicken restaurants, until we zipped past a large, battered, white aluminum sign perched in a traffic circle. This read, "First Sacaba. Municipal Government Working for Development. Onward, Sacabans!" We had reached Sacaba's urban zone (*eje urbano*) that bridged Cochabamba City and Sacaba's provincial town. A large upper-middle-class housing development was followed by a road leading to the Cochabamba Motorcycling Track Association, diesel truck repair shops behind grimy expanses of earth, and an enormous yellow elementary school founded by a deceased Bolivian beer magnate and populist politician. We passed mom-and-pop lumber companies displaying slender eucalyptus logs laid in rows on the ground; a ceramic tile factory; a hotel, its second and third floors still under construction; green fields filled with cows; a store selling steel rebar; a vacant lot filled with trash surrounded by a barbed wire fence; a one-room health clinic; a paint store; a cluster of *chicha* (corn beer) taverns with cauldrons of fried pork bubbling over fire pits, sending up clouds of greasy, savory steam; another field of cows.

The minibus left the highway and entered the provincial town of Sacaba. Hércules Gym fronted a vacant lot where ragged traveling circuses sometimes stopped to perform. The bus passed the spruced-up Sacaba Town plaza, freshly planted with pansies and orange trees, thanks to the influx of funding by the Law of Popular Participation. Plaza benches were filled with men and women hatching real-estate deals and keeping watchful eyes on people entering and exiting the yellow stucco archways of Sacaba's hundred-year-old city hall. The bus wove through Sacaba's crowded outdoor market in which vendors hawked grapefruit, nylon stockings, DDT, and potatoes. Ringing the market were a storefront flour mill, dusty jewelry stores, pharmacies, butcher shops, and money-exchange houses sporting signs that revealed the current exchange rates between euros and U.S. dollars and Bolivian pesos.

At a crush of passenger buses and trucks parked on the highway opposite Sacaba's Transit Police headquarters, long-distance travelers disembarked minibuses from Cochabamba to find transportation to the Chapare. Some of them, women with weary faces and hair escaping their braids in

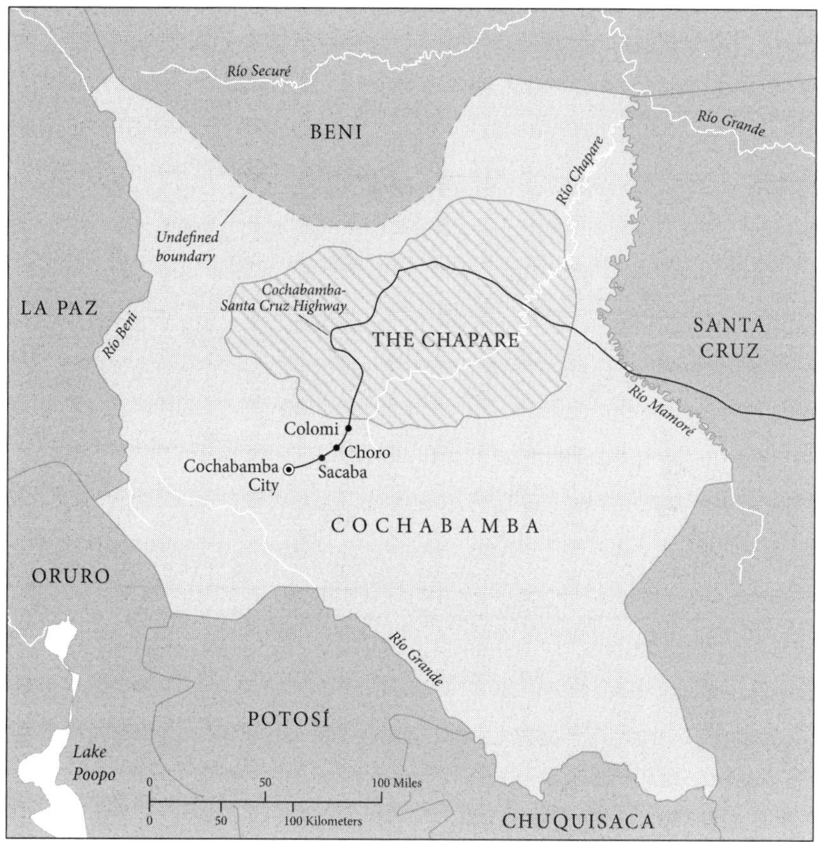


*Figure 1.* Cochabamba Department showing Sacaba and the Chapare.

large wisps, with bundles of clothing and food on their backs and often several small children in tow, had been travelling for days already and were still seven hours from their final destination. Amanda and I bought our bus tickets amid a cacophony of hawkers shouting out the price of tickets. Disheveled boys in shabby, navy-blue slacks called the buses' destinations in exchange for a peso from the bus drivers. They shouted the names of Chapare boomtowns: "Ivigarzama, Ivigarzama, Ivigarzama! Puerto Villarroel!" Women and girls peddled bags of bread and plastic bottles of pink, green, and yellow sodas to passengers through bus windows. The smell of fried chicken wafted over from a restaurant named "Hong Kong," mingling with the smells of diesel fuel, dust, and tripe soup bubbling over gas burners

*Figure 2.* Bolivia.

in small kiosks. Our bus was relatively high priced in exchange for well-padded seats, good shock absorbers, a gleaming exterior, and the presentation of a horror film.

After waiting an hour for passengers, the bus wound up the twisting highway through Amanda's hometown of Choro, one of Sacaba Municipality's rural localities. Despite its designation within Sacaba Municipality as a peasant community (*comunidad campesina*), few Choro residents worked solely in agriculture and few resided exclusively in Choro. From the bus, Choro appeared as a thick sprinkling of cement and adobe houses lining the highway, many marked by poles with small white cloths fluttering in the wind, signaling that their occupants sold *chicha*. Rolling hills were painted in a checkerboard of green, yellow, and brown. Large swaths of dry, brown, unirrigated land punctuated the verdant, irrigated potato, onion, and fava bean fields.

The steep grades of the highway beyond Choro were the terror of long-distance truckers; the groaning of the brakes on their secondhand Norwegian Volvo semis and tractor-trailers could be heard at all hours of day and night as they passed through Choro to deliver their cargo of tin roofing, natural gas, or tropical lumber to Cochabamba City. There were frequent accidents on nearby hairpin curves, and truck carcasses dotted the sides of the highway, attesting to the frequency with which brakes failed or drivers succumbed to sleepiness or alcohol.

Choro's 2001 census count of roughly 1,400 inhabitants masked the constant ebbs and flows of this population during different seasons and during the periodic fluctuations in the price of the coca leaves and cocaine in the Chapare. Many houses remained empty for significant periods of time; at other times they filled to capacity when people returned for holidays, school, or to try their luck making a living back in Sacaba. People waited alongside the highway for bus rides to their coca fields in the Chapare, bundles of blankets and occasionally a bound sheep at their feet.

The bus groaned up through smaller hamlets and large herds of sheep. Increasing elevation thinned the trees and vegetation and chilled our toes. Eroded orange hillsides interspersed with green gave way to desertlike, spiky bromeliads and cactus. At a high pass through these foothills of the Andes, in the chilly market town of Colomi, Amanda bought a bag of boiled, salted fava beans and sheep cheese patties. As we turned down the eastern flank of the Andes and entered tropical elevations, the air that had been wintry became moist and warm. The roar of rivers penetrated the windows of the bus that had been closed against the dust. Lush greenery began appearing on the steep hillsides and our hair sprang to life in the humidity. The bus's brakes squealed with effort as it miraculously clung to the twisting road. Amanda pointed happily and wordlessly to a thunderous river whose waters roiled and crashed against gigantic boulders, as if just seeing rushing water quenched the thirst of living in Cochabamba's arid valleys.

When we arrived at the checkpoint that marked the entry to the Chapare, heralded by a plaster Virgin encased in glass, members of the drug control armed forces in olive and camouflage military uniforms were inspecting the contents of a long line of trucks and buses. Before the election of Evo Morales, travelers feared the checkpoint as a principal node of interdiction in the drug war. A bus passenger could be arrested for carrying items recently declared contraband because they could be used in cocaine production—sulfuric acid or even seemingly innocuous elements of cocaine base paste production like toilet paper and onions. Passengers leaving the Chapare feared arrest for carrying small amounts of cocaine for sale or unregistered stashes of coca leaves for their own consumption. Past the checkpoint, the bus then entered the flat tropical plain of the Amazon basin and sped along an arrow-straight highway flanked by lush vegetation until we arrived several hours later at the boomtown of Puerto Villarroel. We stayed for one day to attend the coca growers' meeting as representatives of Amanda's father, who owned a coca field nearby, and then hopped on a bus back to Sacaba. Amanda's speedy round-trip journey along the highway, between Cochabamba, Sacaba, Choro, and the Chapare, was typical of the frenetic movement of Sacabans between places, between officially designated rural and urban spaces, and between identities, in their quest for upward mobility.

## Middle-Class Political Culture in Bolivia

The conundrums of Sacaba's new middle classes followed three threads that I examine in this book. First, I explore how middle-class people in central Bolivia confronted conflicting moral imperatives: the imperative to achieve individual upward mobility and therefore superiority over their poorer friends and neighbors, and, on the contrary, the imperative of social equality. The moral value of "bettering oneself" (*superarse*) was widespread, but so was the sanction on snobbery, as when neighbors and relatives accused the upwardly mobile of "selfishness" or when the MAS party's powerful political movement declared its formal platform based on the redistribution of wealth, social equality, and indigenous power. Second, I trace the ways in which Sacabans attempted to reconcile multiple, sometimes conflicting, ideals about how politics should work. These multiple ideals of citizenship have been promoted successively by national leaders since the 1950s, including clientelism (patronage); ideals of anticlientelism shaped by free-market principles and Bolivia's 1994 decentralization reform, the Law of Popular Participation (LPP); and the MAS party's platform of anticlientelism, indigenous rights, and redistribution of wealth. Third, I examine how middle-class aspirations conflicted with the romanticized ideals of peasant communities that guided local governance in Sacaba in the late twentieth and early twenty-first centuries. The LPP had promoted the idea that rural Bolivian civil society could avoid the political conflicts and self-interest of earlier patronage politics. Yet this romantic vision bumped up against actual practices and ideals of community held by Sacaba's middle class.

### Highlighting the Presence of Middle Classes in Bolivian Politics

My principal aim in this book is to highlight the significance of middle-class experiences for social and political life in Bolivia. Bolivian politics are commonly characterized as a struggle between "two Bolivias" comprising the wealthy and white, on the one hand, and the poor and indigenous, on the other hand (for a critique, see Dunkerley 2007). This depiction is true, but incomplete. In fact, a significant segment of Bolivians possesses aspirations, wealth, and lifestyles in between those of the very poor and the very wealthy. In Chapters 1, 2, and 3, I trace many middling Sacabans' active reflections on the long-standing racial and class hierarchies of Bolivian society. Their perspectives enrich our understanding of what it means to be middle class in a Third World country whose government has promised the imminent, massive redistribution of wealth from elites to the poor. Middle-class hopes and concerns have been little acknowledged but are significant in shaping politics in the local arena of Sacaba and in the country as a whole. Their discussions can help us understand the place of middle classes beyond Sacaba and to rectify their surprising absence in much anthropological scholarship on the Third World and in Bolivia.[8]

Bolivian middling groups' responses to the rise of MAS and its platform of social equality were filtered through their diverse experiences during recent economic and political transformations. Though Bolivia is blessed with abundant natural resources from silver to timber, Spanish colonialism and the small exclusionary elite that governed the country since its independence in 1825 left a ravaged, deeply unequal economy. Bolivia is rare in that a majority of people speak an indigenous language. New middle classes in Bolivia, many of whom speak indigenous languages, emerged in the wake of a social and economic opening permitted by the 1952 Bolivian Revolution and 1953 Agrarian Reform. This nascent rural and provincial middle class expanded further with the explosion in the price of cocaine in the United States and Europe in the 1970s that led to a boom in the price of Bolivian coca leaf. In central Bolivia, where coca grew, a new cohort of prosperous farmers, merchants, and professionals arose. The coca and cocaine booms presented unprecedented opportunities for upward mobility until the U.S.-led war on drugs partially squelched the boom in the 1990s. The drug war and the subsequent decline of the coca and cocaine markets spelled frustrated expectations for many people in the Sacaba region, even as many hung on tenuously to a new middle-class identity as professionals or as well-to-do merchants.

Free-market neoliberal reforms in the 1980s led to a deepening of Bolivia's massive unemployment, as the influx of goods from foreign industries and foreign-subsidized agriculture outcompeted the products of Bolivian factories and small farms. Mass layoffs among miners and workers at other state-owned industries that were required under the terms of Bolivia's free-trade policies contributed to further job losses. This unemployment, coupled with the decline in state spending on social services under free-market reforms, contributed to a bleak economic climate for many Bolivians that has lasted until the present, though for a while mitigated by the coca boom.[9]

The historically unprecedented election of Evo Morales in 2005 on a platform of redistribution of wealth and social equality has led to dilemmas of self-identification for this new middle class in Sacaba. President Morales became a prism through which many Bolivians reimagined their own identities. For upwardly mobile Sacabans, Evo's political persona as an indigenous and poor leader provoked opposition as often as it did pride and approval. A cohort of first-generation doctors, lawyers, teachers, and prosperous merchants wrestled earnestly with how to distinguish their identity as professionals from those of the campesinos and Indians who were their parents, brothers and sisters, cousins and neighbors—and their new president. Some people greeted Evo's and the MAS party's rhetoric with dismay. They rejected the new government's promotion of indigenous pride, social equality, and the redistribution of wealth. Other Sacabans with similar levels of wealth and aspirations for upward mobility began to tout campesino, working-class, or indigenous roots and trumpeted the government's rhetoric of social equality; still others praised the new government's promise of an end to corruption while continuing to assert their own social superiority.

Middle-class identity in Sacaba was experienced as ambiguous in part because little language existed to name it. As a result, many Sacabans alternated between identifying themselves with wealthy national elites and with poor indigenous campesinos and the working class. I highlight the ways in which identification with rural and urban spaces was a critical binary axis along which Sacabans struggled to define themselves and their political actions. Given that markers of class and race had been historically fluid, Sacabans often found it difficult to define their own and others' social status, even as MAS and its allied political movements rhetorically asserted that there were clear dividing lines between elite and subaltern.

Political conflicts in Sacaba fed in part on this poor fit between existing social life in the municipality and the popular vision of Bolivian society polarized between the indigenous poor and the white superelite. Following Morales's election and the precarious realignment of national power after centuries of elite rule, a fundamental uncertainty existed regarding who held political and social power in Bolivia. On a national scale, MAS supporters held the executive branch of government while right-wing, very wealthy elites controlled the vast majority of wealth and most Bolivian television, radio, and newspaper outlets. On a municipal scale, Sacaba's urban districts were home to the wealthiest residents and received the majority of municipal government resources, but the agrarian union members, the base of support for the MAS party, gained strength from their strong relationship with President Morales and the national MAS leadership. On both national and municipal scales, then, the rise of MAS upset historical imbalances of power without establishing a new hegemony: power relations were fundamentally unstable. These public conflicts were the product of and contributed to private self-questioning and social repositioning amidst Sacaba's new middle classes.

### Hybrid Political Cultures

Divergent ideals about how to be a good citizen and political leader also created moral dilemmas and conflicts of interpretation of other people's motivations. Sacabans' middle-class aspirations shaped this diverse political culture. I employ the concept of political culture to mean the repertoire of practices, meanings, and languages through which people struggle over power and attempt to act collectively. I draw on Sidney Tarrow's (1998) concept of "repertoires" of political action to emphasize the ways in which

Sacabans conducted their political conflicts through patterned forms of action that were familiar to each other. Moving beyond an understanding of national political culture as consisting of uniformity and unanimity, in this book I join a growing number of scholars who emphasize the essential contested quality of culture (e.g., Jacobsen and Aljovin de Losada 2005; Haugerud 1993; Glick Schiller 2003). As Angelique Haugerud notes, national political cultures are neither monolithic nor consensus driven, but rather consist of public rituals and symbols that are arenas of contest as well as acquiescence between people of unequal social and economic standing (Haugerud 1993:8).

Three principal political ideals circulated in Bolivia in the early twenty first century. First, clientelism (*clientelismo*)—patron-client reciprocity of gifts, favors, jobs, and votes—was a legacy of colonialism and of Bolivia's revolutionary government that took power in 1952 and promised national economic development delivered through patronage networks. Next, liberalism, the emphasis on free markets and individual responsibility, reemerged in the harsh free-market reforms instituted in 1985 and in the state decentralization reform of 1994, the LPP. The LPP created new powers and resources for local governments and promoted multiculturalism, while LPP reformers condemned clientelism as antidemocratic and archaic.[10] At the same time, the LPP's increased funding and expansion of salaried positions for over three hundred municipal governments created new arenas for graft and competition for public-sector jobs and for development resources. This political competition often erupted, as in Sacaba municipality, in repeated municipal conflicts between factions of people seeking upward mobility by vying for municipal bureaucracy jobs and elected posts as mayor or city council members. Third, a model of grassroots democracy coupled with the rhetoric of socialism and indigenous pride gained force with the rise of MAS during the late 1990s, and became the official platform of government with Morales's election in 2005. Morales and MAS officials also vehemently denounced clientelism as a legacy of elite dominance and heralded a new nation free of clientelism. In the late 1990s and throughout the 2000s, MAS political leaders and development workers called publicly for Sacabans to reject politicians' stealing of public funds, nepotism, vote buying, and the seeking of jobs and other favors through clientelism.

Many ordinary Sacabans agreed in theory with this condemnation of clientelism and expressed the hope that MAS or the LPP—or both—would deliver an end to clientelism. Sacabans, like MAS leaders, often termed clientelism as "selfishness," individualism, and "envy," because they deemed the seeking of patronage favors as the cause of local political struggles that obstructed local governments. Furthermore, many Sacabans—though not all—agreed fervently that clientelism maintained the dominance of Bolivia's superwealthy and had to be extinguished for racial and economic equality to be born.

Yet in practice many Sacabans sought jobs and resources from the municipal government and were accused by others of clientelism. Often, this was the only path to finding a job and therefore, a route to middle-class status. Sacabans' political practices in fact often blurred the theoretical line between clientelism, the liberalism promoted by the LPP, and grassroots democracy promoted by the MAS party. The widespread condemnation of clientelism as "selfishness" signaled the theoretical clash between political frameworks that many Sacabans combined in practice: liberalism, grassroots democracy, clientelism, and the imperative to enter or remain in the middle class, often through securing a patronage job.

Self-interest, like collective interest, is a central human motivation. When MAS leaders and development workers perceived that their attempts at political transformation had failed, they often blamed citizens' moral failure. MAS leaders expressed disappointment when citizens were unable, in their view, to properly assume an attitude of public-mindedness over private interest. Such language of blame ignores both the structural constraints on Bolivians' realizing their own middle-class aspirations and the practical ways in which individuals drew on multiple frameworks in participating in public life. These observations lead me, like Ernesto Laclau (1992:9), to argue that self-interest and individual interest often blur in political practice, despite the widespread assumption in political theory that we can analytically distinguish between the two (see also Seligman 1992).

In practice, many Sacabans described their hopes for the future in ways that combined individual middle-class aspirations, collective prosperity for indigenous and poor Bolivians, and the uplift of Bolivia from its subordinate position in the global geopolitical community of nations. Many prosperous Sacabans who fervently supported MAS in the early years of Evo's government described themselves as members of the historically excluded indigenous majority and therefore asserted that their individual interests *were* the interests of the nation.[11]

I suggest that these paradoxes are not confined to Sacaba but have broader reach. MAS leaders have claimed to have ushered in a new post-neoliberal era in Bolivia,[12] three decades after scholars began analyzing the impact of neoliberal free-trade policies around the world and the ideologies that accompany them—such as the Law of Popular Participation's depiction of clientelism as a form of immorality that public-minded citizens can root out (e.g., Comaroff and Comaroff 2001; Carrier 1998; Ferguson 2006; Greenhouse 2010; Phillips 1997). Anthropologists have begun to pose the question of whether some societies, such as Bolivia, are indeed creating post-neoliberalism (e.g., Gustafson 2009; Fernandes 2010; Goodale and Postero 2013). What might post-neoliberalism look like? Chapters 4 and 5 follow middle-class Sacabans' own debates over these questions about whether a deep societal transformation was possible and whether clientelism could be stamped out.

### Definitions of Community Shaped by Middle Classes

Concerns about clientelism as the expression of individualism and selfishness also emerged repeatedly in Sacabans' intense frustrations at what they saw as a lack of collective action at the local level—a failure of community. My third aim in this book is to show how ideals of community became a central focus of political debate in Sacaba in the context of rising middle classes. In Chapter 6, I trace the mismatch between idealized definitions of Sacaba's rural communities as organized civil societies or as indigenous campesinos, promoted by LPP reformers and national MAS leaders, respectively, and the more heterogeneous ideals and practices of community enacted by Sacaba's new middle class. Bolivia's LPP reformers often depicted rural communities as rigidly bounded geographically, and governed by indigenous communal institutions of solidarity that had remained little changed since pre-Columbian times. National MAS leaders, meanwhile, defined communities as agrarian unions composed of campesinos and organized politically in networks with regional and national unions to defend the interests of Bolivia's peasant-indigenous (*campesino-originario*) majority. Measuring actual local communities against these standards, many Sacaba municipal officials and development workers regularly deplored what they saw as a lack of strong collective action in Sacaba's localities. I contrast these idealized, rigid ideals of harmonious peasant community with the other forms of collective action that emerged in response to middle-class aspirations in Choro. Finding funding and building vital infrastructure like a sewer and a new high school, fervent goals of development workers, required intensive collective effort that conflicted with many Choro residents' other ambitions. For example, when coca leaf prices were high, many Choreños sought upward mobility by joining in the highly organized coca growers' union in the Chapare region where coca was grown, seven hours away, withdrawing their time and attention from collective organizing within the boundaries of Choro. The desires of upwardly mobile professionals, coca growers, merchants, and truckers resident in Choro diverged from poorer people who could less easily afford to buy services such as health care and education in urban areas like Sacaba or Cochabamba City. Community, like clientelism, was an important genre of political debate.

## My Position in Bolivia

Finally, as is always the case when conducting ethnographic research, local perceptions of me as a researcher mattered in shaping the stories that I was told and can tell. When I had a baby part way through my fieldwork, I became newly privileged to conversations with other parents in which they expressed concerns about their children's health and safety, their upward mobility, or their quest for jobs. As a red-haired *blancona* (light-skinned woman), I heard plenty about race from Sacabans, who often expressed the wish that their hair and skin were lighter. When I became a mother toting a red-haired, *blancón* infant with me, I began hearing plenty from parents who expressed the wish, often in front of their children, that their children's hair and skin were lighter. As a graduate student, I was received as a kindred spirit by many in Sacaba's first-generation middle class who aspired to or had recently earned professional degrees. As a foreigner who spoke Quechua, I was greeted with great warmth and generosity. As a citizen of a wealthy country, I was often seen as a potential patron: a supplier of funds for home improvement, medical bills, and community centers. Finally, as a citizen of the United States, my presence elicited the longings of many Bolivians for the prosperity and power the United States symbolized, on the one hand, and intense resentment at the U.S. government's heavy-handed interventions, on the other hand, particularly regarding free-market policies and the war on drugs that had squelched the coca and cocaine booms.

One story that Sacaba friends often asked me to retell conveys the mix of generous hospitality, fascination, wariness, and resentment with which I was viewed in a region that owed its prosperity, even more than other regions of the country, to the coca and cocaine booms. As a college student studying abroad, I had traveled in 1995 with a group of U.S. students on a guided tour of the Chapare. Led by our leftist study abroad program directors, we toured modest "alternative development" projects—a palm heart plantation, a dairy factory—funded by USAID as an anemic sideline to the United States' military focus in the drug war. We also had a cordial meeting with several Chapare coca growers (*cocaleros*) union leaders who invited us to a *cocalero* protest. Arriving in the boomtown of Villa Tunari for the protest, we watched, awestruck, as thousands of men and women marched by in well-practiced formation. They carried banners that read "Long live coca, our sacred leaf" and "Long live coca, die Yankees [*Kausachun coca, wañuchun yanquis*]" in Quechua, Bolivia's most widely spoken indigenous language. A few marchers began shouting at us, "*Wañuchun yanquis* [Die, Yankees]!" Though we could not understand their words, the marchers' meaning was clear. Our program directors hustled us onto our bus and whisked us away.

When telling this story in Sacaba, I attempted to make clear my opposition to the drug war by emphasizing that we students had cheered along vigorously with the protesters in Quechua, "Long live coca [*Kausachun coca*]!" And when the protesters shouted, "Die, Yankees [*Wañuchun yanquis*]!" I narrated to my always-rapt audience, we students echoed "*Wañuchun yanquis!*" before realizing what the Quechua words meant. I mimicked our embarrassment once we understood. This story was a hit. It always elicited shouts of laughter and a clamor to tell the story of "*wañuchun gringuitos* [die, little gringos]" once more.

When close friends in Choro requested this story time after time for an appreciative audience of their relatives and neighbors, they were giving me the opportunity to demonstrate my support for the coca growers' unions, to which many of them belonged. At the same time, the ridiculous picture of twenty college students haplessly condemning ourselves in Quechua provided an opportunity for my friends to poke fun at an intrusive foreign power and express their anger at U.S. meddling in Bolivia. The U.S. government had created an area of intense violence in the Chapare and directly curtailed Chapareños' possibilities for upward mobility while also deliberately protecting the wealth of the United States at the expense of Bolivians, many Bolivians believed.

These mixed sentiments—of admiration of the United States as a symbol of economic power to which Bolivians aspired for themselves as a nation and as individuals, and frustration at the continual squelching of these aspirations by foreign powers such as the United States—are common among Bolivians of many social classes but are particularly emblematic of new middle classes. The next chapter traces the origins of Sacaba's middle class through historical shifts that provided opportunities for upward mobility and challenges to this mobility. I examine this cohort in the context of the Third World, Bolivia, and the regional space of Cochabamba.

# The Formation of a New Middle Class

Marisol, a Sacaba pharmacist, provides one example of the difficulties the MAS government faced in convincing most Bolivians to identify themselves as indigenous members of the working or *campesino* (peasant) classes. In August 2009, four years after Evo was elected president, Marisol was thirty-three years old. She had opened her pharmacy five years before in Sacaba's busy provincial town plaza after becoming the first person in her family to go to college. Marisol wore her straight, jet-black hair long, in the style of many working-class women in Bolivia's cities and provincial towns, and she was always immaculately groomed. The three large glass cases in which she displayed her medicines for sale were kept shining and dust free, no easy feat given Sacaba's year-round wind and dust. Despite her fastidious cleaning, however, business was often slow; Sacaba was filled with competing pharmacies. Furthermore, the stalls of local street vendors—a key element of the informal economy that had sustained the majority of Bolivians since the beginning of free-market reforms nearly twenty-five years before —had gradually expanded to fill the street in front of the pharmacy. The pharmacy entrance was now almost hidden by rows of stalls selling school supplies, bootleg DVDs, and baby clothes. On most days when we chatted, Marisol and I faced only occasional interruptions by customers seeking a pregnancy test or aspirin.

On this particular day in 2009, as Marisol sniffled through a winter cold, she explained vehemently to me that she strongly opposed the Morales government's promise to redistribute large landowners' vacant property to landless campesinos. She did not believe the MAS government's contention that the vast inequality of land tenure in Bolivia was caused by prior military governments' illegal gifts of millions of acres of land to already wealthy families. Instead, she asserted, those landowners who owned hundreds of thousands of acres must have earned them through hard work and sacrifice, as her parents had earned a modest ten acres when she was a baby by moving from the drought-stricken central Bolivian countryside to settle a tropical homestead in eastern Bolivia. About the large landowners' potential losses in Evo's proposed land reform, she maintained,

> What this government wants to do is take control of this land . . . and give it to other people. . . . That's not good. . . . The campesinos are supporting him [Evo] blindly, but in the future, these laws will affect them [prejudicially], too. . . . Those people who have large landholdings, it's not right [to take their land away] because they have perhaps bought it with their sacrifice or inherited it from a relative. What he [Evo] says is that they have stolen it from other people during previous governments. But to me, this doesn't seem true. I believe that Evo just wants to make them appear bad, those he calls . . . what's that term he uses? "Capitalists"?

Marisol asserted that the Bolivian superelite had gained their land lawfully and that campesinos had been duped. Campesinos were "blindly" supporting land reform even though they could suffer by having their tiny holdings confiscated in the future. Her characterization of land inequality as resulting from the hard work of the superwealthy contrasted with a barrage of scholarly studies that showed Bolivia's land inequality rising dramatically during the previous forty years directly owing to government handouts of land and agricultural subsidies to the very rich (e.g., Prudencio Bohrt 1991; Gill 1987; Fabricant 2012). By 1984, 3.9 percent of landowners had come to own 91 percent of agricultural land through such government favoritism (Weisbrot and Sandoval 2008:2), and no land redistribution had taken place since. Marisol also disagreed with the assertion by social movements and the Morales government that Bolivia's extreme inequality represented a moral wrong that required a remedy by the government.

Marisol instead narrated Bolivia's history through the framework of her own family's experience of modest upward mobility. Her parents had taken advantage of a 1960s-era government program for small-scale farmers from western and central Bolivia to receive free land and tools if they moved to the tropical lowlands to grow soy, cotton, sugar, and peanuts. It was through their hard work, Marisol and her father had told me, that her parents had built up prosperity measured proudly by their ownership of a mechanized tractor and enough disposable income to send her to the university. She and her parents had worked hard so that she would not share their self-identification as a campesina who spoke the indigenous language, Quechua, but rather as a middle-class professional. And they had succeeded: she was a pharmacist married to an agronomist who was also among the first from his rural community to earn a college degree.

Marisol's views coincided closely with the statements of Bolivia's tiny, light-skinned, superwealthy class. Kiko Aguilera, one of Bolivia's wealthiest men, owner of thousands of acres of tropical ranch land and leader of an elite right-wing political opposition movement, declared in 2006 soon after Evo's election: "I've worked hard for everything that I own. . . . We haven't stolen anything from anyone. We worked for our land with the sweat of our brow. We won't return it to anyone. Death, first!" (quoted in Leidel 2006).

Yet as Marisol reaffirmed her middle-class status by distinguishing herself from campesinos she also complained about her own lack of resources: the dearth of clients in her pharmacy, the difficulty of living for several years with her husband and daughter in a small rented room while they saved money to build their own home, and the challenge of taking care of her six-year-old daughter with little help while running her own business.

Why did Marisol so vehemently set herself apart from campesinos if her parents were small farmers themselves, and why did she argue that government redistribution of wealth was itself a moral wrong, given that her family had benefitted from prior government largesse? Her prosperity, significant by Bolivian standards, was by no means equal to the lifestyle of Bolivia's tiny upper class, marked by enormous wealth, country club membership, plastic surgery, live-in maids, and often, college education at Harvard or Texas A&M. Their social circles in no way overlapped with hers. In spite of limited purchasing power, dark hair and skin, and knowledge of Quechua learned from her parents—all of which would lead a foreigner or a Bolivian census taker to classify Marisol as indigenous—Marisol drew firm distinctions between herself, a middle-class professional, and Bolivia's poor and indigenous campesinos.

Marisol was not alone in Sacaba Municipality in framing her relatively modest and sometimes uncertain means as acquired in comparable fashion to the fortunes of Bolivia's tiny wealthy elite. Throughout Sacaba, many first-generation lawyers, doctors, pharmacists, and newly prosperous merchants argued that their prosperity was available to all Bolivians willing to work hard, and, conversely, that poor people had probably been lazy or imprudent. They, like Marisol, asserted that campesinos and *indios* (Indians) had been tricked into supporting their socialist president and his promises that his government would redistribute wealth more equitably.

The very act of drawing such distinctions mirrors the practices of middle-class people throughout the world (see Liechty 2002; O'Dougherty 2002; Bourdieu 1984). Yet, in other ways, Marisol's response to inequality and her self-identification within hierarchies of race and class were particular to the Third World. In still other ways, she drew distinctions particular to Bolivia, and to the particular social world of a provincial municipality in central Bolivia. Marisol's experience exemplified patterns shared by many in Sacaba whom I am terming the new middle class. At times Marisol, a first-generation pharmacist, allied herself rhetorically with Bolivia's wealthiest elite. Yet in other moments she expressed discomfort when faced with wealthier, lighter-skinned, or generally more elite Bolivians. She conveyed a sense of anxiety over her social status and she alternated between professing values of egalitarianism and superiority and between subaltern and elite social identities.

This alternation between elite and subaltern identities was common in Sacaba, as a sample of incidents I witnessed reveals.

A doctor chastised me, as we ate roast guinea pig (a rural Andean delicacy) he had prepared, for not eating the skin. He declared with heat, "I'm poor; I eat the skin." On another occasion, he told me proudly that his children insisted on his buying them cakes from Dumbo's, Cochabamba's most expensive bakery, for their birthday parties.

A lawyer remarked wistfully that he always felt out of place in law school because of his rural origins. He declined to marry his common-law wife, however, because her identity as a campesina and indigenous person from the countryside did not fit with the middle-class image he wished to project.

A rural family that had become wealthy through a trucking and logging business vied for superior status with their cash-poor but highly educated neighbors.

Marisol did not, in fact, call herself middle class; nor did most Sacabans. The term "middle class" (*clase media*) in Bolivia was most often reserved for well-established urbanite professionals and business owners. Like most other college-educated Sacabans, Marisol referred to herself as a professional (*profesional*) to convey her proud ascension of the Bolivian social ladder. Other prosperous but non-college-educated Sacabans similarly did not attribute to themselves any particular explicit term for being in the middle. Middling Sacabans instead, like Marisol, alternated between calling themselves subaltern—in terms like *pobre* (poor), campesina, and *popular* (working class)—and making statements of comradeship with Bolivian superelites. They also shared her anxiety over social status and alternation between ethics of social superiority and equality. Those I am calling Sacaba's new middle classes also differed in their experiences and status from the prosperous urbanites termed "middle class" in the Bolivian press, political polling, and public debate because they were deeply shaped by the social connotations of living in or near a provincial town, a place viewed by many Bolivians as one step away from stigmatized rural spaces. I am calling them "middle class" because they had achieved some of their aspirations for upward mobility, because many elements of their experience were similar to experiences of self-identified middle classes elsewhere in Bolivia and the Third World, and because their self-presentations, preoccupations, and aspirations differed from the explicitly campesino-indigenous rhetoric of political leaders. These aspirations conditioned their political ideals and their relationships with their families and fellow townspeople.

Like members of middle classes elsewhere, Marisol made an effort to distinguish herself from poorer people through moral and intellectual, as well as economic, superiority (Bourdieu 1984; see also Ehrenreich 1989; Frykman and Löfgren 1987; Liechty 2002; O'Dougherty 2002). She rhetorically marked her intellectual superiority over Bolivia's campesinos, who "blindly" believed in the Morales administration's rhetoric of redistribution of wealth. She also aligned herself sympathetically with people much wealthier than herself when she suggested that Bolivia's richest people, the large landowners, must have gotten that land through their own or their families' hard work and "sacrifice" rather than through government handouts, as she suggested campesinos were attempting to do.

The notion that people who prospered did so due to their own hard work and sound money management, and that poor people remained poor because they lacked those values, were common sentiments among upwardly mobile Sacabans. Deysi, a schoolteacher from the rural community of Choro, similarly argued that her own and other first-generation professionals' superior management of their lives came from the intellectual insight gained from a university education and from the moral worth gained by having "sacrificed themselves" to attain those professional degrees. "As a *profesional*, you know how to budget from your paycheck," she declared in 2009. By contrast, her neighbors, "people from the countryside [*gente del campo*] . . . don't know how to budget their money well. [They buy] a case of beer, then another case of beer. Meanwhile, a professional knows what he has sacrificed for his money; he isn't going to waste it." Her neighbor, a coca farmer who became a music teacher, echoed many upwardly mobile Sacabans in his criticism of poorer neighbors when he argued in 1998 that "if a person wants to work, he can prosper; if a person doesn't want to work, he won't . . ." Such sentiments mirror the "pull yourself up by your bootstraps" narrative prevalent in the United States that presents the middle class as more virtuous than the working classes and poor.

To be middle class was not an identity based solely on economic standing. Sacabans' race and class identities were based as much on symbols with deeply charged meanings—a kitchen sink with running water, a trip to the orthodontist, a university diploma—as on a particular income or assets. As Mark Liechty reminds us, middle classness is a frame of mind, a set of behaviors, a "cultural project or practice . . . rather than a social category or empirical condition" (Liechty 2002:21).[1] Middle classness is often defined by the practice of drawing distinctions between oneself and others who are poorer and using moral explanations for one's success (O'Dougherty 2002:6). Marisol's placing of herself in opposition to campesinos is emblematic of middle-class strategies for assuming social superiority.

Despite these similarities with middle classes throughout the world, many elements of Sacaba's new middle classes' identities are not shared by middle classes in places like the United States or Europe but are distinctive to the Third World. Given that impoverished people who struggle daily to earn enough to feed and house themselves make up a larger percentage of the Bolivian population than in the United States, new middle-class Bolivians experience more anxiety. The newly prosperous in Bolivia are faced continually with a grim reminder—in the 50 percent poverty rate—of what will happen to them if they fail in their quest for upper mobility (World

Bank 2013; see Liechty 2002:10–11; Dickey 2000; O'Dougherty 2002; Cahn 2008). Like middle classes from Brazil to Nepal, newly middle-class Sacabans vigorously identified themselves with modernity and development and associated poor people with backwardness and underdevelopment. Bolivia's superwealthy agribusiness landowners, the national class and racial elite, represented modernity and development, and Marisol, from her struggling pharmacy, placed herself with them.

Furthermore, the middle class does not define national identity in the Third World to the same degree as it does in the United States and Europe, where most people term themselves middle class. In the First World, middle classes became a large segment of the population in the mid-twentieth century as a result of industrial expansion that employed large numbers of unionized skilled laborers, middle managers, engineers, doctors, and teachers (Bledstein and Johnston 2001). By contrast, in Bolivia and much of the Third World, economies based on natural resource exports rather than industry supported a much smaller proportion of the overall population as a middle class. In early twentieth-century Bolivia, these were skilled craftspeople, medium-scale landowners, and doctors. Following the 1952 Bolivian Revolution, which expanded the functions of government, the middle class grew. As education became available in the countryside, new university graduates were hired as white-collar workers in rapidly expanding government offices and state-owned enterprises, for example in mining, telecommunications, and railroads. In large Bolivian cities like Cochabamba and La Paz, middle-class neighborhoods filled during the midcentury with boxy, modernist, cement houses, with perhaps a Brazilian-made Volkswagen Beetle parked in front. With Bolivia's free-market reforms of 1985, government offices and state-owned companies saw mass layoffs, shrinking the ranks of the urban middle class. Internationally funded development organizations (NGOs) became a fallback, but less secure, middle-class employer. Throughout the twentieth century and into the twenty-first, the slice of the Bolivian population calling itself "middle class" has grown but never become a majority.

Another important aspect of middle-class identity in Bolivia, as in much of Latin America, is the overlap in the meanings of racial and class terms (de la Cadena 2000; Weismantel 2001). In Bolivia in the early twenty-first century, explicit class terms like *pobre* (poor) and campesino carried the racial meaning of "indigenous," just as racial and cultural terms that indicated indigeneity (*indígena, indio*) connoted poverty. This overlap stemmed in part from the Bolivian revolutionary government's decree in 1953 that *indios* (Indians), a racist term to describe the majority of the country's people, would be called campesinos and that all Bolivians shared the same *mestizo* (mixed indigenous and European) race. Pejorative racial meanings persisted in class terms: Sacabans often identified each other as belonging to the "campesino race" and defined campesinos as ignorant, uneducated, unintelligent, or ugly, drawing on racial ideologies of the colonial Spanish and Bolivian elites. These racist meanings have persisted alongside the assertions of racial and cultural pride promoted by social movements and the Morales government during the past three decades. Most terms of identity in Bolivia, whatever their dictionary definitions, connote race as well as class. Middle classness was therefore experienced as racially—as well as economically, morally, and culturally—intermediate.

## Class and Race Among Middling Folk in Cochabamba

Some elements of the experiences of members of the new middle class in the Cochabamba region were distinct from other regions of the country, owing to Cochabamba's particular history as a crossroads of migration and commerce. Tracing this distinctiveness can help us understand why many Sacabans alternated between identifying themselves with the wealthiest and with the poorest Bolivians and how they confronted simultaneous social pressure from their neighbors and family members to treat others as both equal and inferior. Cochabambans historically possessed unusually fluid identities relative to other regions of Bolivia; individual people identified themselves by different racial and class identities in different social contexts (Larson 1998:350). The roots of this fluidity can be traced to political and social patterns established as far back as the fifteenth century A.D. when Inca armies conquered the Cochabamba valleys and forced most native Cochabambans to move to other parts of the Inca Empire (Larson 1998). They resettled the Cochabamba valleys with subjects from other regions of the empire. When the Spanish conquered the Incas in the 1530s, many people returned to their home communities as far afield as modern-day Ecuador and Colombia. In the power vacuum that ensued after this exodus, some ambitious indigenous leaders cobbled together new communities from the Cochabamba residents who remained, collecting taxes and conscripting labor for Spanish colonial mines. Compared to highland communities, whose residents the Inca rulers had left in place and where community identity tended to be strong, Cochabamba community leaders' authority was always more tenuous and community identity was historically weaker. Cochabambans readily left their natal communities to escape Spanish taxes, deadly forced labor in Spanish mines, and abusive indigenous leaders. Many became merchants and traveled between the valleys and highlands selling food and clothing to miners (Larson 1998:80, 323).

Cochabambans' geographic mobility as a strategy for gaining freedom had enduring effects on their class and racial identities. The Spanish colonial government had created two legal classes of people throughout Latin America: urban residents were known as the Republic of Spaniards while rural residents were the Republic of Indians. In Spanish colonial times, the racial terms *indio* (Indian), *mestizo* (mixed race), and *blanco* (white) were primarily legal categories rather than based on physical appearance. Indians were taxpayers and laborers who resided in legally designated Indian rural communities. That is why geographic mobility and social mobility were intertwined: when individual Cochabambans moved from rural communities to towns or cities to avoid taxes and forced labor, they deliberately jumped from the Indian category to become mestizos (Larson 1998:375). Unlike in most other parts of the country, in Cochabamba self-defined mestizos became the majority of the population, and Cochabambans generally held less rigidly defined social and economic status than in other regions of the country.

On winning independence from Spain in 1825, Spanish-descended elites attempted to deny indigenous people a livelihood and a legitimate place in the new Bolivian nation. In the Bolivian highlands, indigenous people contested elites' oppression with militant battles and identified themselves as the oppressed descendants of powerful indigenous empires such as the Inca and Tiwanaku (Hylton and Thomson 2007). In Cochabamba, by contrast, Indians and mestizos often attempted to join the ranks of the local elite. While barriers of wealth and racial inequality were strong in Cochabamba, they were not insurmountable. Free-trade laws passed by elite Bolivian governments during the late nineteenth century that robbed highland indigenous communities of their land actually helped small-scale mestizo and Indian farmers to buy land in Cochabamba. As Cochabamba elite landowners were unable to compete with the cheap grain imports from Argentina and Chile following free-trade reforms, many Indian and mestizo Cochabambans determinedly bought their lands, freeing themselves from servitude on large estates. By 1900, 60 percent of land in the Cochabamba valleys was owned by self-identified mestizo and Indian small-scale farmers—a dramatic difference from anywhere else in Bolivia and from other Andean countries (Larson 1998:311; Jackson 1994).

By buying land, some new campesino landowners rose to a position in the middle of Cochabamba's social world. And in keeping with their new-found wealth, they asserted a higher social status by wearing urban clothing and following elite social norms. For example, when elites argued that mestizos were morally degenerate because they were nonwhite or rural born, mestizos countered that they could move up the class and racial ladder by following elite moral norms of decency (*decencia*) (Gotkowitz 2003; see also de la Cadena 2000:180).

With these transformations in Cochabamba, by the early twentieth century urban and rural social norms and identities blended even further. Small-scale farmers who owned their own land often split their time between tending their own plots, during which time they identified as mestizos, and laboring as serfs on haciendas, identified as *indios*. Although self-styled mestizos regularly asserted superiority over Indian people, and whites asserted superiority over the other two groups, the vibrant weekly markets throughout the region, coupled with the rising market for *chicha*, cottage-industry corn beer, provided many opportunities for interaction between people of different social backgrounds. This emerging fluidity of rural and urban identities differed from the rigid social separation in the Bolivian highlands. Paradoxically, however, the Spanish colonial idea of rigidly separate rural and urban people and spaces persisted, despite the relative changeability of individual people's identities.

Sacaba's new middle class in the twenty-first century also had roots in the *chola*, a central social figure in the Cochabamba region since the late nineteenth century. Understanding the history of *chola* as a social category helps uncover the anxieties and aspirations of contemporary middle classes, as well as the ways in which these contemporary middle classes attempted to set themselves apart from rural, indigenous, and campesino status. *Chola* was a mestizo social category that reflected both the ideology of firm racial division mapped onto rural and urban geography in theory, and the more fluid identities of daily practice (e.g., Poole 1997; Weismantel 2001; Seligmann 1989; de la Cadena 2000; Albro 2000; Paulson 1996). *Cholas* were women who wore long, pleated skirts (*polleras*) adapted from Spanish colonial women's clothing, petticoats, and stovepipe or fedora hats; they wore their hair in two long braids. Like new Bolivian middle classes more broadly in the late twentieth and early twenty-first centuries, *cholas* have, since their emergence in the late nineteenth century, portrayed themselves as socially superior when interacting with people who identified as Indian but have taken on socially inferior Indian status during interactions with elites (Weismantel 2001; Seligmann 1989; de la Cadena 2000).

Despite some room for upward mobility for aspiring *cholas*, however, being a *chola* was fraught with anxiety (Gotkowitz 2003:115). *Cholas* wielded more economic and social power than Indians, but they were always subject to challenges to their middling social status from people who claimed to be above or below them. The 1952 revolutionary government's declaration that Bolivia was a mestizo nation rather than a European-descended nation with an excluded Indian hinterland specifically recognized *cholas* as a socially legitimate intermediate group.

Following the revolution, class and racial identities and ideologies shifted further, though in contradictory ways. Education became more widely available after the revolutionary government ended the earlier restrictions on education for the children of rural serfs. Although the national government failed to deliver high-quality education in rural areas, and less than one-tenth of rural students remained in school through sixth grade (Luykx 1999:47), by the late 1970s the first generation of rural-born university students had earned professional degrees. These graduates began to challenge the longtime association of rural origins, including *chola* identity, with a denigrated Indian identity.

Yet as education became more widely available and the ranks of middle classes broadened in Bolivia, the meaning of *chola* identity inched down the class and racial hierarchy in the Cochabamba region, from an aspiring middling group (Gotkowitz 2003) to indigenous or campesina. Girls who attended high school were legally prohibited from wearing *polleras* and braids, the central symbols of *cholas*. Teenage girls throughout the region dropped their *chola* status by donning pants or straight skirts in pursuit of upward mobility through education. This prohibition held until the Morales government passed legislation in 2006 to remove this law. Within the Cochabamba region, though some individual *cholas* who wore expensive earrings, elaborate *polleras*, and immaculate braids might be recognized as prosperous or even wealthy, *chola* was often used synonymously with campesina and *india* (Indian) (see also Albro 2000). A wealthy farmer in Choro marveled approvingly in 2004 that a former president, General René Barrientos, had correctly foreseen the disappearance of *cholas* in the late

1960s. In a populist speech to Choreños, Barrientos had assured them that by the end of the twentieth century, Bolivia would have achieved such progress and prosperity that *cholitas* would have been replaced by *chotas*: girls and women wearing straight skirts and pants and presumably better educated and more prosperous.

From my perspective, the *chola* identity of the early twentieth century in the Cochabamba region established the anxieties and aspirations of those I am terming the emergent Sacaba middle class in the early twenty-first century. Both the early twentieth-century *chola* and contemporary new middle classes were relational categories: individual people experienced different statuses depending on whom they were interacting with in a given moment. Members of the contemporary middle class, like Marisol, defined themselves through alternating binary categories of socially superior or inferior, campesino or elite, poor or wealthy, Indian or mestizo. Both Sacaba's early twentieth-century prosperous *cholas* and early twenty-first century *profesionales* occupied a middle race as well as a middle class, but this was an ambiguous, anxiety-provoking, and fluctuating position.

Economic and political convulsions during the second half of the twentieth century further shaped the emergence of intermediate social groups throughout Bolivia. These convulsions included massive foreign debt (1953–present); hyperinflation (1981–1985); extreme droughts and floods (1983, 1998, 2010); the coca and cocaine boom (the late 1970s to 1998); the sudden, massive drop in the price of tin, which had formerly served as the mainstay of the Bolivian economy (1985); and free-market reforms (1985 to 2005). The free-market reforms of 1985 caused severe hardship for most Bolivians, including middling groups (Healy 1986; Hylton and Thomson 2007). The reforms led to mass layoffs from government offices and government-owned companies, including mines, telecommunications, and railroads. Increased imports of cheap clothing, cosmetics, and food from neighboring countries that subsidized their industries also created stiff competition for Bolivian industries and led to widespread unemployment in private manufacturing industries and lost income for small-scale farmers.

Cochabamba Department was the epicenter of coca and cocaine production, which provided a temporary cushion in the region from the hardships caused by free market reforms in the 1980s. Coca farming drew people from rural areas throughout the country. Many coca growers saw their incomes jump dramatically. Some families' yearly income from coca growing could reach tens of thousands of dollars and those who engaged in cocaine production or trafficking could earn many times more. This far surpassed what peasant farmers earned from potato or vegetable farming. Those who benefited from the boom did not feel the economic pinch from free trade reforms until 1998. That year, Bolivian antidrug forces under the supervision of the U.S. Drug Enforcement Agency eradicated thousands of hectares of coca plantings and arrested many low-level cocaine producers, transporters, and bystanders. The drug war contributed to the volatility of the price of coca leaves and cocaine and increased the risks for those involved in illicit cocaine production.[2] This drew the final cushion out from under the Bolivian economy and led to another recession. In 2005, on the eve of Evo Morales's election, the national poverty rate stood at 60 percent (Interamerican Development Bank 2008). The official unemployment rate was 10 percent, while real employment unemployment was widely recognized to be much higher.

## A New Middle Class in Sacaba

Sacaba municipality's proximity to the Chapare coca-growing district facilitated its status as a transit zone within the Cochabamba region. Sacaba residents flocked in large numbers to the Chapare, a mere seven-hour bus or truck ride from their homes. Many Sacabans fulfilled their aims to use their coca earnings to launch a business or pay for their children's college educations and thus allow them to enter the middle class. But not all were able to partake in the coca boom's bounty, given the need for start-up funds to invest in seedlings and land purchases, and the rapid erosion of soil fertility. This inequality fostered bitterness and invidious distinctions between newly prosperous and newly educated middling families, on the one hand, and still-poor laborers and farmers, on the other.

The coca boom also deeply shaped political culture in Sacaba. When a twelve-year-old girl in Choro told me confidently, upon meeting me in 1995, that there would be "a civil war and coup" unless the government ceased the militarized interdiction of coca growing, she was expressing the militancy of the coca growers' (*cocaleros*) union to which her family—like nearly all coca growers—belonged. She was also echoing many Sacabans' belief that their earnings from coca had saved them, or could in the future save them, from a life as destitute campesinos. Many in Sacaba saw coca as the means to achieving the dream of modernity and middle-class upward mobility that the Bolivian state had promised, but not delivered, since the 1953 Revolution. The frustration of these expectations following the drug war echoed the deep frustrations of people throughout the world confronting the bust of a boom economy, licit or illicit (e.g., Ferguson 1999; Shipton 1989). While some families managed to hold on to enough wealth to pursue their plans in higher education or commerce, the drug war made their project of upward mobility more precarious. The middle-class hopes and anxieties fed by the coca boom in turn sparked the rise of the MAS party in the late 1990s and helped propel Evo Morales to the presidency.

In the first decades of the twenty-first century, the principal dimensions of middle classness in Sacaba, as shown by Marisol were ambiguity, anxiety, alternation between elite and subaltern identities, and tension between an ethic of equality and an ethic of social superiority. The expression of these hopes, frustrations, and ambivalence in intimate relationships between family members, friends, and neighbors is the subject of the next chapter. Tracing these intimate politics is crucial to helping us understand the everyday experience of members of the new middle class and their roles in Bolivia's rapidly transforming political culture.

# The Intimate Politics of New Middle Classes in Sacaba

Doña Saturnina Ramírez was in her late sixties in 2013, a plump, formidable woman.[1] She had many godchildren, evidence that she was held in high esteem by many people in her hometown of Choro, even as some of Choro's poorest residents were intimidated by her sometimes severe manner and by her children's astounding professional achievements. Doña Saturnina's family trajectory illustrated the sudden windfall that the coca boom had meant for many Sacabans. She wore a full *pollera* skirt and her hair, streaked with gray, in two long braids. As a *chola* in early twenty-first-century Bolivia, she identified herself as rural and campesina. Three of her four daughters, meanwhile, wore jeans and straight skirts and identified themselves as professionals. Seven of her thirteen children had died in infancy or early childhood of the gastrointestinal and respiratory diseases that afflict the very poor; five of her six living children, by contrast, had earned professional degrees or were attending university.

Like Marisol the pharmacist, Doña Saturnina's children described themselves as an island of professionals amid a sea of campesinos in Choro. They often declared, "We are the only family in Choro in which all the children have studied." While other local families had, in fact, produced several university students or graduates, many Choro residents echoed the family's refrain about their uniqueness. They marveled at Doña Saturnina's ability to raise a brood of "all professionals" (*puro profesionales*) or grumbled that Doña Saturnina's children were snobbish (*creídos*) because they were professionals. Edgar, the eldest and in his forties in 2006, was a lawyer. Deysi, the next eldest, was a rural high school math teacher with a master's degree from a prestigious private teachers' college, while her younger sister Amanda was a lawyer. David was a pediatrician. The youngest, Celia, was nineteen and studying for an architecture degree. The refrain, "all of us have studied" excluded Julia, in her mid-thirties, a coca farmer and small-time cattle rancher before she set off for Spain (prior to the Spanish recession of 2008) to work as a home health aide. Doña Saturnina's children spoke to each other at home in Quechua, Bolivia's most common indigenous language. Yet like many speakers of indigenous languages in Bolivia and other Andean countries, they did not (usually) identify themselves as indigenous (see Canessa 2007; García 2005; de la Cadena 2000).

Doña Saturnina's family, like Marisol and many other residents of Sacaba Municipality, struggled to establish and maintain a middle-class position in Bolivian society. They held fierce ambitions for their family's prosperity and social mobility to "get ahead" (*salir adelante*). The coca boom sparked these ambitions among many in the Cochabamba region, inspiring them to shift their dreams to upward mobility through education or commerce rather than through agriculture, to imagine a future as a professional or affluent entrepreneur rather than a campesino. These middle-class dreams were coupled with intense anxiety, however, in part because they feared skepticism from wealthier or more highly educated people. They also faced equally vexing accusations of selfishness and snobbery from poorer and less highly educated friends, family members, and neighbors. My term "intimate politics" highlights both the prevalence and intensity of power struggles occurring at this most personal of levels between close family members, neighbors, and friends. Struggles for belonging and companionship, competition for social supremacy between husbands and wives, sisters and brothers, friends and neighbors grew from long-standing hierarchies of class, race, and gender in Bolivia as well as uncertain prospects in the free-market, post–coca boom economy.

In this chapter I look in detail at these intimate politics and the broader conflicting moralities that surrounded them, based on conversations with members of two dozen upwardly mobile extended families with whom I became close during my research. They included logging company owners, truckers, market sellers, cocaine producers, and, among younger generations, teachers, lawyers, agronomists, and doctors. I also draw upon years of conversations with people frustrated at their own poverty. I focus particularly on the experiences of Doña Saturnina and her grown children because the diversity of their perspectives and my long-term relationship with them provides a window onto the experiences of conflicting class and race identities that characterized new middle classes in Bolivia and, I suggest, in much of the Third World.

Doña Saturnina and other members of Sacaba's provincial middle class attempted to assert their distinction as upwardly mobile through their moral virtue—hard work, sexual propriety, thrifty money management, and high academic achievement. They also sought to avoid accusations of snobbery or of having profited at other people's expense "from the ribs of others" (*a las costillas de otra gente*). Envy was a common language for talking about conflict over inequality; discussions of envy marked the clash between ethics of individual upward mobility and ethics of equality. In practice, in their intimate lives, they espoused alternating ethics of social equality and superiority.

Upward mobility for people in Sacaba provoked anxiety, in part because the language of race and class was polarized between binary oppositions —of wealthy and poor, indigenous and nonindigenous—in ways that left little space to assert an intermediate wealth and social status. As in Marisol's account in Chapter 1, the prevailing characterization of Bolivia was that of a society split between a dominant white elite and marginalized indigenous majority; there were few words in Sacaba through which people could identify themselves in any way as "in the middle" (compare to Liechty 2002; O'Dougherty 2002). More commonly, they alternated between elite and subaltern terms of identity, alternating, for example, between calling themselves *profesionales* and campesinos or rarely, *indígena* (indigenous).

Newly prosperous people in Sacaba often defined their identity in relational fashion, depending on the social context. This dynamic was similar to that of *cholas* for most of the twentieth century in Bolivia, who took on working-class and Indian identities when confronted by social superiors, and local upper-class and white identities when talking to social subordinates (see Weismantel 2001; de la Cadena 2000). Many newly prosperous Sacabans shared aspirations for upward mobility, fierce social competition, the practice of drawing moral distinctions, anxiety about their social position, and a sense of social fluidity with middle classes in many places in the world (Liechty 2002; O'Dougherty 2002). At the same time, they also shared the experience of relational identity and the alternation between binary opposites of elite and subaltern race and class with people who inhabited the Andean social category of the *chola*. That the language of class and race in Bolivia did not fit their actual middling economic and social experience added an additional layer of ambiguity about their status in social life.

Doña Saturnina's family narrative of escaping campesino and Indian status was emblematic of many Sacabans' aspirations for upward social mobility as individuals and families and contrasted with the MAS party's formal rhetoric of collective uplift as indigenous campesinos. Doña Saturnina's children told me that their parents had worked single-mindedly for many years with the sole aim of sending them to college to escape the everyday social stigma of Indian and campesino identity. They repeatedly recounted a pivotal moment in their family's history when a policeman had yelled viciously (*abusado, maltratado*) at their father, Don Prudencio, who felt powerless as an uneducated man to shout or fight back. Don Prudencio reputedly vowed at that moment, "My children need to study and become lawyers to defend themselves." He and Doña Saturnina thus described their quest as aimed at upward social mobility, an escape from the humiliation of social subordination, as much as material prosperity.

Don Prudencio had earned a decent income while working throughout the 1960s and early 1970s as a driver for a wealthy truck-owning relative. But after several trucking accidents left the family in debt, Doña Saturnina and their children forbade him to drive. The price of coca and cocaine was just then booming, in 1975, and so Don Prudencio and Doña Saturnina decided to turn their efforts toward growing coca in the tropical Chapare region, seven hours away. Over the next twenty years, Doña Saturnina and Don Prudencio put four children through university largely on the proceeds of their coca farming. They were helped by the veteran's pension of Don Prudencio's mother, whose late husband had fought in the 1932 Chaco War with Paraguay, and by Doña Saturnina's earnings from selling *chicha* and dry goods from their home.

Owing to the cost of the children's education, Doña Saturnina's family lived in a home whose symbols of status and comfort were only at the median for houses in Choro. In 2009, it had cement floors, excepting a dirt-floored kitchen that housed a small fridge. They had only recently replaced a small color television bought in 1995, whose channel dial had fallen off and could only be changed with a wrench. On the rough floorboards of the upstairs bedroom, shared by Doña Saturnina, her grandson, and Amanda, stood several varnished wooden wardrobes and a glass case that held a few decorative dishes and mementos from travels to the Bolivian capital, La Paz. They often lamented that their house lacked the flush toilet and shower owned by several more prosperous families in Choro. They had paved their interior courtyard with cement and built several new rooms during the previous few years. Rebar poked out of the roof of their new second story, some of their cement floors were crumbling, and the privy behind their house remained half-dug. In the context of their locality of Choro, their perpetually under-construction house gave off an air of modest prosperity.

The relationships between Doña Saturnina's immediate family and her two daughters-in-law, the wives of Edgar and David, illustrated the family's shifting articulation of their social position between social dominance and social inferiority. These relationships were characterized by both the hopefulness and social anxiety that afflicts middle classes in many places in the world. Of all Doña Saturnina's children, Edgar, the eldest, expressed most explicitly a sense of uncertainty about his social standing. Most people in Choro, including Edgar himself, considered him to have been the first person from Choro to get a university degree. He had lived at home since finishing his law school degree at the public university in Cochabamba in 1995, except for one lucrative year practicing law in Ivigarzama, a boomtown in the Chapare. When the massive Drug Enforcement Administration–sponsored crackdown on coca growing and cocaine production in 1998 ended the boom in the Chapare and sparked a national recession, Edgar moved his operations to the provincial town of Sacaba, a short bus ride from Choro. He rented a tiny one-room office and opened his law practice. Since then, he earned a living but felt his income to be precarious.

Edgar often alternated between asserting an urban, professional identity and a rural, campesino identity. In keeping with his professional aspirations, he told me several times over the years that he was seriously considering moving to the city of Cochabamba. Edgar often bitterly denounced "backward" Bolivia and Choro and extolled the "advanced" nations such as the United States; he said that he could not wait to escape Bolivia. This was why his sisters called him by the nickname "Yanqui" (Yankee), an affectionate reappropriation of the term that among coca growers' union or indigenous movement activists typically served as a harsh denunciation of U.S. intervention in Bolivia.

Despite these vocal longings to be a prosperous professional, Edgar signaled in other ways that he also remained drawn to a campesino identity. When he came home to Choro from his Sacaba office every evening, he immediately changed from the oxfords worn by urban professionals into red vinyl sandals in the rural style of many of his local friends who had not finished high school. On the weekends, he often went drinking with these friends; he socialized often with rural folk. He continued to live at his mothers' house rent-free and ate his sisters' and mother's cooking. While this was certainly a way to save effort and expense, Edgar sometimes said that he relished the relative quiet and the clean air of Choro as compared to the bustle and pollution of the town of Sacaba or the city of Cochabamba. Edgar also told me wonderingly how he still remembered feeling like a "freak" (*un bicho raro*), out of his element, when he had begun attending the public university in Cochabamba during the late 1970s. At that time, he had been one of the only students from a rural background. Edgar appeared often bemused, as if he felt that his life embodied an unshakeable paradox. In 2009, he suggested for the first time in my hearing that he might remain living in the countryside for the rest of his life after all, because it was calmer (*mas tranquilo*) than urban living.

By day, Edgar sat at his desk in his small rented office several blocks from the Sacaba central plaza. He shared the office with his sister Amanda, who had obtained her law degree several years after him. Their clients, many of whom discussed their cases with Edgar in Quechua, appeared to feel more comfortable in this environment—with its cracked and stained walls, shabby chairs, manual typewriter, and piles of worn manila files— than in nearby law offices whose proprietors attempted to lure clients with computers and shelves of shiny legal tomes. During slack periods between clients, the lawyers played cards with Sacaba neighbors at Amanda's desk. Both Amanda and Edgar complained that they earned much less than they had during the coca boom, despite having many clients, because few people could pay high legal fees without their boom-time earnings.

In part because of his reduced income, Edgar expressed ambivalence about having become a professional. It was only once he began practicing law full-time, he told me, that he realized that he had missed his true calling—to become an accordionist specializing in regional Cochabamba music. Edgar began traveling long hours on his days off to take lessons from elderly accordion masters living in provincial towns throughout the Cochabamba valleys, whose scratchy recordings he and his brothers and sisters played during parties and when they sold their mother's *chicha*. Most evenings, the strains of Edgar's accordion practice could be heard wafting from his bedroom on the second floor of his mother's house. While the earnings and social status of a successful accordionist's life could be a step up from those of his parents, only the most successful musician could hope to rival a lawyer's prestige and earnings and Edgar never, in fact, left his law practice.

Edgar's longing for an urban life and higher status showed marked similarities to members of other striving Third World middle classes, to their ethic of rising socially and their longing to take part in transnational modernity (e.g., Liechty 2002; Dickey 2000). Yet Edgar's pleasure in the "calm" (*tranquilidad*) of rural life, in going out drinking in Choro *chicha* taverns with less-well-educated friends, in wearing old clothes and cheap sandals, in listening to provincial music, and in living in his hometown rather than renting an apartment in Sacaba or Cochabamba, also marked him as ambivalent about which lifestyle to pursue and which class and race to identify with.

Edgar's anxiety about upward mobility, his apparent conflict between wanting to join the professional middle class and simultaneous comfort in lifeways defined locally as those of campesinos and Indians also emerged in his relationship with his common-law wife, Doña Cinda.[2] Doña Cinda was a *cholita* like Doña Saturnina: she wore her hair in two braids and wore a *pollera*.[3] Doña Cinda worked as a part-time housekeeper for a wealthy local family and also washed clothing for prosperous families in the town of Sacaba. She and Edgar began their relationship in 1995 and had two children together. Most Sundays, if he was not drinking *chicha* with friends, Edgar spent his time with Doña Cinda, who lived about a mile down the highway from Edgar's mother's house.

By 2006, Edgar's sisters and mother had been nagging Edgar for years to baptize his daughter, Claudia, who was then six years old. Most parents with rural origins baptized and named their children on their first birthdays; urban middle-class parents usually baptized their children as tiny infants.[4] Like the rest of his family, I took Edgar's failure to baptize Claudia as a symptom of cruel disregard for his children and their mother. In 1998, he had taken his eldest son, Teo, away from Doña Cinda's care to Doña Saturnina's home, claiming that Cinda was irresponsible. His mother and sisters took primary responsibility for raising Teo. Edgar had often explained to me that Cinda was "not my real wife" and that his children with her—including Teo, with whom he lived—were "not my real children." He often said, half defiantly and half longingly, that he expected to find another woman who was not *de pollera* at some unspecified future date, one who would be more suitable to his station as a *profesional*. Edgar was echoing the notion that professional-class men should have liaisons with *cholas* but not marry them, a widespread maxim among elite Bolivians for several centuries (see Albro 2000).

Such cruel statements about Doña Cinda and his children seemed to express Edgar's sense of uncertainty about his social standing; they also sometimes angered his sisters and mother. On Christmas Eve in 1998, as we sat in a state of semi-stupor after our enormous holiday meal, Edgar expressed misgivings about having recently brought his son to Doña Saturnina's house. He exclaimed in a tone of mild irritation that he did not want Teo to hang around him because Teo would likely speak to him in Quechua in front of Edgar's friends (presumably lawyers). His sister Deysi harrumphed and burst out to me in private a short while later, "It looks like he doesn't care about his son! If I had a child, I would be working only for him." His sisters Amanda and Deysi often rolled their eyes and grumbled angrily at what they saw as Edgar's neglect of his family. He sent only Teo to Sacaba schools in the urban provincial school district. His other child, Claudia, attended the Choro elementary school in the rural, and inferior, school district. In exasperation, the sisters urged Edgar to either marry Doña Cinda or leave her definitively.

But they did not like her either. Amanda and Deysi often lampooned Cinda's heavily Quechua-accented Spanish in falsetto voices, echoing racist television comedy shows from the 1990s in which middle-class male actors cross-dressed as *cholas*. The sisters laughed gleefully when Teo insulted his mother. Once, for example, when Teo was nine years old and had not lived with Doña Cinda for six years, they laughed encouragingly when Teo exclaimed scathingly, allying himself with them and against her, that he would never return to live with "that washerwoman" (*esa lavandera*). Sometimes they protested to me that, while they sympathized with Teo's mother when Edgar insulted her as a *cholita*, Doña Cinda showed poor moral character and was not worthy of their respect. "She's nuts [*loquita*]! She says bad things about us to other people," Edgar's sisters told me, seemingly in an attempt to justify their mockery.[5]

Deysi, Amanda, and Doña Saturnina explained that Doña Cinda had begun a campaign of malicious gossip about them after Doña Saturnina had visited Cinda one day to warn her that Edgar might never marry her. Doña Saturnina, in their telling, hoped Cinda would leave Edgar because he neglected her and their children. Cinda was young—nearly ten years younger than Edgar—and fair-skinned and pretty; she could find a better husband. But Cinda, instead of being grateful, blew up at her, raging that Doña Saturnina's true concern was that Cinda was not a *profesional* like Edgar. She threw Doña Saturnina out of her rented house.

When telling me this story several years later, Doña Saturnina sighed and said in a resigned tone about Doña Cinda, "She is dying to marry him [*Pay wañurisan casarinanta*]." Cinda held on to Edgar because he was a lawyer, even as she was furious that he contributed only minimally toward her and her children's expenses and spent very little time with them. Deysi chimed in with irritation that Doña Cinda often bragged to others in Choro, "My husband is a lawyer," implying that this bragging was uncouth and demonstrated Cinda's lower status. When I asked why Edgar did not finally marry her, given that so many years had passed during which he had never carried through with his threat to marry a professional, Deysi replied with a weak smile, as if discomfited at expressing snobbishness explicitly: "It's that it's not so acceptable [*no es tan aceptable*] for a *profesional* to be married to a *cholita*." She continued that if the *cholita* were someone *decente* (morally upright) perhaps it could be done. But Doña Cinda was not *decente*: she was a gossip and had a child from a previous relationship. With this comment Deysi demonstrated how middle classes often assert distinction using a rigid morality, in addition to dress, wealth, language (a Quechua accent), and education (see Liechty 2002; de la Cadena 2000; Gotkowitz 2003). Deysi implied that Cinda's moral failings as a gossip and promiscuous woman confirmed her rightful place in a lower class and racial category. By implication, in the relational logic of class and race in Bolivia, all of Edgar's family raised themselves socially by criticizing Doña Cinda for being immoral and a *cholita*. And yet it seemed, if Doña Cinda was bound to Edgar, despite her anger, through her longing to associate with a professional and through her economic dependence on him, Edgar was also bound to her in ways that he could not bring himself to admit directly: his discomfort with fully adopting an urban lifestyle and professional status.

The occasion of Edgar's daughter's baptism brought to the surface Edgar's conflicting hopes and anxieties about his middle-class status and brought to a head Doña Cinda's unfulfilled aspirations for upward mobility through her relationship with Edgar. Both Edgar and Doña Cinda appeared to want earnestly to baptize Claudia but also appeared unsure about whether or not they wanted anyone to attend the event and the party afterward—usually an opportunity for joyful drinking and dancing with the parents' friends and relatives. For example, while Edgar and I planned the logistics together, Edgar shied away from my suggestion that he have his daughter baptized in the large, ornate provincial church in Sacaba. All the other Choro families I knew, wealthy and poor alike, had baptized their children there. Instead, Edgar insisted on the rural church in the nearby village of Muyu. When I asked why, since the Sacaba church was only a few blocks from his office, he admitted sheepishly, "Because my friends are pains in the ass [*fregados*]."[6] He explained that if they found out about the baptism, they could reproach him with the question, 'Why did you wait so long [to baptize her]?' His long delay would be taken as evidence that he lacked proper fatherly concern for his children. But, he added, he also worried they might tease him by saying, 'It turned out that his wife is a *cholita!*' His wife's status, when publicized among other professionals, could unmask him as other than the upwardly mobile persona that he hoped to convey.

And so, the Saturday afternoon of Edgar's daughter's baptism found only four of us winding up the highway between Choro and the Muyu church in Edgar's purple Mitsubishi, a car he had bought used to try to enter Cochabamba's auto resale market as a sideline to his law practice. Edgar sat up front with his best friend, a cousin who hadn't completed high school. I brought up the rear with my teenaged goddaughter, whom I had roped in to keep me company. The churchyard was deserted when we arrived, apart from Doña Cinda and six-year-old Claudia sitting huddled together against the wind and harsh afternoon sunshine on the church's yellowed front lawn. Claudia seemed shyly pleased at the pale green dress I had bought her and gamely tried to wear the black patent-leather shoes that were clearly too big (I had never met her).

Only one other child was being baptized that day; in the Sacaba church on Sundays, by contrast, hundreds of babies routinely were baptized together. Claudia, my new goddaughter, was so much older than most baptized children that the priest-in-training who officiated did not realize that she was to be baptized and excluded her from the beginning of the ceremony until we called out urgently to him from a rear pew.

After the baptism, we returned to Doña Cinda's rented house in Choro. We sat at a battered Formica table and ate chicken she had baked that morning. The wind blew bits of trash across the grey dirt courtyard and rattled the window shutters and doors. It was a desolate scene. Edgar and his friend quickly escaped to a party down the road and my teenaged goddaughter to a youth group meeting, leaving Cinda, Claudia, and me.

Cinda looked sober. Trying to cheer her up, I invited her to my going-away party, which would be held in a few days at Edgar's parents' house. Cinda burst out that she would never enter Doña Saturnina's house and began to sob. "They are all students!" she cried vehemently in Quechua. "I am not a student." She told me about a recent fight in which Amanda, Edgar's sister, had insulted Doña Cinda. "Kiss my ass [*sik'iyta muchaway*]," Amanda had told her in Quechua while accusing her of being unworthy of Edgar.

Claudia's baptism revealed that Doña Cinda's and Edgar's shared ambitions for middle-class status were, in fact, incompatible. Doña Cinda hoped that marrying Edgar, a lawyer, would raise her social and economic standing. Edgar, however, worried that acknowledging Doña Cinda, a *cholita*, as his wife—rather than his mistress—would lower his standing. He had not come so far up in the world that he could afford to have a *cholita* wife. But he also worried that his lack of commitment to her and to their children, when made public, would threaten his moral reputation as a responsible—and middle-class—father and husband.

The contrast between Edgar and David illustrated their intermediate class and racial identities and their classically middle-class anxieties and aspirations. David was acknowledged as the most ambitious and the most successful of the family. Widely regarded as handsome and an enthusiastic dancer at parties, he told me that he had decided to become a pediatrician after seeing seven of his siblings die as infants from easily treatable diseases. He had graduated with excellent grades from a well-regarded public medical school, amassing prestigious scholarships. After several years working as a pediatrician in a large hospital in Sacaba Province, in 2008 he was named hospital director in a Cochabamba clinic, a distinct honor. He also ran a thriving part-time private practice on the outskirts of Cochabamba City. I sat in on several of his medical consultations with Choro children, during which he treated them and their parents with more respect than did urban-based doctors who were often cavalier or downright disrespectful toward their Quechua-speaking patients.

When David talked to me about his own social and economic mobility, he expressed an excitement and confidence that contrasted sharply with Edgar's ambivalence and puzzlement. David seemed to feel that his economic and social plans for upward mobility were coming to fruition. While Edgar characterized himself as feeling out of his element during his entire time as university student, David told me he had quickly outgrown such sentiments. David talked with obvious pride about his close friends who were prominent Cochabamba doctors, his decision to send his son and daughter to private schools in Cochabamba, and his plans to tour Mexico and the United States with his wife and children. Part of his confidence may have stemmed from his more secure job. He had obtained a tenured physicians' post in the public health system, while Amanda and Edgar, as lawyers in private practice, were subject to the vagaries of supply and demand for their legal services. It seemed to me, however, that David's confidence also emerged from his own temperament and from the ways in which in-between, middling status could lead people down different potential life paths.

The relationship between Doña Saturnina's family and David's wife, Eliana, a nurse, contrasts directly with their relationship with Doña Cinda and shows the ways in which the family members were equally anxious and torn between ethics of hierarchy and egalitarianism when they perceived themselves to be playing the lower-status role in a social relationship. As soon as David began dating Eliana, conflicts arose between Eliana and Amanda and Deysi. The sisters claimed that Eliana acted socially superior to them. This outrage contrasted with the sentiment of superiority they expressed in regard to Edgar's wife, Doña Cinda. It seemed that while they saw Doña Cinda as a drag on the family's prestige because she was socially inferior, their sister-in-law Eliana was a drag on the family's standing because she belittled them, albeit subtly.

I had assumed at first that Eliana would be popular with David's sisters because she seemed to share so many of their amusements and their family history. Like them, Eliana was gregarious, laughed easily, loved dancing to Cochabamba valley accordion music, and happily passed her weekend afternoons chatting with friends while they treated each other to round after round of *chicha*. Eliana's parents shared Doña Saturnina's and her husband's background: they were from another Cochabamba valley provincial town, had weathered faces that attested to lifetimes of agricultural work out of doors, and her mother, like Doña Saturnina, wore a *pollera*. Both sets of parents appeared equally rigid and uncomfortable in their lace-up shoes and constricting finery in David and Eliana's wedding photos. Where Doña Saturnina and her husband had sent their children to college with the proceeds of their coca plots, Eliana's parents had sent Eliana to nursing school with the proceeds of their several dozen hectares of soy and cotton in the eastern tropics.

While Amanda and Deysi eventually warmed up to Eliana more than they did to Cinda, they often muttered exasperatedly at her snobbery. Eliana was *altanera* and *creída* (stuck-up), they complained. First of all, they explained, she refused to spend extended periods of time in their family home in Choro. Whereas David nearly always visited home on the weekends and continued to sleep over many Saturday nights in his old bedroom, Eliana almost always went back to her and David's house in Sacaba to sleep. Eliana confessed to me that she felt stifled sleeping in David's small room that stood next to the family latrine. The sisters mimicked Eliana almost as savagely as they did Doña Cinda, exclaiming in Spanish in falsetto voices while pointing to different places in their home, "This is dirty! That's dirty!" With this parody of Eliana, they echoed the widespread concerns of rural residents, inherited from the structural subordination of rural indigenous communities under colonialism, that rural homes, and the countryside as a social and moral space, were irredeemably dirty (Gotkowitz 2003; de la Cadena 2000; Weismantel 2001; Larson 2005). This concern, which they and many other Choreños voiced to me at other times, expressed the fear that the countryside (*campo*) was inherently uncivilized and unbefitting to their professional, middle-class aspirations.

The baptism of Eliana and David's daughter Magaly contrasted cruelly with that of Doña Cinda and Edgar's daughter and illustrated the differences within the emergent middle class. Magaly's baptism, like David's marriage to Eliana, also sparked discomfort among David's siblings when they confronted people who were indisputably of higher racial and class status than themselves. Following the baptism of one-year-old Magaly in the Sacaba provincial church, her godmother, a fair-skinned rheumatologist friend of David from Cochabamba city, drove us in her SUV to a local restaurant. We enjoyed a series of provincial luxuries: we ate roast duck, talked, and danced around a long table in a private room that David had rented, gazing out at a slightly scruffy courtyard rose garden. Throughout the afternoon, friends of David from Cochabamba, mostly specialist physicians and their families, arrived and left the party in a never-ending stream. With their Spanish unaccented by Quechua, their light skin and hair, and their expensive-looking clothes, they displayed signs of class and racial distinction above that of even David and Eliana. The arrival of a family in which parents and their two children shared startlingly pale skin, green eyes, and red hair—all rarities in Bolivia—evoked curious whispers from David's siblings. They asked themselves if they were foreigners or simply very elite Bolivians.

The party following the baptism abounded with signs of class and racial discomfort. Eliana's friends from nursing school, children born to campesinos like her and professionals of a lower rank than physicians, sat

*Figure 3.* Magaly's best friend's sixth birthday in Choro, 2009, with a cake from Dumbo's, one of Cochabamba City's most expensive bakeries. Photo by the author.


at the middle of the table. They joked with each more quietly than did the specialist physicians from the city, who sat at the end of the table, and few conversations arose between the two groups. The nurses' skin was, on the whole, darker; the women's long hairstyles matched those of Eliana, Amanda, and Deysi and attested to a more working-class aesthetic. At the far end of the table, conversing exclusively with the nurses, sat David's sisters, Edgar, his parents, myself, and Edgar's eldest son, Teo.

David's sister Julia, who had dropped out of high school and wore a *pollera*, told me surreptitiously during the party that she felt uncomfortable with David's "high society" (*alta sociedad*) friends. Even Deysi, the math teacher, though she had lived in Cochabamba for several years and had attended an elite, private college, also said she was uncomfortable. She complained while we took a break outside the restaurant that, unlike at a party in Choro where you could relax and have fun, here you had to act "refined" (*refinada*). David's green-eyed friend with her green-eyed children, the one who looked like a *gringa*, had seemed a particular snob (*altanera*), Deysi told me, though she had not actually spoken to her. It seemed to me that part of Deysi's discomfort arose from this challenge to her sense of being on top of her social world as a professional, a privilege she enjoyed more securely within the social space of Choro.

In sum, the relationships between Doña Saturnina's children and their intimate friends and family illustrated many of the aspirations and anxieties of Sacaba Municipality's new middle classes, many of whom built their dreams for a new life on the coca and cocaine booms. They professed fierce ambitions for upward mobility, as well as warring ethics of superiority and egalitarianism. They identified themselves along racial and class binaries— sometimes as campesinos and sometimes as *profesionales*—with few words available to describe being in the middle. And most keenly, they expressed anxiety about this ambiguous social position.

## The Axes of Inequality in Sacaba

Alternation between different poles of identity warrants closer attention to both the language and scale of idioms of inequality. Class and race, in the Cochabamba region and other postcolonial societies, as described in Chapter 1, have historically been intertwined concepts. Furthermore, people experience social status through a series of binary oppositions of race and class terms (Weismantel 2001). Some of these terms emerged from Spanish colonialism while other terms are of newer origin. These terms raise distinctions based on wealth, as in *pobre* (poor) versus *rico* (rich); race, as in *indio* versus mestizo; and geography, such as rural or urban (Table 1).

**Table 1. Common binary terms of unequal race/class in Sacaba.**

| Subaltern | Elite | Formal Bases of Distinction |
|---|---|---|
| *indio*—Indian<br>*lari, salvaje*—savage | *blanco*—white<br>*q'ara*—White urbanite | Race |
| *pobre*—poor<br>*clase popular*—popular class<br>*humilde*—humble<br>*waqcha*—poor and alone | *rico, ricachón, de dinero*—rich | Wealth |
| *campesino, agricultor*—peasant | *rico, ricachón, de dinero*—rich; *profesional*—professional, college educated | Occupation, geography (rural/urban), and wealth |
| *indígena*—indigenous<br>*originario*—native | *blanco*—white | Race-culture (positive evaluation of indigeneity) |
| *analfabeto*—illiterate<br>*no ha estudiado*—didn't study | *bachiller*, professional, college educated | Education |
| *chola*—wears a *pollera* and hair in braids | *chota*—not a chola | Race, class, and education |
| *rural* | *urbano*—urban<br>*citadino*—city dweller | Geography |
| *no chapareño*—Someone who hasn't earned wealth from the Chapare | *chapareño*—earned wealth from the Chapare | Wealth |

Source: Author's fieldwork

The assigning of elite or subaltern categories depended on who was involved in a particular interaction. Deysi clearly considered herself a professional in relation to Doña Cinda but appeared to feel less of a professional when confronted with David's pale, wealthy physician friends from the city of Cochabamba. Doña Cinda herself at times asserted social superiority when speaking of even poorer people.

These binary oppositions were shaped by the particular scale of a given place. Within the rural locality of Choro, Deysi vied for elite status with wealthier but less highly educated people but could assert middle-class distinction over poorer people. When she circulated in the provincial space of Sacaba, she was potentially subject to social demotion, as more highly educated or wealthier people who held stronger associations to urban institutions and social networks could outrank her and inspire her to declare herself a campesina. When she moved in social circles based in the city of Cochabamba, as at David and Eliana's daughter's baptism party, this potential demotion was more pronounced.

While these middling identities were relational—subject to the status of the person with whom an individual was interacting—some important patterns of identification and status were apparent in the social worlds of the community of Choro, the municipality of Sacaba, the city of Cochabamba, and the nation of Bolivia. Within the social space of Choro, I observed local residents define four general categories of people: very poor; professionals or university students like David and Amanda; prosperous merchants such as truckers, business owners, and farmers; and cocaine traffickers (small scale compared to internationally infamous traffickers but wealthier than all others in Choro). On the scale of Sacaba Municipality, two additional class and racial categories emerged in conversations among local residents: urban-based professionals, who lived primarily in the densely populated corridor along the highway between Sacaba and the city of Cochabamba; and provincial elite families whose members had been known as *vecinos* (townspeople, literally "neighbors") since colonial times. Their families had been medium- to large-scale landowners, professionals, or wealthy merchants before Bolivia's 1953 Agrarian Reform. They identified themselves as emphatically not campesino and not Indian, though their physical appearance and wealth were not always distinguishable from that of rural residents. When the social environment widened to include the city of Cochabamba, as at David's daughter's baptism, people of greater wealth, lighter skin, and elite transnational connections entered: people who had obtained master's and Ph.D. degrees from Spanish, U.S., Mexican, or Argentine universities or who identified themselves as belonging to the small European-descended population in Bolivia.

If many Sacabans used alternating binary opposites as terms of identity, some people seemed to wrestle actively with the question of whether or not rurality and urbanity represented sharply separated, unequal worlds and identities. The vision of rurality connoting poverty, cultural otherness, and backwardness is exceedingly common in postcolonial places like Bolivia (e.g., Pigg 1992; de la Cadena 2000; Kearney 1996; Subramanian 2009).

Certainly, there were differences in access to amenities between officially rural Choro and officially urban Sacaba Town. I ran out of Doña Saturnina's house one afternoon in 2004 to try to find a head of garlic and a packet of mayonnaise—common items in corner stores in the provincial town of Sacaba—to cook dinner. Of the four tiny stores located in private homes in Doña Saturnina's sector of Choro, all were either closed or sold out of both items. When I arrived home empty handed, Celia, the twenty-two-year-old architecture student and the baby of the family, greeted me with a scowl. "This is the furthest corner of the world [*el último rincón del mundo*]," she exclaimed in mock despair, as she lolled in front of the television on her mother's bed, amid the blare of highway traffic. "I'm sure that where you live, there are lots of supermarkets—there are *hyper*markets [hiper*mercados*]," she said, surely thinking of IC Norte, a chain of enormous grocery stores in Cochabamba City. Such complaints presented Choro as a rural space walled off from and inferior to urban ones, despite its many amenities that distinguished it from more remote hamlets.

Yet this notion of rural and urban as separate vied with everyday evidence of movement and fluidity: the long history of relational identities and geographic mobility; the economic ties between farmers, merchants, and urban consumers through regional markets; more recent waves of migration since the 1970s coca boom; and the administrative linking of rural to urban areas within the same municipalities through the Law of Popular Participation in the 1990s. The actual state of infrastructure and services in much of Sacaba Municipality was better than in many officially designated rural areas of Bolivia. The construction of a major highway in the 1960s had permitted widespread electrification and running water for all but the poorest Choro households by the 1990s. Public transportation from Choro to Sacaba and Cochabamba was available during the day to anyone who could afford bus fare.

The most perplexing issue for Doña Saturnina's family, however, was not the paucity of services in Choro. They spent most days in Sacaba or Cochabamba and, like other prosperous families in Choro, could purchase mayonnaise there and could, more significantly, afford to pay for urban doctors and schooling. Rather, their urgent questions centered on the extent to which they and others identified them with the countryside.

Sacabans often divided the possession of middle-class distinction—described in Spanish by the adjective *culto* (cultured) and the nouns *criterio* (discernment) and *civilización* (civilization)—along rigidly separate rural and urban lines.

A variant of this local conceptual model posited the qualities of middle-class distinction as ebbing in concentric circles along a gradient from urban to rural areas. A bus driver and urban neighborhood leader whose parents had been Sacaba provincial elites, Don Álvaro, explained to me earnestly that Choro residents rarely left Choro and Sacaba Town residents rarely left the provincial town center. While giving me a ride one day between Sacaba Town and Choro in 2005, he affirmed that people in the town of Sacaba had more "*criterio*" than those in Choro. Pointing through the car window to mechanics' garages, half-built restaurants, and cornfields that sprawled along the highway, he argued that the *criterio* of the inhabitants of each locality decreased gradually the closer one got to Choro. He struggled to define *criterio*, explaining that, whatever it was, *criterio* existed in a person as a function of the amount of time he or she had spent in the town of Sacaba or the city of Cochabamba. *Criterio* thus seemed to mean a classed and raced form of good taste, akin to Bourdieu's use of the term "distinction" to depict middle-class notions of propriety, discrimination, morality, and intelligence (Bourdieu 1984). Don Álvaro's depiction of people residing in officially designated rural areas as motionless, as stuck in place, was so striking because it was readily contradicted by the couples we passed at that very moment waiting by the side of the highway for rides to the tropics, bundles of clothing at their feet, and by the stream of minibuses that zoomed past us in both directions and which Don Alvaro himself had driven for many years. Sacaba, like the region of Egypt studied by Amitav Ghosh, "possessed all of the busy restlessness of an airport's transit lounge" (Ghosh 1994:173). Don Álvaro's notion of a clean rural-urban gradient of identity, however crude and ill matched to the reality, was still more nuanced than the binary divisions between rural and urban identities used by many other Sacabans.

Race and class intertwined with geography, furthermore, in the binary hierarchies of power. Racial insults persisted despite the revolutionary government's declaration in 1952 that *indios* would be identified henceforth as campesinos and that all Bolivians would henceforth term themselves as socially equal, mixed-race mestizos rather than as subordinate *indios* or superior whites (*blancos*). Racial meanings that slipped into explicitly

class-based terms like campesino were also woven into geographic terms like rural, countryside, urban, and city (Klein 2003; see also de la Cadena 2000; Weismantel 2001).

Bolivian public and private talk also remained liberally peppered with explicitly racist epithets in 2006. Some regions of Bolivia experienced more severe racial polarization, for example, in eastern Bolivian regions such as Santa Cruz. Choreños who had traveled or settled there sometimes reported that easterners sometimes called them "Indians" or "shitty highland Indians [*kollas de mierda*]" (see Fabricant 2012; Postero 2007). According to reports I heard from several people from various regions of the country in 2009, such insults increased immediately following the election of Evo Morales in 2005, as eastern elites saw their social and economic supremacy challenged (see also Schultz 2008).[7] Many Sacabans, in turn, referred to western highland residents as *laris*, a term that combined the racism of the Spanish epithet *indio* with the rural connotations of the English class term *hick*. *Lari* signified uncivilized backwardness and moral inferiority. "If you sit down with [*laris*] they won't share even a morsel of food with you!" exclaimed Bald César, a sawmill owner residing in Choro. "They are not civilized people, they are savages!" similarly exclaimed Don Felipe, a man whom neighbors at times insulted behind his back as a *lari* himself, because he was poor and was widely criticized as having too many children. A desperately poor teenager, whose home lacked electricity and running water, explained why her father refused to live with her and her mother in Choro. A neighbor in Choro "called my dad a *lari* and that's why he doesn't come. As if *he's* a *lari*! Her son-in-law, well, he's a little *lari* [*larisito*] himself!" Amanda, in a moment of frustration with the elected leaders of Choro's community council, exclaimed that they were "*laris*" because "they are very disorganized!" Disorganization, imprudence ("too many" children), poverty, lack of generosity, as well as highland origins could thus elicit racist epithets of Indianness.

In Sacaba, racist insults between intimates hurled in moments of anger were often couched in irony or joking, though they appeared to sting their targets deeply nevertheless. One day, for example, a married couple was having an argument while drinking with friends in a Choro chichería. The wife spat "*Lari!*" at her husband and explained to me with a tense smile that she only insulted him with that term when he went on a drinking binge. He emphasized to me, by contrast, his face also rigid and tight lipped, that she insulted him in this way because he hailed from a highland town. His grim expression attested that he felt this racial insult from his wife sharply. As with Edgar, who explained that he was justified in treating Doña Cinda with disregard because she was a *chola*, racist insults between intimates appeared to be deeply wounding.

Racialized teasing was also very common. For example, Deysi and Amanda were extremely fond of Edgar's son, Teo, whom they had help raise, but did not spare him their sharp tongues or biting humor. Since he had come to live with them at age three, his aunts often mockingly shouted the same epithets at him that they used on their brothers when they did something that annoyed them: "*Negro, indio, feo* [Black, Indian, ugly]!" Although they always assured me that they were joking, Teo repeated these outbursts in other contexts, making the racism of these insults more explicit. For example, once when he was eight, while watching *Sábado gigante*, a Saturday-night TV variety show broadcast from Miami throughout Latin America, Teo gazed raptly at the bikini-clad, high-heeled hostesses who often performed dance routines. As one Afro-Latina hostess entered the screen, Teo screamed, "*Negra, fea!*" I was shocked at this harsh expression of prejudice, particularly since virulent racist epithets in Bolivia were usually targeted at Indians, rather than at Afro-Bolivians, who comprise about 1 percent of the population. Afro-Bolivians were usually the targets, instead, of an objectifying, paternalistic exoticism. The entire family, including Teo, adored Doña Saturnina's Afro-Bolivian godson and often remarked with wonder, rather than scorn, at the contrast between his green eyes and skin darker than theirs. It seemed that Teo had picked up on the barbed quality of his aunts' banter but not yet learned to direct it precisely nor to cloak it in the guise of humor.

Even the kindest people participated in such racialized banter and expressed the finely tuned color-consciousness of Bolivian society, couching their remarks in irony or joking. A few months before becoming ordained as a Catholic priest, a gentle friend of the family named Denis had Doña Saturnina's children in stitches recounting his recent clever play on words. Their cousin Wilson was known to be very sensitive about the fact that his four-year-old son was dark skinned. "Your son is very *choco*," Denis had told Wilson mischievously. *Choco* was the local colloquial Spanish term for light skinned and blond. When Wilson turned on Denis, furious, insisting that Denis was insulting his child by deliberately saying something that everyone knew was not true, Denis had retorted, "I wasn't insulting him. He is very *choco*: he is *choco . . . late!*" (a pun on "chocolate" brown). Denis grinned roguishly at us while retelling the exchange and Doña Saturnina's children roared with laughter. They repeated his joke many times during the subsequent weeks and marveled at his wit.

People also turned racialized disgust on themselves. Amanda, like many other women I knew in Sacaba, often lamented that she was ugly because her skin was "too dark." Once Amanda, after a long, introspective discussion with her brothers and sisters after we had finished dinner, looked up seriously at me and told me that she had not yet had children (she was then thirty-eight years old and single) because she was afraid of passing on her dark skin to her child. "It was a joke, a joke!" she exclaimed when she saw my horrified expression. She insisted that she was teasing me precisely because she knew how earnestly I always tried to talk her out of such sentiments. Sometimes people extended this internalized racism to their children, like the many strangers on Sacaba buses who lamented to me that their children were "dark and ugly" when they saw my pale, redheaded baby. These were melancholy variants of more lighthearted but still racialized exclamations to me and my blue-eyed son: "Lend me your eyes! [¡Prestáme tus ojos!]" or sometimes, with a flirtatious chuckle, "Lend me your [strawberry blond] husband so I can make a blond baby!" Skin and hair color were common sources of nicknames such as Negrita (Blackie) or Choca (Blondie, light skinned).[8]

These examples show racialized thinking alive and well in Bolivia, despite the government's declaration in 1952 that racial consciousness would disappear by fiat. Racial signs, such as skin color and dress, could at times be synonymous with subordinate class signs, while at other times they diverged. Dark skin did not prevent Amanda from becoming a professional, but she appeared to fear that it constrained her options for finding love and forming a family. Meanwhile, Amanda also declared that light-skinned and fair-haired Doña Cinda was socially subordinate in terms in which race and class were indivisible: Cinda's Quechua-accented Spanish, her *pollera* and braids, and her purported immoral gossiping and unwed motherhood, demonstrated her lower class and race. That some comments about race were couched in jokes—"black, Indian, ugly!" and "chocolate"—suggests that, like in the United States, Bolivians felt some restraint in making racist comments as a result of government and social movement condemnation of racism. That people often uttered harsh racist epithets in moments of anger at spouses and children also shows how racist speech could channel antagonism and tension; explicit racism marked the momentary lessening of self-control.

By the late 1990s, in response to the national government's promotion of multiculturalism and the rise of the MAS, some Sacabans had begun to take on explicitly racial terms as badges of pride. "Around here, we are *indios, laris,*" said a taxi-bus driver in an affirming tone in 1998 as he sped along the road between Choro and Sacaba Town. Yet such self-identification with a term that had racist connotations—rather than the more positive *indígena* and *originario*—was rare in Sacaba.


**Snobbery and Egalitarianism**

The clash between the ethic of upward mobility, which Sacabans often feared was necessarily tied to snobbery, and the norm of equality created personal dilemmas. Deysi, Doña Saturnina's math-teacher daughter, in her mid-thirties, was an astute analyst of local social relations and a vivid story-teller. On many occasions, she described the social quandaries created by this clash that she began to navigate as she became a professional and attempted to shrug off her status as a "person from the countryside."

One moment in which Deysi asserted her own middle-class distinction while also condemning snobbery occurred on July 2, 2006, the night of the election for Bolivia's Constitutional Assembly delegates. Deysi came back to our shared bedroom at her parents' house with her sometime-friend Norah's husband. Norah was also a rural teacher, but unlike Deysi, who had a master's degree from an elite urban university, Norah had earned a combination high school diploma and elementary school teaching certificate (*bachiller pedagógico*) from a rural boarding school run by Catholic nuns. Norah had been lucky to graduate and find a teaching job in the late 1990s before the Bolivian job market flooded with teachers. Though many people who had earned the less rigorous teaching degree a few years later were at that moment unemployed, Norah had a steady job.

Norah's husband, Chavo, a successful auto mechanic, was telling Deysi about his long-running arguments with Norah and her mother. He was tearful and his voice was slurred from their recent round of postvote drinking. He, Norah, and their two small children had recently returned to live in Choro from the town of Sacaba in order to keep Norah's mother company because she was a widow who lived alone. But his mother-in-law constantly claimed that he was taking advantage of her. She insulted Chavo as a bad provider, telling him: "I'm supporting you, here," and asking pointedly, "And you, what do you have?" "It's true," Chavo said defiantly to Deysi. "My father is a poor farmer [*pobre agricultor*]," while Norah's mother was a prosperous vegetable merchant who had inherited large plots of farmland from her grandparents. But Chavo's mother-in-law's taunts rankled mostly because Norah took her mother's side, reproaching Chavo for his lack of earning power, saying scornfully, "I'm a teacher! I earn money." Norah had told Chavo that her salary maintained the two of them and their two small children more than did his income as a mechanic. I was momentarily surprised at the fine distinction that Norah had drawn, since many Bolivians believed that rural teachers, particularly those with Norah's high school degree, were not true professionals (see Luykx 1999). But Norah asserted her middle-class distinction in her fights with her husband. Chavo had hit Norah in anger, he told Deysi, and he regretted it.[9]

After Chavo left, Deysi lay on her bed, looking up at the ceiling. She wondered aloud in a thoughtful tone why she seemed to have so much "fear of getting married." I replied that it did not seem to be such a mystery, given the dire example of Chavo and Norah. I reminded her that she herself had often told me that, as a single woman in her late thirties with a steady, relatively well-paying job, she had quite a bit of freedom—to go to parties with friends and relax on weekends. So many husbands she knew drank heavily, beat their wives, tried to forbid them from leaving the house, or abandoned them to raise their children alone.

I had also noticed, though I refrained from mentioning, that during the years that I had then known them, both Deysi and Amanda had often seemed ambivalent about whom to date. They appeared to continually wonder whether their potential boyfriends were appropriate matches based on their status. It is possible that she, like Edgar, was perplexed about the way in which marriage would constrict her present ability to play with different identities. In 1995, when Deysi was a first-year college student in her early twenties living in Cochabamba, she had confided in me that she would only date men from Choro, never from Cochabamba. This provided a quite small pool of potential boyfriends: though Choro consisted of roughly four hundred families in 2006, few Choreños her age had college degrees.

On election night in 2006, Deysi emphasized the dilemmas created by perceived class differences. She continued, "Around here, it's mostly this situation: one spouse comes from a family with more wealth and wants to put down [*despreciar*], to humiliate [*humillar*] the other one. You know, they say that it's better for professionals to marry each other and for people from the countryside to marry each other [*es mejor casarse entre profesionales o entre gente del campo*]." Deysi was thus reaffirming the local hierarchy by which class and racial identity were defined in geographical terms: professionals, among who she counted herself at that moment, were inherently urban, while poor and uneducated people were by definition "people from the countryside." She repeated that Chavo's parents were indeed very poor. He shouldn't have hit Norah, but, on the other hand, Deysi seemed to imply, Norah was engaging in emotional abuse when she touted her class origins as being above Chavo's. Norah was a snob (*altanera*), Deysi said, for accusing Chavo of being only a mechanic and not even a high school graduate.

People are, of course, inconsistent. They are the targets of accusations that they also lob at others. On the one hand, Deysi argued that Norah was a snob for belittling her husband because she was a professional and he was not. Deysi had criticized David's wife and his physician friends on similar grounds of snobbery. She resented Norah as snobbish in relation to herself as well, explaining that Norah was never willing to "share" (*compartir*): to sit with friends, drinking *chicha* and chatting. The common term Deysi used to describe such conviviality, *compartir*, conveys the widespread norm in Sacaba that socializing was an expression of generosity—the opposite of selfishness—as well as a pleasure. On the other hand, Deysi herself had argued that Doña Cinda, Edgar's wife, was socially inferior to Edgar because of her immoral character in addition to her status as a *cholita*. Doña Cinda had similarly accused Deysi and her sister and mother of being snobs for not accepting Cinda's relationship with Edgar.

David on one occasion attempted to insert more nuance into these binary oppositions of rural and urban, campesino and professional. When I asked him in 1998 whether he considered himself a campesino, he replied, "I'm a campesino because I live in the countryside, but I'm not poor like a campesino." His was a rare assertion that a professional with close ties to both rural and urban areas could potentially assert a rural identity that was also prosperous and professional.

Deysi and Amanda sometimes called themselves campesinas, too, in moments when they pointedly criticized others' snobbishness and promoted social equality. Their statements, like the examples of overt racism and classism described above, drew on fine local nuances of food, clothes, accent, or birthplace to connote race and class. One day in 2003, for example, Doña Saturnina and most of her children had gathered for a festive lunch while watching the Sacaba municipal anniversary parade from the rooftop of David and Eliana's apartment building. Amanda handed a plate of fried chicken to David's seven-year-old son, Alejandro, from a previous relationship. "Me and my mom don't like to eat chicken skin," Alejandro said mildly, as he began to peel the skin off his drumstick. "Well," Amanda replied with mock severity to her nephew, "you and your mother are classy people [*gente decente*]. We [his aunts and uncles] eat chicken skin because we are campesinos." Her comment echoed the complaints of Choro parents that their children refused to eat the skin and entrails that Choreños had eaten during leaner times before the coca boom. Similarly, in 2005, David admonished me for not eating the skin of a roasted guinea pig, an Andean delicacy to which I never became accustomed, which he had prepared at his mother's house. "I am poor [*soy pobre*]; I eat the skin!" He declared pointedly to me. Both Amanda and David were teaching cultural beginners —a child and a foreigner—to be egalitarian.

If Doña Saturnina's children expressed irritation when they perceived that I, Eliana their sister-in-law, or David's city physician friends belittled them, they also complained angrily when nonprofessional and *de pollera*, but wealthier, neighbors asserted a higher status than them. Such complaints surfaced, for example, when I lamented that a well-to-do, *cholita* neighbor who owned a trucking business with her husband hadn't come to my son's baptism party, which we threw at Doña Saturnina's house in December, 2005. Amanda remarked in a sharp, ironic tone, "She's loaded [*ricachona*]! She only goes to rich peoples' parties. Because we are poor [*pobres*], she didn't come." Amanda explained that this woman's discriminatory thinking was "clear from where she goes and how she speaks. For the weddings of rich people [*ricachones*], she shows up with presents; for poor people, she doesn't show. These people are *creídos* [snobs]." Years earlier, in 1998, Amanda, Deysi, and David similarly condemned another wealthy *cholita* neighbor who owned a successful *chicha* tavern. The neighbor had reputedly proclaimed that she would reserve expensive bottled beer and cocktails for "rich people [*ricos*]" at her daughter's wedding, while serving poor guests only *chicha* and making them leave early. Amanda, Deysi, and David did not expect the neighbor to treat them as poor and refuse to serve them the expensive drinks; indeed, they partook freely. They nevertheless expressed these episodes as an affront to them personally—they had less visible wealth and cash on hand than their wealthy neighbors—as well as an altruistic concern for the many Choreños who were even poorer. Their protests also illustrate the intense social competition within this middle group in Sacaba, between professionals with little disposable wealth and wealthy merchants and truckers with little formal education. In a manner emblematic of middle classes throughout the Third World, they jockeyed intensely for the social supremacy to be recognized as a middle class, in this case through competing claims of distinctions based on wealth versus education (Liechty 2002; O'Dougherty 2002). Finally, these complaints by David and Amanda also demonstrate how in the social world of Sacaba Municipality, this rivalry for moral superiority could entail, paradoxically, making claims to egalitarianism.

In fact, the sisters termed themselves campesinas and rural and asserted an ethic of egalitarianism in some situations when they were called out as being snobs. In 2003, for example, Deysi recounted a painful episode in which she and Amanda had unexpectedly lost a valued friend. During a party at their home, they had teased their friend, a fellow university student who hailed from a rural town in the Bolivian highlands, that he had no right to criticize them: "Don't forget that you're an Apaza!" Apaza is a common indigenous Aymara last name that immediately signals a person's origins in the rural, Aymara-speaking Bolivian highlands. Deysi and Amanda were subtly marking Bolivia's racial hierarchy, in which highland Aymara speakers have been viewed as more Indian than, and inferior to, Cochabamba valley Quechua speakers.[10] In effect, they had admonished him, in mock severity, not to be an "uppity Indian." He became angry and told them that they had insulted him with a racial slur, left the party, and never returned to Choro to visit. Thinking back on this event several years later, Deysi said that she and Amanda had spoken in a spirit of fun, but they had been too free with their characteristic, biting humor. "I regret it so much. We were joking around [*bromeando*], but we shouldn't have said that. . . . It must have hurt him to the bone [even though] it was just a slip of the tongue. Surely he went and told his mother what we said to him, and his mother must have said, 'How could they say such a thing, being campesinas themselves!'" In an assertion of empathy and equality with her friend, Deysi implied that Doña Saturnina could easily have just as easily found herself listening to her own children's stories of racial and class discrimination. Deysi's analysis of the joke gone awry seemed to be that she and Amanda had been justifiably reprimanded for asserting racial superiority. Doña Saturnina's family, in sum, alternated between identifying with superior and inferior racial and class categories and between professing superiority and egalitarianism.

## Envy (*Envidia*)

The common language of envy (*envidia, qhawanaku, miramiento*)[11] in Sacaba marked the clash between the widespread ethic of egalitarianism and the equally widespread ethic of upward mobility. When David, for example, expressed a concern that his old friends and neighbors in Choro resented him as snobbish, he said that they were envious (*miramiento*) of him. He explained in an interview with me in 1998,

> I treat my people well. I speak with them in their language . . . in Quechua. . . . In fact, I try to change them, right? I say "You shouldn't do this. . . . We need to develop," . . . or "Instead of spending your money on this thing, you could do another thing," always thinking about how they can progress. . . . I haven't kept myself apart from them . . . but people talk, you know? I mean . . . I'm a serious person, I have a calm demeanor, and people peg me as stuck up [*creído*]. But it's *they* who are separating themselves from me, it's not because I'm stuck up. . . . People my age say, "He's a doctor, so now he won't say hello to us." Who knows what they're saying! So, sometimes when we pass by on opposite sides of the road, they just . . . say "good morning" and go by, they don't come up to me. . . . I think that they feel . . . I'm not sure . . . mmm . . . humbled, ashamed.

David described, with apparent pain, that he was misunderstood as being snobbish; that his intentions were egalitarian but his Choro neighbors and old friends misperceived him as acting socially superior since becoming a professional. In this instance, David did not condemn his former friends' envy as a moral fault but rather lamented that their ill-will emerged from a misperception of his thoughts and intentions. The implication of their perceived criticism was that David, by believing in his own social superiority, was socially selfish. He suggested that his old schoolmates harbored particular rancor for him, beyond what they might feel toward a snobbish stranger, because they saw him as rejecting them despite belonging to the shared social community of Choro. David countered with the implicit argument that he was not selfish but actually generous, because he tried to contribute to the progress of those old friends by offering them helpful ideas for how to become upwardly mobile themselves. He found, however, that his efforts to present himself as egalitarian had been unsuccessful.

The accusation of envy was an exceedingly common idiom in social life in Sacaba, as in much of the world, to denounce these types of social and economic inequality, suspicion, competition, and conflict (see Taussig 1980; Taussig 1986; Herzfeld 1981). The specific types of conflicts characterized as envy in Sacaba varied widely. Sometimes, Sacabans said that envy described other people's mutual relationship of suspicion or resentment. An impoverished widow exclaimed that wealthier and poorer teenagers "had envy of each other [*qhawanakunku*]," as expressed, for example, when a rich teenage boy beat up her son and falsely accused him of being a gang member. A middle-aged *de pollera* woman complained that her neighbors envied her (*envidia*) because she held a well-paying job as a housekeeper at a wealthy foreigner's home.

Concern about envy suggested that when people became upwardly mobile, no matter how modestly, they feared that other people would respond with anger and resentment. A prosperous and *de pollera* farmer who had inherited abundant irrigated land explained that she never hired day laborers to harvest her valuable long-stem roses for market because they had *envidia* of the dependable wealth she earned from her rosebushes and might deliberately trample the flowers. She exclaimed in frustration about Choreños who were poorer than she: "They don't want anyone to get ahead; they want everything equalized. They want only equality [*no quieren que nadie se alce; quieren todo igualado. Igualya munanku*]." The flower farmer thus denounced equality as a social norm; she rejected the ethic of egalitarianism by rejecting the legitimacy of the envy she imputed to her neighbors. In a classic lament of a new middle class, she implied that she had gained her wealth from a combination of luck and her hard work, and that people who remained poor—by definition, a result of their ill luck or laziness—were unfair to resent her.

As David suggested in his own experience, however, and as will emerge in narratives of extremely impoverished people below, the flower farmer faced other people's accusation that she was selfish: that she had succeeded through illegitimate means, retaining wealth unfairly without sharing it, or acting socially superior. As in David's presentation of his envious former classmates' perspective, the flower farmer implied that the envious (*envidiosos*) particularly resented her wealth because she was a member of their community and should therefore share. Doña Saturnina's children themselves often told me that other Choreños legitimately envied a wealthy cocaine trafficker because he got his riches "at other people's expense [*a las costillas de otra gente*]." They explained that the trafficker's exploitation consisted of his refusal to pay his lower-level cocaine suppliers full market price for the drugs that he resold. Yet it seemed from their own resentment of the trafficker's purported snobbery and by similar comments I heard from other Choro residents, that it was as much annoyance at his snobbery and the very fact of his wealth that inspired David and his siblings to claim that he was envied legitimately because he was selfish.[12] Ultimately, when David or the flower farmer complained about being envied, they were implicitly marking a conflict between the moral norm of equality within a social community, on the one hand, and the competing moral norm of "getting ahead" (*salir adelante*) to become middle class, on the other.[13]

David's and the flower farmer's concerns about envy conveyed that more privileged people worried about less privileged people's resentment at unequal wealth and status. In most cases, a person who feared that others envied him or her believed the envy to be unjustified. In David's case, he saw himself as promoting social equality rather than snobbishness. In the flower farmer's case, she viewed her inherited wealth as something beyond her control and within her right to maintain.

## The Coca Boom and Social Hierarchy: Frustrated Expectations of Upward Mobility

The sudden opportunities presented by the coca boom in the early 1980s had a dramatic effect on the ways in which Sacabans' sense of their status was based in part on expectations of a rising future class and race for themselves and their children, what Nancy Abelmann terms "class horizons" (Abelmann 1997:399). The coca and cocaine booms, in addition to expanding class horizons also presented surprising challenges. Local inequality increased when the boom permitted some, but not all Choro coca growers to join the new class of prosperous, upwardly mobile people of rural, sometimes destitute, origins. The volatility of earnings from the boom and risk of confiscation or imprisonment also made class and racial identity even more ambiguous than before. Furthermore, the illegality of cocaine and some of the coca production sparked rivalry between families wealthy from legal businesses such as trucking and professional work and people who worked in illicit cocaine production.

The coca boom certainly sparked strong aspirations for a middle-class lifestyle and social status throughout Sacaba. Since 1995, when I first arrived in Bolivia, Choreños overwhelmed me with stories about how the material conditions of their lives had changed during the previous decade, and most credited their increased purchasing power to coca growing; occasionally, they admitted to working as small-time cocaine producers or traffickers. The boom had brought electrification and potable water.[14] Televisions, medical care, a decrease in the number of babies who died from communicable diseases, college education, meat as daily fare rather than only on holidays—these were still miracles to many people I met in 1995, more than a decade after this dramatic shift began. "Before [the coca boom], we were lucky if we ate an egg once a week!" a Choro coca grower exclaimed to me in a common refrain in 2005. "Now we eat meat all the time." Photos of children's parties taken in the early 1980s, filled with scenes of hired clowns, store-bought birthday cakes, and children brandishing kazoos, support this claim of suddenly increased prosperity. The coca boom had permitted "civilization" to arrive in the region, in the words of Edgar and many other Sacaba residents. "People didn't used to know how to read or write; they didn't know to watch television; there was no electric light; they didn't know Cochabamba City. Now, by contrast, the children are sharp [*pícaros*]! Before, they only spoke Quechua. Now . . . five- and six-year-olds speak Spanish—they speak better than I do!" Edgar often exclaimed.

The coca boom had fostered an expectation—though unattainable for many people because of lack of capital—of getting ahead (*salir adelante*), to rise socially and economically (*superarse*) and to "become someone in this life" (*ser alguien en la vida*). As with Doña Saturnina's family, the dream of graduating from high school (*salir bachiller*) and from the university or at least a trade college (*salir profesional*) that had seemed far-off prior to the boom became a tantalizing dream for many people. The majority of Choreños, including some of the very poor, hoped their children would study agronomy, medicine, business administration, or elementary education. At 8 A.M. on weekday mornings, the streets of Sacaba Town filled with the small, uniformed figures of children arriving by public taxibus and minibus from dozens of surrounding communities like Choro to attend the better provincial urban schools. Parents migrated to grow coca or produce cocaine in the Chapare while leaving their children with grandparents to attend the better public schools in and near Sacaba.

Yet many people in Choro also remembered the height of the boom in the early 1980s as a time of moral, economic, and social disorder. They spoke about coca and cocaine with ambivalence: fondness for an era of lost prosperity and alarm at a society morally adrift because they believed that cocaine work was inherently "corrupting." Narratives recounted by the many people in Choro who claimed to be the select few who never worked in cocaine production or trafficking described the height of the coca/cocaine boom as a time in which most people were "crazed" (*alocados*). Their behavior and morals temporarily were altered from both the sudden influx of cash and from ingesting *pijchicata*, cocaine base paste.

Raquel, a prosperous *cholita* in her mid-thirties, often served beer to truckers at her father's truck stop in Choro. One windy afternoon in August 2004 she reminisced to us about the mid-1980s. "There used to be a lot of involvement in drugs [*droga*] around here. People were crazy from drugs [*loca por la droga*] and also crazy from all that money. People were different then," she said, mimicking someone staggering, as if on the verge of passing out in a drunken stupor. "I've seen it! One time, my mother went down by the river and saw . . . a pile of money in the river, just spilled there. And I saw in the bathroom here at the restaurant that people were wiping themselves with [U.S.] dollars."

Raquel argued, however, as did many Choreños, that this wealth did not translate into permanent upward mobility for many people. Those who were involved in cocaine production or trafficking [*pijchicata*] did "nothing" with that money. It was "only for their stomachs." After years of wild parties fueled by beer and hard liquor, they now had nothing, less than they had before the coca boom. Raquel listed several Choro families that had squandered, in her opinion, their cocaine earnings. "Why do you think people were that way?" I asked. Raquel paused thoughtfully and then replied: "They must have thought that there would be money like that forever; they must have thought that it would never end."

Doña Saturnina's family criticized their neighbors in identical terms. Sometimes they even used their daughter and sister Julia as a prime example. Julia had dropped out of high school but had earned a lot of money during the coca boom. She then had frittered it away—in their opinion—by buying alcohol and cars that she and her husband then wrecked in drunken accidents. When Julia migrated to Spain in 2004 to work as a home health aide, Doña Saturnina speculated, as many Choreños did about other neighbors and relatives who migrated abroad, that Julia would not waste the money she earned in Spain because that money was earned with "sweat," in contrast to coca and cocaine's "easy money" (*dinero fácil*). Such concerns about the corrupting power of quickly earned money are common to boom economies, whether licit or illicit (e.g., Shipton 1989; Parry and Bloch 1989).

Such descriptions also point to the ephemeral quality of wealth during this time and a pervasive thread of frustrated expectations. The image of restaurant patrons wiping their bottoms with U.S. dollars—and Raquel was one of several people in Choro who recounted such scenes to me—conveyed vividly the sense of coca and cocaine wealth as inherently impermanent. The Bolivian economy's hyperinflation, in which the value of Bolivian pesos plummeted in the early 1980s, may have added to Raquel and others' impressions of social chaos. It is quite possible that the "dollars" used as toilet paper in Raquel's tavern were in fact the near worthless Bolivian currency. Deysi similarly told me that many people during the boom time carried around money "in bundles [*bastones*] to inspire envy" in their neighbors. These people burned through the money, in her telling. another example of the evanescence of cocaine wealth.

### Rivalry Among Middling Folk

Raquel's stories also convey a lack of consensus about who counted as socially superior. By implicit contrast to those who had improvidently frittered away their wealth, Raquel asserted that her own family's wealth was accumulated legally and thus was more morally sound and longer lasting. She was therefore suggesting that her family constituted a genuine middle class, while those who earned wealth from cocaine production or trafficking were brief and illegitimate aspirants to a middle status. This was supported by comments I often heard in Choro that Raquel's family had been prosperous since the 1953 Agrarian Reform, as her grandparents had been landowners with holdings large enough to support several indentured laborers. Their *chicha* tavern was one of the older and better established of the half-dozen truck stops along the highway.

If Raquel asserted her middle-class distinction as a member of a family that had gotten its wealth legally rather than illegally, Doña Saturnina's family argued to me that their professional status signified an even more legitimate middle-class identity than Raquel's mother's wealth. Other people openly involved in cocaine production or trafficking asserted a third competing claim to distinction: that absolute wealth should be the measure of hard work and prudent money management. This emerged in the ongoing friendly, though barbed, rivalry between Doña Saturnina's family and the wealthy family of "Bald César."

Many Choreños pointed to Bald César's personal history as a parable of the hoped-for possibilities of the coca and cocaine booms. As a small child, everyone agreed, he was *waqcha*, a Quechua term for "orphan" that points simultaneously to his parents' early death, his lack of an extended family, and his utter economic destitution. He had worked first as a trucker's assistant, then as a truck driver, and then steadily built up his wealth as a cocaine middleman. Eventually he bought a fleet of tractor-trailer trucks and passenger buses and launched a medium-sized tropical timber business and lumber mill. In 2009, however, Bald César was found shot to death along a lonely dirt road, seemingly in retribution for reneging on part of a cocaine transaction. Choreños appeared shocked by the unusual event of an adult's violent death but not completely surprised, given the widespread assumption that he was involved in higher-level cocaine trafficking than other Choreños.

In 1998, when I first met Bald César, his house appeared opulent compared to other homes I had seen in Choro. His kitchen contained an interior sink and tiled countertops, while his dining room sported matching dining table and chairs of varnished wood. A bathroom boasted a bathtub and flush toilet, all rarities in Choro. The courtyard held a cage with two large and beautiful macaws. The families' several sport-utility vehicles, enormous Volvo trucks for transporting lumber, and heavy machinery for cutting and processing tropical hardwoods stood in the driveway. Several people in Choro referred to his home as "that luxury house" (*esa casa de lujo*).

When I visited in the years before his death, Bald César and his family usually saw fit to tell me with clear satisfaction that Doña Saturnina had "squandered" (*malgastado*) her coca earnings, while he had used his prudently and effectively to build up his prodigious timber and transport business. He was certainly regarded widely as a hard worker. In 1998, the morning after a major festival in Choro when many people were sitting on their patios bleary eyed, attempting to recover from hard drinking the night before, I rode a bus that passed Bald César driving his huge truck loaded with enormous tropical logs down the steep highway toward Cochabamba. "Bald César, damn!" the bus driver exclaimed. He marveled that Bald César was such a hard worker that he did not even attend the festivities. This comment reflected a widespread opinion that Bald César was wealthy in part because he was a hard worker, but also that so much work was a bit unnatural. The driver sounded impressed, but also a little disgusted that Bald César had given up the festival in order to work.

"But Bald César did not know how to take advantage of [*aprovechar*] his money!" Doña Saturnina's family often retorted to me, using me as a proxy for their argument with each other. "None of his children has studied." Whenever I returned to Doña Saturnina's house after visiting Bald César's family, Doña Saturnina's children treated me to the same scathing refrain: Bald César's home might be more luxurious than theirs, but their own extraordinary levels of education made them morally superior and gave them greater earning potential in the long term.

Amanda and Deysi complained that other Choreños who were actively involved in cocaine production or transport had also ridiculed them for spending their time and money on education instead of building a business, or even simply having fun, particularly during the boom years of the 1980s. Amanda recalled that when Edgar was studying for his law degree in the mid-1980s, his friends who worked in cocaine production would walk by and tease him: "Throw away those law books—what are they good for? Come work with us." But they repented after the boom was over, Amanda added with satisfaction. They came back to Edgar and said, "You were right, we should have studied." Amanda thus expressed superiority both for the legal manner and the route of education through which her family had achieved upward mobility.

We cannot rule out, as well, that the stagnation of the regional economy since the early 1990s, in which many professionals despaired of finding work, inspired Amanda to argue fiercely that her family's strategy had, in fact, been the wisest. The frustrated expectations of the coca and cocaine boom that Raquel described—"They must have thought that there would be money like that forever"—were echoed even by Amanda and Edgar about their own professional careers. They often complained that their earnings from their law practice were dwindling because customers could no longer pay the high fees of the height of the boom. Thousands of agronomists, lawyers, and architects were packing their bags to become nannies and construction workers in Spain before the Spanish economy collapsed in 2008. Several Choreños remarked in disappointment to me that "education no longer yields as much prosperity" (*el estudio ya no rinde tanto*) as they had once hoped. Truckers and merchants of licit goods similarly complained that they faced increasing competition and diminished earnings as the economy continued its decline.[15] The competition for middle-class legitimacy between professionals, merchants, and cocaine entrepreneurs was paired with a shared sense of frustrated expectations.

## Disillusionment of Impoverished Folk

Some Sacaba families, through all the ups and downs of the price of coca and the ambiguities of status, however, remained unambiguously identified by themselves and others as socially subordinate because of poverty. Bald César and his wife asserted their middle-class distinction by taking their children to an orthodontist; Doña Saturnina's children asserted their middle-class distinction by touting their education as professionals; other people could rarely afford bus fare, running water, or an electric hook-up. Their babies died from easily treatable infectious diseases. While the wealth of individual families had long been unequal in rural Bolivia, the coca boom and market liberalization furthered inequalities of wealth and consumption. Those who did not acquire land to grow coca during the beginning of the boom in the late 1970s were often unable to find land later, because rising land prices accompanied the rise in price of coca and cocaine (Healy 1986; Flores and Blanes 1984).[16] Others earned wealth in the boom but lost it owing to accidents, illness, or the military's confiscation of their product in the drug war. And so, while some Choreños like Bald César described their rise from rags to riches with pride and wonderment, others recounted continual frustration, often explaining their misfortune through their lack of access to coca.

The suffering of poverty is social, as well as economic. If wealthier people's assertions of racial and class superiority were painful for Doña Saturnina's children, the poorest people in Choro suffered the most. These poorer people were often the targets of outright insults couched in racist and classist language. Doña Gladys, a mother of six children in her late forties, still wept in 2006 whenever she remembered the slights she received at the age of sixteen when she moved to her husband's family home in Choro from a nearby highland community. She still spoke Spanish heavily accented with Quechua, having left school early to tend her family's sheep. Her husband's mother and sisters had scornfully called her "shepherdess" (*ovejera*). Her illiteracy and halting Spanish were readily available mannerisms for them to belittle in racialized terms.

These barbs were still fresh for Doña Gladys when I knew her, thirty years later, in large part because of her dire economic situation as a widow. She was nearly destitute following the Bolivian drug control army's confiscation of her $30,000 savings from coca or cocaine earnings, in addition to her furniture and refrigerator, in 1997. She often remarked on how her wealthier sisters-in-law would scorn the watery, nearly meatless, soups she prepared as only fit for dogs. Her daughters dropped out of school when she couldn't afford to pay for their bus fare and uniforms. Her poverty was all the more bitter because she had come to believe, during the flush time of the boom, that she had left the poverty of her childhood behind. Doña Gladys's family and others like them in Choro and throughout Sacaba served as a constant reminder to Amanda and other professional families of what they had escaped. These were also the people whom Amanda and her siblings criticized for improvidence in managing their money and worried would accuse them of being snobs.

Indeed, Choreños who were poorer than Doña Saturnina's family complained of the snobbery of "Chapareños," wealthier neighbors who accused them of laziness for not making their fortunes in the coca boom. For example, Don Felipe, a man who served as the paradigmatic "poor person" (*gente pobre*) among Doña Saturnina's neighbors in Choro, often railed against the Choreños who were wealthier from coca and cocaine work. Don Felipe said that his bitterness stemmed both from Chapareños having many things he lacked *and* from their blaming him for his poverty. He reported in 1998 that some people had asked him scathingly, "Don't you have feet" to migrate to the Chapare? Not only did they argue that he was poor because of laziness and having too many children but also that he lacked the will and entrepreneurial spirit to take the wealth lying everywhere in the Chapare ready for the collecting. Don Felipe told me that he replied airily to the Chapareños, "That's destiny for you!" but that he seethed inside. In fact, he had worked many years on and off in the Chapare and had harvested coca as a renter (*partidario*) entitled to half the profits—an arrangement that did not allow him to amass enough savings to buy land at the highly inflated prices of the boom time. And, like some other people who had not harvested wealth from the Chapare, he said that the Chapare's hot, humid, and insect-ridden climate—a "green hell"—had often made him ill. Don Felipe said in 1998, "People who have land in the Chapare have everything," but those who did not own land, like him, were excluded from prosperity.

Thus, if the coca boom allowed everyone in the Cochabamba valley region to imagine the possibility of becoming middle class as a professional or wealthy merchant, there were enormous differences in their possibilities of making good on this dream, even before the massive coca eradication campaign that began in 1998. The coca boom, along with the expansion of TV and other media images of plenty since economic free trade policies, had sparked intense and bitter frustrations in the accounts of many Choreños like Don Felipe and Doña Gladys. Their intertwined aspirations for higher status and longing for the means to consume caused intense emotional pain when they were surrounded by people who enjoyed relative plenty, like Doña Saturnina and Bald César.

In sum, the coca and cocaine booms deeply conditioned social hierarchies and distinctions as well as upward mobility in Sacaba and Choro. The boom deepened preexisting inequalities of wealth and status. The scarcity of opportunities for upward mobility in Bolivia's free-market economy— as farmers, doctors, lawyers, truckers, cocaine transporters, and as licit merchants—fostered intense competition for status. The boom supported an expansion of class horizons; these expectations were frustrated for some people by the intensification of the drug war in 1998, laying bare a free-market economy stripped of any cushion.


## Conclusion

I have argued that many Sacabans occupied ambiguous social identities. They identified their own and others' racial and class identity through terms that alternated between subordinate and superior. This was in part because the discursive categories of identity were polarized binaries—rich and poor, urban and rural—that did not capture their middling status. The coca boom sowed high aspirations for the achievement of middle-class prosperity by means of a new and, for a while bountiful, cash crop. The visible influx of TV images of prosperity that accompanied free-market policies contributed to these aspirations. Yet many Sacabans' expectations were frustrated in the wake of the war on drugs. Furthermore, the competing claims for social status between professionals like Amanda, merchants like Raquel the tavern keeper, and cocaine impresarios like Bald César elicited alternating expressions of ethics of social superiority and egalitarianism. At the same time, those who aspired to upward mobility feared the resentment of poorer people and accused them of envy. In short, this was a social environment characterized by highly charged intimate politics within families, communities, and the region.

This complex landscape of class and indigenous identity made especially fraught the sometimes contradictory goals promoted by social movements and the MAS party—redistribution of wealth within Bolivia, assertion of indigenous pride, support for limited coca growing, the transformation of Bolivia's subordinate economic status in the global economy—and, under the surface of political rhetoric, individual dreams for the attainment of middle-class status. Often unspoken alongside MAS leaders' pledges to promote indigenous power and redistribute wealth from rich to poor lay the fierce desires of coca growers, central players in the MAS party, for middle-class prosperity for themselves and their families.[17] The multiple aspirations of middling groups explored in this chapter, their ambivalence regarding social and economic equality, and the fundamental ambiguities about their social class and race within the recognized social categories of Bolivian society, had profound effects on governance and political culture under Bolivia's first elected leftist and indigenist MAS government. The next chapter considers how these middle-class aspirations shaped Sacabans' diverse responses to the election of Evo Morales and to the rise of the MAS party and other new Bolivian social movements.

# Middling Sacabans Respond to Evo and MAS

> The distinctive language of identity appears again when people seek
> to calculate how tacit belonging to a group or community can be
> transformed into more active styles of solidarity, when they debate
> where the boundaries around a group should be constituted and
> how—if at all—they should be enforced. Identity becomes a question
> of power and authority when a group seeks to realize itself in political
> form. This may be a nation, a state, a movement, a class, or some
> unsteady combination of them all.
>
> —Paul Gilroy, *Against Race: Imagining Political Culture*
> *Beyond the Color Line* (2000:99)

As she stepped through my front door in January 2006, a week after Evo
Morales's inauguration as president, Amanda fairly pounced on the newspaper on my kitchen table. She asked if it listed Evo's newly announced
cabinet ministers. I opened the newspaper and showed her the chart that
listed the ministers' names and pictures. This line of photos presented a
startling departure from those of prior administrations in that it included
several women. Amanda looked right at the photo of the new minister of
justice, who gazed soberly out from the page; her skin was dark and she
wore her hair in two braids. Amanda made a disgusted sound. I asked her
if she knew the minister and did not like her.[1] I had met her and liked
her, I said. She was Casimira Rodríguez, president of the Bolivian domestic
workers' union, who had successfully pushed the Bolivian government to
pass minimum wage and job protection legislation for maids and nannies
(*empleadas domésticas*) several years before. This had been a landmark legal

victory. Amanda laughed and said that she had not met Rodríguez, but, her voice rising with indignation, she did not like her for three reasons. "First, because she is Indian, second, because she is *de pollera*, and third, because she is not a lawyer, and so what does she know about the law? She doesn't know anything!" Amanda laughed again. She seemed tickled by her own vehemence—and by the succinctness with which she had formulated this tripartite distinction; she repeated it several times over the course of that afternoon.

Amanda's profession of social superiority—her intertwining of racism with the sentiment that higher education was a sign of moral legitimacy and a marker of competence—emerged clearly that afternoon. Yet when denouncing Minister of Justice Rodríguez, Amanda's laughter seemed to affirm, in my analysis, both that she disapproved of the presidential appointment and that she was making fun of herself for being a snob and racist. This double edge of racism and countervailing egalitarianism emerged more explicitly in a similar comment Amanda made in 2009 while criticizing a new MAS government minister of justice, Celima Torrico. Torrico was a *cholita*, like Rodríguez, and a longtime MAS party leader familiar to many people in Sacaba. This was three years after Evo's first-term inauguration, and *cholitas* in high-level government leadership positions were now more common. Amanda was in the midst of reminiscing wistfully to me and Edgar that she herself had enjoyed putting on a *pollera* each afternoon as a child when she returned home from elementary school. She stopped when she became a teenager, though, because it was against the rules to wear a *pollera* to high school and furthermore, "lawyers can't be *cholitas*." A few moments later, Amanda exclaimed that she hated Celima Torrico. When I asked why, she retorted severely, "Because she's a *chola*!" After a moment of thought, she laughed, as if trying to turn her comment into a joke, and added, "No, that's not why. It's because Celima Torrico promoted a law saying that law students can no longer work as legal assistants [*tramitadores*]."[2] Amanda had worked as a *tramitadora* before completing her law degree and sympathized with law students who might suffer economically without the option of this paraprofessional employment. That Amanda described her yearning to wear a *pollera* just before insulting Torrico as a *chola*, and then quickly denied hating the political leader for her *chola* race and class status, suggests that Amanda was ambivalent, repeatedly alternating between the assertion of superiority and egalitarianism. Amanda implied that on this occasion she was calling Torrico a *chola* because she was angry at her for her actions, rather than naming a self-evident race or class identity. This was in a similar fashion to Amanda's insulting her nephew by shouting "*black, Indian, ugly!*" when Teo annoyed her (see Chapter 2).

Amanda, like many other newly middle-class people in Sacaba, alternated between support for principles of superiority and egalitarianism. If the previous chapter demonstrated how these conflicting principles infused many middling Sacabans' intimate lives, in this chapter I show how these anxieties over race and class strongly shaped Sacabans' attempts to define themselves as political actors in the dramatic period just before and after Morales's ascent to power. Sacaba's middling folk struggled to establish how they personally fit into the models of citizenship actively debated in Bolivia in 2005 and 2006. Long-standing, conflicting imperatives to demonstrate both social superiority and egalitarianism were placed in further tension by the rise of Evo Morales and the MAS. As the first national party to claim actual political power for campesinos and indigenous people, MAS put increasing pressure on Bolivians to explicitly compare and contrast their identities to Evo's public persona and to the philosophies of redistribution of wealth and indigenous power. Middle-class Sacabans in 2005 and 2006, confronted with the MAS platform and the figure of Evo, expressed pride, anxiety, disgust, ambivalence, or sometimes a combination of all these sentiments.

Evo's much-touted identity as a subaltern person, in particular, prompted many Sacabans to rearticulate their own identities, but they did so in different ways; class and racial identity did not map onto political sentiments in predictable ways for people in the middle. Though the poorest people in Sacaba tended to be MAS supporters, there was great diversity of opinion and identification among the broad swath of people whose wealth and occupation placed them at the median for Sacaba and Bolivia. For the sake of simplicity, in the discussion that follows, I divide middling Sacabans into three groups based on how they identified themselves, keeping in mind that they did not always identify themselves neatly or permanently. In the first group, middling people identified themselves in opposition to Evo and the MAS party's assertions of indigenous and subaltern pride. In the second group, people allied themselves with MAS but termed themselves local elites. Finally, in the third group, MAS supporters who explicitly called themselves by subaltern categories also identified themselves as (or were accused of being) upwardly mobile in more subtle ways.

Middling Sacabans' attempts to fit themselves into polarized identity categories between elite (such as *rico, profesional, de dinero*) and subaltern (such as *pobre,* campesino, *rural, indio*) unleashed anxiety and resentment from those around them. Amanda and her siblings, for example, were often accused by other people in Sacaba as being untrue to their subalternity by rejecting MAS; some MAS leaders and activists, on the other hand, were accused by other MAS activists of falsely claiming subaltern status when they were really elites. People in all groups held multiple frames of civic engagement through which they imagined themselves as citizens on local, regional, and national scales. For example, some middle-class Sacabans professed to admire Evo immensely as a national leader, yet lamented that rural or poor Sacabans no longer acted subservient to them as members of the provincial elite. Such paradoxes in political life mirror middling Sacabans' anxiety in their personal lives over their social standing and alternating identification of themselves as elite and subaltern.

## Concerns of Middling Folk Who Explicitly Opposed Evo

As the MAS party began gaining power, Doña Saturnina's children espoused one pole of identification claimed by Sacabans, drawing middle-class distinctions in their opposition to the party and to Evo. Amanda and her siblings engaged in particularly active political and personal reflection during the months before and after Evo took power in 2005 and 2006. They drew on two decades of familiarity with him as a *cocalero* leader and an elected congressman from the Chapare, the coca-growing district. They expressed a number of strong reservations.

Some of their concerns about a potential MAS victory were practical. For example, Amanda expressed a resigned frustration regarding Bolivia's weak position in geopolitics, an articulation of Bolivian national identity that both accepted and protested the country's economic dependency and limited state sovereignty. Amanda often worried aloud in 2005 that if Evo were elected, the U.S. government would cut its considerable foreign aid to Bolivia. Such a concern was not trivial, given that the Bolivian government received half of its yearly budget from foreign aid and much of that came from the United States (Andersen and Evia 2003). President George W. Bush and several U.S. ambassadors to Bolivia had made abundantly clear that they abhorred the possibility of Evo's election and supported his right-wing rival, a wealthy, light-skinned Texas A&M graduate named Tuto Quiroga.[3] In October 2005, several months before the presidential election, Doña Saturnina and several of her children were watching campaign ads on television. When I said that I had heard that Evo was leading in public opinion polls, her son Edgar burst out irritably: "I don't want to hear anything more about Evo. They'll never let him be president!" His mother elaborated, "Because he's a campesino." Edgar retorted that it was because Evo would legalize coca and cocaine. "Who would allow that? The United States would invade!" he exclaimed. The two recent U.S. invasions of Iraq loomed large as forbidding examples for many Sacabans, as did the long-running U.S. war on drugs in Bolivia. Many jokes and serious discussions circulated as to whether the United States might ever invade Bolivia.

Another practical issue that concerned Amanda and many others in Sacaba (though it later proved unfounded) was that Evo would win but with less than 50 percent of the vote. Bolivian electoral law mandated that any election in which no candidate received an absolute majority would require that Congress choose any one of the top three candidates. These three candidates would, if history proved any guide, make a "devil's pact," casting aside their ideological opposition to each other in order to form a coalition government. Or even worse, Congress would select the right-wing candidate despite his coming in second or third place, and Evo's supporters would foment violent rebellion, or even a civil war. Such concerns expressed a weariness with decades of infighting and deal making among political leaders that had produced an erosion of parties' ideological platforms. Right-wing and left-wing party leaders had often made deals in order to get high-level government positions when they lost elections.

Amanda also urgently needed a job and this colored her perspective. While she worked with Edgar in his law office, she had little opportunity to develop her own clientele and she was not earning what she considered the equivalent of a full-time professional salary. It was common knowledge in Bolivia (as in most other countries in the world, including the United States), that volunteering on a winning political campaign could yield a paying job after the election; in Bolivia this was one of few routes to a middle-class job. Several of Amanda's friends, also underemployed college graduates from Choro, convinced her to volunteer with them on the campaign of Tuto, the right-wing candidate. Amanda hung Tuto's red PODEMOS party campaign banner in front of her mother's house in October 2005. Throughout November and December, she, Edgar, David, and

Deysi plus their nephew Teo wore Tuto's red T-shirt and baseball caps printed with the party's five-pointed white star logo. When bored, Teo could be found twirling around their cement courtyard brandishing an enormous, red Tuto flag. On the day of the election, Amanda and her younger sister Celia also volunteered as poll staffers for Tuto's party.

Yet this practical decision to support Tuto appeared to cause Amanda some inner conflict, not because of his origins in the superwealthy white elite, but because she doubted that he was looking out for the nation's best interests. In the early morning after the elections, Amanda, Deysi, and Edgar stared glumly at the TV as the results of Evo's resounding victory poured in. While we boiled water for breakfast in their tiny kitchen, I told Amanda that she seemed tired from standing at the polls the entire day before. "More than tired, I'm upset [*molestita*] with the election results, even though I didn't really want Tuto to win," she confessed dispiritedly. She found Tuto untrustworthy, a "*busca pegas*," she admitted, using the common Bolivian criticism of people who sought jobs through patronage relationships.[4] She implied that Tuto was merely hungry for wealth and power, rather than committed to public service. "Like everyone else," she explained, "he's looking out for his personal interest." She had favored another candidate who had ended up a distant third in the polls, Samuel Doria Medina, the millionaire owner of the Bolivian national Burger King franchise, because she thought his wealth made him less likely to steal public money. His status as an already powerful millionaire also meant that he must be seeking public service, rather than naked power. But Doria Medina's poll numbers had been consistently low, and Amanda implied that it had behooved her to invest her time in a party that was more likely to win and therefore to yield her a potential job after the election.

Another of Amanda and her siblings' many practical frustrations with Evo stemmed from their opposition to the road blockades, a form of political mobilization that Evo had often employed as coca growers' union leader and senator, as had many other MAS and social movement leaders. Like small businesspeople and urban residents dependent on interstate commerce (she and Edgar commuted by bus to their shared law office in the town of Sacaba), she often complained that Evo was "a blockader" (*Evo es muy bloqueador*). Doña Saturnina herself often said that she had never felt comfortable with the *cocalero* union's ready use of tumultuous protest and resented that their family had been required to send a representative to often-dangerous *cocalero* blockades.

Far beyond these practical concerns that troubled Doña Saturnina's children, however, Evo's race and class identification and the goals of political transformation that he and other MAS leaders promoted, seemed to trouble them most intensely. The sisters, during and after Evo's campaign, confronted the increasingly insistent demands for societal transformation from Bolivian social movements that centered as much on the premise that most Bolivians were indigenous and campesinos as on ending neoliberalism (Albro 2006; Lazar 2008; Postero 2007). The interests of Bolivia's superelite and social movement participants on a national scale were genuinely opposed. MAS and other social movements were attempting to decolonize one of the world's most unequal countries. Yet these categories of social opposition could be only imperfectly transposed onto the more fluid social environment of Sacaba municipality. Sacabans like Deysi and Amanda had to confront the question of whether their subjectivities—their self-identification in its broadest sense—would conform to the new definitions of a Bolivian citizen as subaltern and indigenous or if they would define themselves in opposition (see Ortner 2005:31; Luhrmann 2006). They could move in either direction, but there was little room for them to assert an alternate, middling identity.

The sisters were part of a cohort of Sacabans who rejected the MAS model of citizenship in their assertion of a middle-class, *profesional* identity. Yet Deysi and Amanda's ongoing process of self-identification was by no means simple. They shared with MAS several cherished ideals and symbols promoted by Bolivian governments and popular movements since the 1940s. As the sisters and others like them in Sacaba began to define themselves in opposition to the ideals promoted by Evo and the MAS, however, they often asserted different interpretations of the symbols used by MAS leaders.

Agrarian unions, deeply influential in Bolivian politics since the 1940s, provided part of Deysi and Amanda's repertoire of symbols in constructing their identities and understanding of Bolivian history. As rural leaders began to organize for an end to servitude of indigenous campesinos during the 1940s—which they successfully accomplished in western Bolivia with the 1953 Agrarian Reform—they also attempted to redefine their followers' identity in ways that would promote collective political action. Agrarian leaders of the 1940s emphasized a series of dichotomies: of working class (*popular*) versus bourgeois, campesino versus large landowner (*patrón*), and rural versus urban. Many symbolic markers of identity that agrarian leaders used in the 1940s and 1950s became common currency throughout western Bolivia. As regional leaders traveled the Cochabamba valleys giving speeches to community groups urging them to form *sindicatos,* local agrarian unions, they emphasized visible symbols of identity through which their audience could define themselves in opposition to large landowners: rubber sandals salvaged from automobile tires in contrast to landowners' leather lace-up shoes; old hats and disheveled hair in contrast to landowners' hair slicked back with pomade (Dandler 1975). In drawing these distinctions, they were influenced by urban trade unions that conceived of societies as divided between capitalists and industrial workers and by the Spanish definition of colonial society as divided between an urban nation of Spaniards and rural nation of Indians. These polarized terms of identity were useful for political mobilization, even as they glossed over many intermediate social identities Bolivians held. In contrast to previous Bolivian power relations, agrarian leaders privileged the language and symbols of class— labeling rural folk campesinos and plebeians (*clase popular*)—and deemphasizing the indigenous race and culture that had dominated Bolivian terms of identification.

MAS leaders of the 2000s continued to emphasize the vision of Bolivia as comprised of two opposed camps while reinfusing revolutionary-era political symbols—like *polleras*—with indigenous racial and cultural meaning. People like Amanda and Deysi, by contrast, in their moments of egalitarianism, identified themselves through revolutionary categories like campesina while emptying them of both racial and political meaning. The sisters' refusal of political and racial content for terms of identity has its history in the symbols and models of citizenship promoted by the MNR, the National Revolutionary Movement (Movimiento Nacional Revolucionario) that governed during the 1950s, and the subsequent dictatorial governments of the 1960s. The MNR government tried to foster racial assimilation by squelching indigenous racial and ethnic terms of identification and promoting a common mestizo identity for all Bolivians. MNR leaders encouraged mobilization around class identities when it benefitted the government, as when they recruited agrarian unions grateful for land reform to repress striking miners. In other ways, however, the MNR government did not acknowledge inequalities in Bolivian society differences, arguing that rural folk were national citizens first and foremost. The revolutionary government and subsequent military governments tried to bind the loyalty of rural Bolivians to the government through clientelism. They downplayed the notion that campesinos and superelites, such as the large landowners that had moved to the eastern tropics and were receiving massive government grants of land and subsidies, held opposing interests. In addition to accepting these politically vacuous meanings for symbols of identity, many middling Sacabans in 2005 and 2006 did not question the 1950s revolutionary government's continuation of the Spanish colonial separation of Bolivia into urban cores and rural hinterlands. This conceptual division of rural and urban social identities was institutionalized in separate—and unequal—rural and urban bureaucracies for education, health, and economic development.

Middling Sacabans like Doña Saturnina's children also drew on the halfhearted government turn toward multiculturalism in the 1990s, during the height of free-market reforms. 1990s government leaders had begun to recognize many Bolivians' indigenous identity for the first time since the 1950s, formally acknowledging Bolivia as a majority indigenous country. They began urging all Bolivians to take pride in the country's cultural diversity as expressed, for example, in clothing, food, and language. This multiculturalism was very limited, despite borrowing symbols and rhetoric from militant transnational and Bolivian indigenous rights movements and from older romantic portrayals of indigenous culture. Critics of the government promotion of multiculturalism argued that political leaders saw the recognition of indigenous culture as an easy substitute for significant redistribution of wealth and power to actual indigenous persons, a way to coopt political movements led by indigenous people, and a distraction from the widespread suffering resulting from free-market reforms (Postero 2007; Paulson and Calla 2000; Canessa 2005; see also Hale 2002 and 2005).[5]

Deysi and Amanda participated actively in the national government's revival of interest in the less political elements of indigenous culture prior to the rise of the MAS. They often framed their enthusiasm through the idiom of patriotism. They were avid fans of what they termed ''national music'' sung by musicians dressed in indigenous clothing and featuring highland indigenous instruments such as panpipes and flutes. On weekends they piled together onto Amanda's or Deysi's bed in front of the television and watched live musical reviews of dozens of groups playing music billed as traditional and representative of each region of the country. The sisters professed disgust for *cumbia*, a pan-Latin American genre of pop-rock, invariably asserting that national music was better. They collected mementos made from handwoven, embroidered wool cloth sold in Cochabamba's tourist markets and displayed them in their bedrooms. Their tastes may well have developed in high school and college, as several of their less highly educated friends and relatives admitted that they felt little affinity for national music. None of this enthusiasm for cultural artifacts and performance challenged Deysi and Amanda's sense of themselves as successful professionals who were attempting to overcome the stigma of being born into a poor, rural, and indigenous family.

The sisters explicitly identified themselves in direct opposition to MAS. They deplored the party and movement's militant rhetoric and most of its demands. MAS leaders and those of allied groups in fact employed many of the symbols and ideals already in circulation in Bolivia—class opposition developed by agrarian revolutionaries during the 1940s, militant indigenous pride of activists during the 1970s and 1980s, transnational indigenous rights rhetoric (Albro 2006; Postero 2007; see also CSUTCB 1987), and 1990s government reformers' multiculturalism and romanticizing of indigenous culture (Postero 2010). But Sacabans like Amanda firmly opposed MAS leaders' depiction of Bolivian society as riven by class and racial injustice that made redistribution of wealth and power to an indigenous majority necessary (see Hahn 1991; CSUTCB 1987; for a critique see Dunkerley 2007).[6]

Doña Saturnina's family and many other middling Sacabans opposed MAS, and Evo as a model indigenous leader, in part because MAS' militant models for campesino-indigenous citizenship challenged their goal of raising their social status and in part because they feared that the new government might initiate redistribution policies to confiscate their hard-won wealth or potential future wealth. When national MAS leaders argued that the structural conflict between elites and subalterns could only be resolved through the massive redistribution of wealth, as well as the equalization of political and social power, people like Marisol, Deysi, and Amanda seemed to fear losing their hard-won prosperity and social prestige. In fact, neither government rhetoric nor policy aimed at middling folk. When Román Loayza, a MAS party leader, for example, argued that *"q'aras"* (white urbanites) should cede political control of the country and allow for the transfer of much of their wealth to the indigenous *"nosotros"* (us), he was not referring to people like Deysi as either the elites or the subalterns (CSTUCB 2006). MAS leaders consistently denounced "oligarchies" of landowners in eastern Bolivia who owned thousands of acres and oppressed landless and impoverished campesinos. MAS and allied leaders marshaled indigenous symbols such as the rainbow *wiphala* flag and the *ayllu*, a highland Andean form of indigenous community organization, to promote indigenous political power and the redistribution of wealth to indigenous people. Movement activists also held up indigenous rebel heroes of the eighteenth and nineteenth centuries as models for action and consciousness (Hylton and Thomson 2007; Villarroel 2008). MAS leaders promoted the notion that all Bolivians should "live well enough" (*buen vivir, sumaq qamana*), that is, live modestly, but not luxuriously (e.g., MAS-IPSP 2005:43). These symbols and demands did not appeal to some upwardly mobile Sacabans like Amanda, and often frightened them. In the mutually reinforcing process through which they developed their political perspectives and their racial and class self-categorization, Amanda and Deysi grouped themselves with elites and feared on their own (and elites') behalf.

The most visible symbol of MAS, and the object of much of Amanda and Deysi's frustration, was Evo's public persona as a subaltern indigenous leader. According to many published accounts and trumpeted by his supporters, Evo was born into a destitute, rural, Aymara-speaking family in the drought-stricken highland department of Oruro (e.g., Stefanoni and do Alto 2006; Sivak 2008). Three of his five brothers and sisters died in infancy from easily treatable communicable diseases. He moved with his parents to the Chapare in the 1980s when the coca boom was at its height, learning some Quechua and rising rapidly in the ranks of coca growers' federation leaders. Speculation ran rife as to whether or not he had completed high school, despite the publication of his high school graduation photo (e.g., Stefanoni and do Alto 2006). His origins in poverty in a remote, rural community; his speech with an indigenous accent; his story of working his way up to high levels of leadership through an agrarian union to the pinnacle of formal political power while lacking a professional degree—all this made Evo a model of subalternity, fitting squarely into the poor, indigenous, rural majority of the "two Bolivias" model. Doña Saturnina's children were appalled.

Their vehement rejection was often expressed in racial terms, which I interpreted as internalized racism and shame at seeing the glorification of the indigenous and impoverished identity that they had struggled so hard to shake off. When the election results began to trickle in at midnight on December 18, 2005, showing that MAS had won more than 51 percent of the vote, Amanda burst out in a shocked tone, "That Indian will govern us!" As Evo's image appeared on the TV screen, she wailed, "How can we have a president with such a face?" To an outsider, Amanda would have belonged to the same race as Evo—her skin, hair, eyes, and facial features were similar to his; she complained of it herself. Her family origins were similar, though her hometown of Choro was less identified with indigeneity than Evo's highland Aymara-speaking hometown. But her racist epithets expressed the force of her disappointment as well as her attempts to assert her middle-class distinction in contrast to Evo's identification of himself as belonging to the *indio* race and the campesino class.

Other self-identified professionals in Sacaba expressed similar sentiments about Evo's and his allies' racial inferiority. "The campesino race [*raza campesina*] doesn't know how to govern!" exclaimed Don Pedro, a middle-aged teacher who lived in Choro, several days before the 2005 election. Don Pedro had been a coca grower with a high school diploma but no college degree before earning a teaching degree in his forties. Don Pedro assured me that the inaction of the few indigenous members of congress elected during the previous electoral cycle boded poorly for Evo's competence as president. His reference to the "campesino race" brought to the fore the way in which the class terms that Bolivian governments since the MNR of the 1950s had promoted in place of racial terms like *indio* had in fact taken on racialized meanings (see also de la Cadena 2000). "Look," Don Pedro exclaimed to me as he rode a public bus from Choro to the Sacaba racquetball club, his gym suit rustling as he waved his arms for emphasis. "Look at all the senators who are from indigenous groups. They have their special clothes, they have their feathers [*headdresses*], but they haven't done anything!" Don Pedro seemed to be simultaneously arguing that the new political leaders who made visible displays of indigeneity were incompetent on racial grounds and that they were substituting the promotion of indigenous culture for substantive legislation.

Amanda's and some other Choreños' opposition to Evo and MAS also stemmed from Evo's lack of a professional degree, a deficiency in which racial and class were inseparable, in which Evo's "Indian face" was simply another facet of his nonprofessional, campesino class status. If Amanda and her siblings had "sacrificed so much" in order to succeed in life, they implied, Evo's refusal to follow this path devalued education as both a moral and practical necessity. Other Choro residents who were students or professionals similarly remarked that Evo's lack of education made him unfit for office. A psychology student living in Cochabamba City, the daughter of a prosperous Choro farmer, told me that she agreed with her psychology professor's recent comment in class: because Evo was not "educated" (*preparado*), his would be a "puppet" government—he would be a figurehead for the elite, nonindigenous professional advisors who would do the substantive work.

An agronomist and MAS supporter who directed a Sacaba NGO that promoted indigenous pride interpreted such statements as internalized shame. He remarked in frustration in early January 2006 that many Choreños had voted against Evo after asking themselves, "How can we vote for that Indian?" He viewed this as false consciousness. This was especially vexing to him because a central goal of his NGO was to try to reawaken indigenous pride in local residents, to help them embrace their indigenous cultural heritage and self-identification (see Chapter 6).

Yet as I showed in Chapter 1, Amanda and many other Sacabans alternated between racialized self-hatred and assertions of social equality. In fact, sometimes she and her sister argued that they opposed Evo because of their own commitment to equality. Evo's supporters included the wealthy and snobbish (*creído*) midlevel cocaine producers in Choro, they said, who snubbed her family as less wealthy and denied that she and her siblings held better claims to upward mobility because they were more highly educated.

The political sentiments of Amanda and other newly prosperous Sacabans who opposed MAS were also deeply shaped by their analysis of the coca boom as a time of moral disintegration. They often expressed fear that Evo, as the longtime leader of the coca growers' union, would bring about a return to the debauchery and social disorder that had reigned during the 1980s. Amanda and her siblings, like their neighbor Don Pedro, repeatedly worried aloud during the lead-up to the 2005 election that Evo's election would mean a "free trade in narcotraffic." On the day after the presidential election, Deysi and Amanda gazed bleary eyed and horror stricken at the television screen on which MAS supporters were depicted as ebullient, celebrating Evo's campaign promise to nationalize the natural gas industry. Deysi announced dramatically, "Now, what is going to be nationalized is . . . narcotraffic!"

Even their moral opposition to MAS because of its championing of coca growing was not straightforward. In fact, they professed a complex stance of both loyalty to and rejection of the coca growers' union. Doña Saturnina and her children had often pointed out to me that they owed their college education to coca even though they resented the stringent demands of the *cocalero* leadership that they participate in the union's frequent and dangerous public protests. I had many conversations with Amanda and her family over the years in which they eagerly debated among themselves the benefits and drawbacks of the coca and cocaine booms for their own family, for friends and neighbors in Choro, and for the country as a whole. Once in late 2005, several months before the election, Amanda chuckled while musing about what would occur if Evo were elected, declaring that her whole family might move back to the Chapare to grow vast quantities of coca. Her tone had been joking and lighthearted, but she then eagerly began calculating the exact income she could earn from various amounts of land planted in coca. Similarly, in 2009, after criticizing friends and neighbors at length because they "didn't know how to take advantage" of the coca boom—had not amassed savings to build a home, start a successful business, or pay for a professional degree—Amanda sighed and said about the boom time of the 1980s, "Ay, I wish those times would return." When I asked why, she laughed gaily and said: "To make myself a little money, of course!" Clearly, such analyses of the harms of the coca and cocaine economies entailed a moral analysis of how coca or cocaine earnings were spent; that cocaine earnings were "easy money" made it especially difficult to save those earnings to invest in a productive enterprise (see Chapter 2). Their evaluations of the new political party in power thus reflected a core element of new middle-class identity in Bolivia: the drawing of moral distinctions to show that one had spent one's money productively on professional education or a prosperous business.

If these middling Sacabans' repudiation of MAS for championing coca growing was not straightforward, they also admitted feeling concerns about their relatives' and neighbors' judgment of them as snobbish and disloyal. Deysi and Amanda often told me with chagrin about receiving flack from friends and neighbors for not supporting MAS, arguing that they should be grateful to the coca growers' union, which had directly benefited them. Some of their MAS activist neighbors also complained directly to me that Doña Saturnina's children were mistaken in believing that they could leave behind their identity as campesinos by rejecting MAS.

There was one more significant reason why Sacaba's middling folk opposed the MAS platform: they hated the idea of redistribution of wealth. As Marisol expressed in Chapter 1 when she explained why she opposed the MAS government's push for confiscation and redistribution of the massive estates in the eastern tropics, many middling Sacabans worried that the principle of redistribution of wealth, and land redistribution in particular, would harm them personally. In 2009, Edgar exclaimed thoughtfully to me while we were chatting, "I don't like socialism; I don't even like the name." He explained that he liked "freedom" (*libertad*), and worried that under socialism, every detail of his daily life would be regimented, from waking to sleeping. This last concern was likely a response to right-wing TV and radio commercials that threatened that Evo's government would make Bolivia "like Cuba" and repress personal liberties down to restrictions on everyday clothing. Supporters of Evo and "socialism" wanted everyone to be "equalized" (*igualado*), Edgar complained. "But in La Paz, Oruro, Potosí [highland regions of Bolivia], there are people who are extremely poor." Edgar continued, "If I owned two houses . . . ," he trailed off. The implication was clear: he feared that the government might confiscate one of his houses to redistribute to those impoverished people. Edgar resumed plaintively, "But I work. A renter who lives in my house would get ownership of one of my two houses and that wouldn't be fair. They [MAS] want to equalize wealth [*igualar*] even though not everyone is working equally. So I like capitalism, not socialism." Edgar's tone was affable, bemused, and a bit introspective. He seemed to be earnestly asking himself why he didn't like the idea of redistribution of wealth. His criticisms echoed those of the prosperous rose grower in Chapter 2, who had accused her neighbors of envy several years before Evo's election, complaining, "They don't want anyone to get ahead; they want everything equalized. They want only equality." In this particular instance, Edgar's middle-class values of upward mobility and economic achievement clashed directly with the MAS party's rhetoric of redistribution of wealth and living modestly.

Surprisingly, even Doña Cinda, Edgar's common-law wife, expressed concerns similar to those of Edgar and Marisol about the MAS platform of redistribution of wealth, even though she had much less to lose economically from redistribution of wealth, and in my view, in her class and racial standing, than did her sometime-husband. When I asked her in 2009 what she thought of Evo's government, she replied in Quechua: "I don't think it's so great [*mana as tumpa waleqchu, nini noqaqa*]." She said she didn't like the idea of the redistribution of wealth (*redistribución*). After having moved repeatedly from one rented house to another during her fourteen years with Edgar, the two of them had finally built a two-room, adobe house together, though Edgar rarely stayed there. They borrowed heavily from a neighbor for the construction. The rooms had dirt floors and no glass in its windows—much more Spartan than Edgar's mother's house—

but Cinda was thrilled to have a permanent home at last. She and Edgar had also bought a plot of land nearby that they had hoped to sell at a $10,000 profit (land speculation was widespread and values were skyrocketing throughout Sacaba municipality). She dreamed this would provide her with a nest egg to launch a small business venture selling used medical uniforms over the border in Brazil. She worried, however, that under the MAS government's proposed redistribution, her currently unused plot of land would be confiscated to redistribute to some poorer person. As with Edgar, some of Cinda's concerns likely responded to the barrage of right-wing denunciations on TV and radio sponsored by superwealthy landowners in eastern Bolivia. MAS leaders had vehemently denied that they intended to redistribute the property of any but the wealthiest Bolivians. Like Marisol, Doña Cinda expressed a sentiment common to people of greater wealth and higher status. It was her aspiration, in this case, rather than her current wealth and social status, that sparked her concern that she would lose what little she had gained after years of financial hardship. And ironically, her financial hardship had been caused in part by Edgar's unwillingness to taint himself by marriage to a lower-status *chola*—precisely the category of Bolivian that the national MAS party was attempting to represent.

## Watching the Inauguration from Deysi's Room

These racial and class fears among Sacaba's new middle class demonstrate how such identities were not simple. The moral distinctions they drew between themselves and those around them shaped their evaluation of the MAS party and indigenous social movements, but many of these evaluations were ambivalent. Their rejection of the MAS platform and of Evo as a campesino-indigenous leader was not utter and total, given the alternation in their personal lives between ethics of egalitarianism and ethics of superiority and between self-identification as campesino or *profesional*.

While these middling folk often denounced the notion of economic redistribution and racial and class democracy and professed shame in campesino and Indian identities, in other moments they expressed puzzlement, uncertainty, and occasionally grudging acceptance. Raymond Williams' (1977) notion of "structures of feeling"—the emotionally intense quality of experience during moments of historical flux, when identities and political sentiments are particularly fluid—captures Sacabans' and many Bolivians' active work on their own identities during this time.

Amanda and her siblings' responses to Evo's inauguration ceremonies in 2006 elicited a discussion of their structure of feeling: the variety of symbols of citizenship they drew from prior political movements and government reforms and their ongoing shock at Evo's disruption of the previous narrative of elite rule. I watched the preinaugural ceremony on TV with Doña Saturnina's children in their home in Choro that January. The preinauguration, a day before Evo's swearing-in was to be held in the Bolivian Senate, had been billed as the "Andean inauguration ceremony." It was broadcast live from Tiwanaku, a pre-Inca indigenous ceremonial site and popular tourist destination in the Bolivian highlands. Amanda, Deysi, and their youngest sister, Celia, sat on the bed in Deysi's room, cuddling together for warmth under handwoven wool blankets in front of the TV, as they often did on weekends.

When Deysi tuned in, Evo was standing in the midst of a group of people dressed in white tunics with brightly colored designs clearly intended as re-creations of pre-Conquest indigenous Aymara royal regalia. Evo wore a red tunic with multicolored block pattern in black, yellow, and white over his trademark blue and red striped sweater. A square skullcap with orange, white, and red embroidered geometric patterns perched on his head. He held an intricately carved wooden staff inlaid with gold and copper that was taller than he was. Around his neck hung a luxurious garland of white and purple flowers. The people around him were lighting ceremonial incense bundles similar to those sold in Bolivian open-air markets, and the camera showed close-ups of the burning of a llama fetus, a common element of indigenous Andean ritual. A crowd of several thousand people stood at the base of the ancient ruins, next to several small adobe houses and a rural schoolhouse. Behind them stretched the Altiplano, an expanse of flat green and yellow plains bordered by low hills painted in a patchwork of small farm plots.

Evo then gave a speech while standing at the Puerta del Sol, an imposing and intricately carved rectangular stone door that was regularly pictured on tourist pamphlets. He extolled the pre-Columbian accomplishments of Andean peoples such as the Inca and Aymara. Deysi and Amanda, like most Bolivians, usually agreed with this kind of valorizing of the grandeur of ancient Andean civilizations. When a television commentator stated that Evo was "giving respect back to [*revindicando*] *indios*," however, Deysi rejected Evo's racial claim. Countering with the language of the 1952 revolutionary government, which had attempted to end indigenous racial identification by declaring all Bolivians to be patriotic mestizos, Deysi declared "We are not *indios*! We are *Bolivianos*." Evo described how *indios* had been marginalized since the time of the conquest, through Bolivian independence in 1825, to the present: "In 1825, when Bolivia was founded, Aymaras, Quechuas, and Guaranis were excluded and marginalized from the new republic, which had achieved its independence thanks to the struggle of thousands or millions of indigenous people. That is why the native peoples [*pueblos originarios*] clamor to refound Bolivia through the Constitutional Assembly" (MAS 2006: 15). This claim of long-term exclusion left the sisters unmoved, or maybe, ashamed. Amanda poked fun at the way that Evo pronounced "twenty-five," complaining that he had an Aymara accent and could not speak Spanish well.

After Evo's speech, a series of people whom the TV commentators identified as "international indigenous representatives" struggled up the steep stone steps of Tiwanaku to stand next to Evo at the top. Each made a statement extolling his inspirational leadership of indigenous peoples throughout the Americas and handed him a symbolic object. Their presence reflected the expansion of transnational indigenous rights movements since the 1990s. These movements' rise entailed a shift throughout Latin America from political organizing around campesino identity, as agrarian unions had done in the 1940s and 1950s in Bolivia, to organizing around ethnicity and culture since the passage of the influential United Nations (International Labour Organization) Indigenous and Tribal Peoples Convention in 1989 (Jung 2003; Postero 2007; Hale 2005; Warren 1998; Jackson and Warren 2002, 2005). While representatives from Ecuador, Mexico, Colombia, Canada, the Philippines, and Argentina clambered up the steps, Amanda, Deysi, and Celia were distracted, giggling and elbowing each other. They were calling each other *ch'utillas,* a Quechua term meaning "imitator of foreign ways." Collapsing in gales of laughter, they teased Amanda for being, like Evo: an "*india ch'utilla*," an uppity or pretentious Indian. It seemed that they were projecting their disapproval of or shame at Evo's bold claims for indigenous power, and for himself as an indigenous leader, into a joke on their sister. Deysi complained that George W. Bush would be contemptuous if he saw Evo's preinaugural ceremony. With mock dismay, she drew on her catechist training to paraphrase the Bible, imitating what she would say to the then-U.S. president, in Quechua: "Forgive them; they know not what they've done [*Mana yachankuchu imatachus ruasqankuta*]!" Her sisters burst into more gales of laughter at her ironic expression of embarrassment that Bolivia's head of state was presenting Bolivian modernity as deeply shaped by indigenous tradition.

Yet Deysi and Amanda expressed support for a circumscribed version of indigenous cultural expression, in keeping with the mild multiculturalism of the Bolivian governments of the 1990s. After the preinaugural ceremony ended, the scene moved to a TV studio. Three commentators faced the audience, including two slender women who looked like most Bolivian television newscasters, with light complexions, sleek hair, and form-fitting clothes. They sat next to a man whose clothing was uncommon among newscasters on the conservative Bolivian news channels: he wore a neatly trimmed beard; glasses with round, John Lennon–style frames; a vest woven in an indigenous pattern. He was speaking in Aymara. Deysi and Amanda commented in an interested and approving tone that the television channel would translate the entire inauguration ceremony the next day into Aymara, Quechua, and Guarani—the three most commonly spoken indigenous languages in Bolivia and rarely aired on television. Their approval of multilingual news broadcasts suggested that they supported depoliticized cultural expressions of identity. Moments earlier, they had rejected Evo's depiction of them as *indios* and affirmed instead with nationalist fervor that they were "Bolivians" when Evo argued that the interests of *indios* were in conflict with those of Bolivian elites. The Aymara television interpreter, by contrast, did not elicit this conflict.

Their support for a circumscribed indigenous culture separated from class, race, and politics emerged again shortly afterward when they switched channels to watch some Bolivian folkloric music videos.[7] The first video showed a group of about forty men and women singing and dancing in the middle of a vast field in the Bolivian highland Altiplano, accompanied by llamas. The women dancers and singers wore black, calf-length dresses belted at the waist and their hair in cornrows, costumes meant to invoke the Chipaya, a small indigenous group based in the Bolivian Altiplano often reputed to be the "most indigenous" in Bolivia. One of the sisters praised the song and video enthusiastically. This was yet another occasion in which they listened avidly to Bolivian folkloric music. They regularly bought and borrowed DVDs of music videos and watched weekly folklore shows on TV. Deysi's bedroom walls held several posters of Bolivian folklore groups that used native Andean instruments such as guitarlike *charangos* and panpipes.

The next day, Deysi and Amanda explained to me, as we prepared to watch the formal inauguration together from Deysi's bed, that they opposed MAS out of resentment at the local MAS activists they knew personally in Sacaba. They laughed while telling how Edgar had scolded them for taking down the right-wing PODEMOS flag, which had hung outside their house for several months. Deysi explained to me that part of the reason they had removed the flag was because they received flack from the many MAS supporters they knew. Several neighbors had confronted her, saying, "As if you all are not Chapareños?" implying that the family was ungrateful to Evo and the MAS for the money they had earned as coca growers for many years that had put them through college. They reiterated to each other—as much as justified to me—that they had supported Tuto mostly because of their outrage at the actions of local MAS leaders. Jaime, the MAS congressman representing this district, had helped his hometown steal Choro's irrigation water rights and had starved Choro of development projects by funneling regional development funds exclusively to his hometown. Overall, they argued to me, he had accomplished "nothing" in congress. The Sacaba MAS mayor had similarly accomplished nothing. They added that MAS supporters in Choro wanted to "force" (*obligar*) everyone to go to party rallies and vote for the MAS. These pushy MAS activists were not motivated by ideological zeal for the MAS platform but were merely (like Tuto himself) *busca pegas*: self-interested job seekers. These neighbors attempted to rally Choreños to show up for MAS events in the hopes of getting a municipal patronage job in the MAS-controlled Sacaba municipal government. And this was especially unfair to Amanda, since she was at that moment underemployed as Edgar's legal assistant. The sisters implied that they would have respected MAS supporters if they had thought that their support came from ideological beliefs rather than economic self-interest. Several years later, for example, Deysi told me that she admired a new friend who was a MAS supporter "*por convicción*" (out of conviction) in contrast to most other supporters she knew, who joined MAS "just to get a job."

As the TV focused in on Evo and the vice president–elect Álvaro García Linera slowly approaching the Senate building through streets lined by cheering crowds, Amanda returned to her sentiments of racial and class shame during the previous day's preinauguration. "I'm embarrassed" that Evo was not wearing a suit and tie, she said. Deysi countered knowingly, "But the campesinos would kill him" if he wore a tie. National and local

MAS activists had, indeed, long denounced "tie-wearing" (*corbatayoq*) elites for their oppression of poor people. Women and men from Choro who were not party activists, and therefore not immersed in party rhetoric, also complained bitterly that *corbatayoq* men and women in city and provincial offices discriminated against them for wearing *polleras* or speaking haltingly in Spanish. Evo's frequent declarations in recent months that he would never wear a tie as president spoke to the potency of ties as a symbol.

When, however, Evo came into view wearing a custom-made, long, black leather jacket with a woven wool strip in natural creams, browns, and grays displayed across the front, Amanda seemed to change her opinion. She exclaimed in an impressed, mildly surprised tone that Evo was "holding his own" (*se está defendiendo*), which literally means "he's defending himself." She used the same term (*defenderse*) with which, in their family narrative, her father had vowed to educate his children after he was insulted by a policeman in his own youth, and which Sacabans commonly spoke of as a primary benefit of education (see Chapter 2). Amanda appeared to agree with later public commentators that Evo had arrived at a suitable level of formality, projecting the appropriate gravitas of a president and deftly escaping the fraught symbolism of suits and ties (e.g., Stefanoni and do Alto 2006).

As Evo and his procession entered the Senate building, the camera panned over an enormous crowd filling the Plaza Murillo, La Paz's largest public space and a traditional site of marches and protests. These staunch MAS and Evo supporters contrasted with Doña Saturnina's children in their wholehearted support for indigenous pride and redistribution of wealth. Some in the crowd carried *wiphalas*, flags composed of squares in rainbow colors, the emblem of Andean indigenist social movements. Many also waved the Bolivian flag and the MAS party flag of blue, white, and black, illustrating the diversity of the ideological roots—indigenist, union, nationalist, party based—that had brought Evo to the presidency.

Amanda's brief moment of admiration for Evo's inaugural clothes soon shifted to outrage, however. When Evo took his oath of office, he held up his left hand rather than the customary right hand; Deysi and Amanda both cried out in surprise and irritation. They asked each other why he could not make the sign of the cross with thumb and index finger, as was standard for Bolivian leadership swearing-in ceremonies. Evo was swearing the oath of office to the Pachamama, the Andean Earth Mother, rather than to God! They, like other Choreños, half-reverently toasted the Pachamama while

*Figure 4.* Evo Morales's inaugural portrait, 2006. Source: Movimiento al Socialismo, 2006.

drinking with friends, and poured alcohol into the soil "to the Pacha-mama" when planting and harvesting. They also, like many Choreños and Cochabamba residents, often sanctified their home by burning incense and clay figurines to the Pachamama on the first Friday of the month. But Deysi and Amanda implied here that invoking an indigenous deity like the Pachamama, lighting incense, or burning llama fetuses could be acceptable for private moments but was shocking, and perhaps, shameful, to feature in public affairs of state.

Evo then gave an extemporaneous speech lasting an hour and forty-five minutes in which he declared that 62.2 percent of Bolivia was indigenous and that indigenous people had been marginalized since the Spanish con-quest. As she had the day before, Deysi questioned Evo's assertion that those who had been termed campesinos since the 1950s should now identify themselves as indigenous and that they needed to shake off colonial oppression. Deysi looked at me with a puzzled expression, and said slowly that the issue was not that "they [elite Bolivians] have marginalized Indians." Really, it was just the current economic recession, "*la crisis.*" Where Evo diagnosed widespread structural racism as causing poverty, Deysi maintained that all Bolivians, wealthy and poor, were experiencing shared and temporary economic suffering. Deysi's puzzlement suggests that she did not connect the MAS party's opposition to racialized discrimination to the policeman's insults to her father on the fateful occasion that he decided to send his children to college. Nor did she connect discrimination to her continual joking about her brothers being "dark" and "ugly," described in Chapter 2, and which, only the day before, she had expressed in teasing her sister Amanda as being an "uppity Indian."

The sisters' attention was waning; they were chatting with each other when Evo declared that he was proud that urban "professionals" had voted for MAS in droves. These members of the established Bolivian middle classes had surprised many pundits by voting overwhelmingly for Evo. He and other MAS leaders had made a deliberate decision to appeal to them by choosing Álvaro García Linera, a very light-skinned intellectual from a wealthy urban family, as his running mate. García Linera had been a longtime ardent leftist and fighter for indigenous rights but did not identify himself as indigenous or poor. With a characteristically militant speech-making expression on his face that revealed his longtime union leadership, index finger jabbing emphatically toward the ceiling, Evo continued that middle classes and wealthier elites must continue to give up some of their historical social and economic privileges:

> We all have the right to live in this life, on this earth. . . . [T]he result of the national elections . . . is the combination of social conscience with professional capacity. Here you can see that the native, indigenous movement is not exclusive; it is inclusive. I hope, I hope that others will also learn from us.[8] . . . I invite you to feel proud of the indigenous peoples, who are the moral reserve of humanity. (MAS 2006:30)

Evo was formally inviting urban middle-class professionals, and in veiled language, the superwealthy of eastern Bolivia, to respect indigenous culture and indigenous people. Such a widespread sea change in attitudes would entail an enormous redistribution of social and political power, he implied. Meanwhile, Doña Saturnina's children were expressing in multiple ways the lack of resonance that Evo's proposal to middle classes held for them—of indigenous pride, of excitement at subalterns achieving formal political power, of the commitment to coca growing.

Yet their tone softened moments later, revealing ways in which Evo's public persona also encapsulated some of their own fierce narrative of individual upward mobility. Their father entered Deysi's doorway. Just over eighty years old, Don Prudencio had suffered a brain injury during an accident several years before. Even after major surgery, his speech was indistinct and he was often disoriented. He watched Evo's speech intently for several moments and then remarked with uncharacteristic lucidity that Evo had improved his accent (*Ha mejorado su habla*). His three children laughed fondly and explained that their father knew Evo personally. In this country of only ten million people, and particularly in Sacaba, home to many coca growers, politics was intimate; many people knew Evo. Don Prudencio had listened to Evo's heavily Aymara-accented Spanish since the 1980s, when Evo had been first elected secretary of sports of a local coca growers' union. Their fond laughter conveyed an echo of his admiration at Evo's ability to diminish his Aymara accent. In keeping with their own determined focus on upward mobility through hard work, they had mentioned on several occasions the need for a person to reduce his or her indigenous accent in order to "move ahead" in life (*salir adelante*). This was another of many moments in which they espoused multiple perspectives simultaneously. Deysi and Amanda indirectly and grudgingly lauded the president for having achieved the moral ideal of climbing the class and racial ladder even as they firmly rejected his racial self-identification and denied that structural racism existed in Bolivia.

Deysi and Amanda continued this admiring tone while discussing several ways in which they appeared to feel a kinship with Evo. Deysi reflected that as a teacher, she had met Evo several times when he marched with the rural teachers' union to provide support from the coca growers' union. She said that the coca growers' union almost always joined the marches and protests of other unions. In the case of teachers, in particular, *cocaleros* justified their support by stating that teachers "are our children," pointing to the reality that many children of *cocaleros* were teachers like her or studying to become teachers. Deysi was acknowledging that *cocaleros* followed through on their aspirations to move their children from campesinos into the professional middle class by rallying politically in solidarity with them. Finally, Evo declared in his speech that he would create jobs so that Bolivians working in Spain and the United States—many of them first-generation lawyers, agronomists, and MBAs—could come home; the sisters cheered enthusiastically.

Throughout their moment-by-moment commentary while watching Evo's inauguration ceremonies and implicitly comparing themselves to him, Deysi, Amanda, Celia, and their father alternated between sentiments of egalitarianism and social hierarchy. The sisters several times vehemently asserted social superiority, paired with shame at Evo's promotion of militant indigenous pride. Deysi and Amanda called Evo an "uppity Indian" and denounced his promotion of indigenous symbols in ceremonies of state. They also drew on several strands of citizenship from Bolivian political history in rejecting most of Evo's symbolic stances in the inauguration, such as his promotion of the Andean deity, the Pachamama. They rejected his analysis that Bolivia suffered the continuation of colonial racism and deep economic inequalities when they affirmed that all Bolivians were suffering equally in the present economic downturn. Also contrary to Evo's stance, they adamantly affirmed the racial assimilation model of citizenship promoted by the MNR government of the 1952 Bolivian Revolution, which had declared that *indios* would henceforth be termed *campesinos* and that if all Bolivians were identified as equally mestizo, racism would immediately end. Doña Saturnina's daughters also, in their vocal appreciation of Bolivian folkloric music, implicitly supported the narrow multiculturalism of 1990s neoliberal government, with its promotion of indigenous culture as long as it was not tied to demands for the redistribution of wealth or political power.

On the other hand, the sisters also professed enthusiasm for social equality, for example lauding Evo's support for teachers' unions as an instance of solidarity between the different social classes of campesino and *profesional*. The sisters asserted egalitarianism in their complaint that they opposed Evo because Choro neighbors in his party pulled social rank over them and excluded them economically and politically from local government jobs. Finally, they praised him as a model of hard work to assimilate toward a professional ideal (losing his indigenous accent). This last statement expressed the classic coca grower's yearnings for individual upward mobility. They shared this individual dream of progress, fueled by the coca boom, with the many middling Sacabans who otherwise differed dramatically in their political sentiments, who enthusiastically supported MAS and embraced Evo as a campesino-indigenous leader.

## People Who Identified as Middle Class and Supported Evo and MAS

Sacabans of middling wealth or education responded in many different ways to the MAS platform. Amanda and Deysi's opposition to Evo and to the national MAS party placed them in the minority in Choro and within Sacaba municipality more broadly in 2006.[9] Sacaba was a MAS stronghold, in part owing to its residents' extensive ties to the coca growers' union, which formed a central support base for the national party. Sacaba municipality voted 64 percent for Evo and MAS in 2005; in the rural districts in which Choro was located, Evo received more than 80 percent (Corte Nacional Electoral 2005). Many people looked at me incredulously when I asked them in December 2005 for whom they would vote, answering, "For Evo, of course." Their support, like Amanda's opposition, was based on a variety of considerations: the cultivation of shared identity, specific networks of friends and family, predictions about whether they could tap into local MAS party patron-client opportunities for jobs or development projects, hopes for an end to political leaders' theft of public funds, and opposition to foreign-imposed free-market reforms and the drug war.

Many Sacaba MAS supporters came from backgrounds similar to that of Doña Saturnina's family; like Amanda, they identified with the social category of *profesional*, but they did not feel their status to be threatened by the prospect of an equalization of social, political, and economic relations. For example, a few days after the inauguration, I ran into Amanda's friend Marlene in Sacaba's crowded open-air market. Marlene was a rural schoolteacher who lived near the Sacaba town plaza and had opened a long-distance call center on the first floor of her house. Marlene's home boasted more consumer comforts than did Doña Saturnina's house. Her living room contained several sofas, a varnished dining room table, a large stereo and TV, and a computer. Despite the similarity of Marlene's home decor to that of longtime members of the Sacaba provincial middle class, however, Marlene's mother and Doña Saturnina hailed from similar rural origins and Marlene's mother also wore a *pollera*. I had witnessed the first meeting of the two families during Marlene's son's baptism in 2004. They had quickly established their common ground in a mix of Spanish and Quechua. Marlene's mother danced with Doña Saturnina to Cochabamba valley regional music. They passed casks of *chicha* around the table, recounted similar stories of upward mobility from campesina roots, and traded tearful stories about neighbors who envied their children's academic and economic successes.

On the day after Evo's 2006 inauguration, when I encountered her in the marketplace, Marlene exclaimed happily to me that she had watched the inauguration on TV. She confessed, laughing, that she had cried while watching it. "I'm very sentimental," she explained, and added that she also cried when she heard the Bolivian national anthem. When I asked her whether she thought that the new government could "make a change," she looked surprised and said earnestly, echoing several other people I heard during this time, "There has to be a change [*Tiene que haber un cambio*]." Marlene described a social transformation that would effect a national economic transformation. If elites rejected their assumption that they were superior to subalterns, Bolivia could finally achieve economic prosperity as a country. Inverting the status hierarchies that her friends Amanda and Deysi passionately supported, Marlene argued that nonprofessionals were *superior* to the professional elite, even though she termed herself a professional.

Marlene had recently come to this conclusion on overhearing another teacher, a stranger, on a Cochabamba city bus. "Evo isn't even a professional," the teacher had declared dismissively, while counseling a teenage student. "You, on the other hand, need to study so that you can get a professional degree." The teacher was criticizing the president for having attained only a low level of education, Marlene exclaimed earnestly. But the teacher's statement in fact showed the "ignorance" and impotence of Bolivian professionals! Professionals had been in power for so long in Bolivia, but "they haven't accomplished anything!" Marlene said. Clearly, it was time for other groups to take power. Although she did not state this explicitly, it seemed to me that Marlene was arguing that economic and social transformations must be intertwined. The rejuvenation of the economy— defined in recent years in public opinion as the nationalization of Bolivian natural gas, which Marlene supported and which had been one of Evo's campaign promises—could only take place in tandem with the equalization of everyday power relations. People like Marlene thus explained their support for the MAS platform by pointing to the need to create equality in the broadest sense.

What accounts for the difference between Marlene's and Amanda's family's different self-positioning? While it is impossible for me to know all of her motivations, I suspect that Marlene's championing of the MAS platform may have stemmed from her more secure prosperity. Having grown up in the town of Sacaba rather than in a formally defined rural community, and owning a more visibly comfortable home, perhaps she did not need to assert superiority. It may have also been that her brothers, who were MAS party stalwarts, had convinced her. Most of all, I suggest, the betwixt-and-between status of Marlene and Amanda as members of a middling class and racial provincial group provided them with the potential to identify with a wide range of political leaders, movements, parties, and ideologies. Personal experiences had led them in different directions—at least for the moment. Their positioning was neither total nor permanent, reflecting the multifaceted nature of all people's political identification, the middling status of this particular group, and the dynamic political formations during this moment in Bolivia.

MAS supporters in Sacaba who identified themselves as *vecinos*—provincial elites who traced their origins for several generations to the provincial town of Sacaba—on the other hand, more often supported MAS based on Evo's reputation for being personally incorruptible.[10] The wealth and social status of these provincial elite MAS supporters might be termed "lower middle class" relative to Bolivia's superwealthy or to sociologists' definitions of middle class as professionals and wealthy businesspeople based in Bolivia's cities. But they were recognized as a local elite in Sacaba. They explained their enthusiasm primarily in terms of the hope that the MAS party would avoid the graft and hunger for personal power that they, like most Bolivians, believed plagued other political parties. For them, nostalgia for the rigid social hierarchies of the past could coexist with support for Evo and the MAS party.

One such local elite family whose members supported MAS consisted of Vilma, a MAS municipal official, and her husband, Remigio, a nurse. Throughout 2005 and 2006, Vilma and Remigio often eagerly told me about their central role in founding the Sacaba MAS party. They counted Evo as a personal friend, having hosted him during many campaign meetings since the mid-1990s. They praised him for being incorruptible and "very capable" (*muy capaz*), like several other well-known self-identified indigenous national MAS leaders. They also marveled that Evo treated everyone he met as a social equal, even after becoming a congressman in the late 1990s.

Yet one day in September 2005, over a lunch of chicken soup with rice and afterward, relaxing on slipcovered couches in their cavernous dining room, the two of them also expressed frustration at the ebbing of their own social status as elites within Sacaba municipality. They complained that they had discovered that "people from the countryside are disloyal [*infiel*]" during Vilma's campaign for city councillor several years before. Remigio told me, with quiet outrage, that as a political candidate, "You have to spend money, go to communities with things to give people, like baseball hats, food, and *chicha*. People [in rural areas] ask for a lot and take what you give them, and then they vote for someone else!" They explained that Vilma won her city council position with the support of the provincial townspeople rather than "people from the countryside" (*gente del campo*).

The couple resented campesinos' changed attitudes not only because they had nearly cost Vilma the election; they also mourned the loss of their social status in day-to-day life. Remigio and Vilma continued reflectively that "people from the countryside" had lately lost "respect" for professionals, including lawyers like Vilma. When her father had been a wealthy *vecino* merchant during her childhood in the 1960s, she remembered, campesinos had always doffed their hats respectfully to him, bowed their heads, and begged for his attention with a polite and deferential "excuse me" (*disculpa*). But no longer. "[Rural] leaders are demanding [*Dirigentes son exigentes*]!" Doña Vilma exclaimed. People from the countryside "have gotten power [*se han apoderado*]," they remarked together ruefully, using a phrase that connoted the positive meaning of the English cognate "empowerment" and simultaneously an illegitimate usurping of control (see Gotkowitz 2007:46). "They no longer have respect," Vilma lamented.[11]

Why did Vilma and her husband support MAS and deeply admire its leaders such as Evo, but express frustration that rural folk were no longer subservient to them as a provincial elite, that they were too "demanding" and "disloyal"?[12] I suggest that this apparent contradiction points to the way Remigio and Vilma imagined themselves through multiple frames of reference: as citizens of Bolivia and as residents of Sacaba municipality. While imagining themselves as citizens of Bolivia, they were pleased to have established a close relationship with a powerful, intelligent—and, critically for them, morally uncorrupted—indigenous leader like Evo. They could feel proud of their open-mindedness and ideological positions on the cutting edge of Bolivian politics. On the national scale of wealth, their at times uncertain income placed them below that of the superelite; on the national scale of race, their dark skin and moderate knowledge of Quechua separated them from the light-skinned, Spanish-speaking national superelite.

Yet Remigio and Vilma also identified themselves within Sacaba as local elite *vecinos*, urban residents of a provincial space, who have historically viewed themselves as a mestizo bulwark against a backward Indian-campesino rural hinterland surrounding the provincial town (see also Chapter 1). When Vilma and Remigio placed themselves in their mind's eye in this municipal space, they attempted to assert their class and race distinction by declaring superiority to campesinos. From this perspective, they also regarded as intolerable rural residents' demands for them to divest themselves of some of their social and political superiority.[13]

Like Amanda and Deysi, Remigio and Vilma expressed their middling status by alternating between ethics of superiority and egalitarianism. Their multiple frames of self-identification also illustrate the dynamic flux of social and political relations in Bolivia at this time. Finally, their alternating expressions of superiority and egalitarianism reflect the polarized, binary language and concepts of identity based upon national-scale inequalities, which provided little room for articulating a middling status.

Don Álvaro, the leader of a Sacaba neighborhood council in the urban sprawl adjacent to Cochabamba City, similarly coupled support for the national MAS party platform with demands for entitlement as a provincial elite, though in even more strident language. Don Álvaro, who argued in Chapter 1 that Sacaba's urban residents had more *criterio* (elite taste and knowledge) than rural residents, was the son of an impoverished rural laborer and a wealthy landowner's daughter. He had built extensive political connections during a decade serving as an elected leader of the powerful Cochabamba regional bus and taxi drivers' union. He made his living buying and selling land parcels during Sacaba's real estate boom. Don Álvaro explained to me in 2006 that he had switched from the free-market MIR (Movimiento de la Izquierda Revolucionaria, Left Revolutionary Movement) party to MAS several years before, after becoming fed up with Bolivia's massive inequalities, "because these gentlemen [MAS] are fighting for the dispossessed people, for the poor people" of Bolivia. Such a vision reflected a national view of Bolivian society. Yet, like Remigio and Vilma, Don Álvaro expressed dismay when rural leaders in Sacaba asserted social or political equality. Don Álvaro recounted a fight he had picked with El Chino, a former Sacaba mayor, in 2002. El Chino had been the first Sacaba mayor to hail from a rural community rather than the provincial town of Sacaba or the urban corridor (*eje urbano*) running between the provincial town and the Cochabamba city limits. El Chino was accused by urban leaders—and lauded by rural ones—of favoring rural communities with municipal Popular Participation Law funding, while starving urban districts.[14] Don Álvaro told me how he led his urban neighborhood constituents in 2002 to occupy the Sacaba City Council headquarters when El Chino refused to let Don Álvaro's neighborhood group borrow municipal funds to pave their neighborhood streets. He quoted his own angry tirade against El Chino to me. While he and his neighbors bodily pushed El Chino out of the city council headquarters, Don Álvaro had shouted, "I'm demanding [money for] my streets, because these streets already have sewers, potable water: all the basic services. The only thing that we need is asphalting so that we can live like real people [*como la gente*]—or do you want us to live the way you live up there?" Don Álvaro thus had declared publicly that El Chino and his rural neighbors did not deserve to live with the urban amenities of sanitation and paved roads as Don Álvaro and his urban neighbors did. Like Vilma and Remigio, Don Álvaro was a prosperous, provincial elite supporter of the national MAS platform of equality who nonetheless denigrated rural residents of his own local space when they challenged his access to resources and social superiority in local matters.

Admiration for Evo among self-identified provincial elites like Don Álvaro, Remigio, and Vilma was based to a large extent on his reputation for incorruptibility and the hope that the MAS party could usher in a new era of good governance. When the president and his party tarnished this reputation later in his term of office, these self-identified local middle-class supporters quickly abandoned him and his movement. Their commitment to the rest of the platform—redistribution of wealth and political power— was ambivalent and fluctuating.

This possibility emerges clearly, for example, in the statements of a self-described "European" Bolivian, my landlady in Cochabamba City. Doña Amelia would conform to what Bolivian sociologists termed the middle class (*la clase media*). Residing in the city and owning her own home, she was a fair-skinned widow of an engineering professor and proudly identified both of her grandparents as European: Italian and Greek. She was not in the Bolivian upper class, however. She lived on her deceased husband's pension and the $200 per month rent from the small apartment behind her house. Her daughters were having trouble finding work as engineers in the United States. Doña Amelia often railed against upwardly mobile university students of indigenous backgrounds. "Those people don't have any culture yet!" she exclaimed in frustration when students at Cochabamba's public university went on strike demanding better teaching practices, and locked their professors—including her son, a computer science professor—inside their classrooms. Like many middle-class urbanites, she also complained often about her Quechua-speaking maid's low standards of cleanliness. Yet Doña Amelia allowed her maid to convince her to vote for Evo the day before the 2005 election on the grounds that Evo's government would be less corrupt than that of his right-wing rival. When Evo won, Doña Amelia announced to me with a small voice of satisfaction, "It's good. We needed a change already. There was so much robbery," referring to her widely shared suspicion that political leaders of other parties stole public money. Doña Amelia's support for the MAS platform of national transformation centered primarily on anticorruption—the hope to throw the bums out. Her cooler support for social equality than that of provincial elites like Don Álvaro and Vilma made her less ambivalent, and presumably, less patient with any deviation from MAS leaders' campaign promises.

## Middling MAS Activists and the Authenticity of Subalternity

A significant cohort of Sacaba's MAS supporters identified themselves proudly as subaltern: as *pobre*, campesino, *rural*, *indígena*, and *chola*.[15] Among economically struggling people, MAS support was nearly universal. A young and impoverished MAS party activist in Choro reputed to work full-time in cocaine production told me in 2005 that if Evo were not elected, there would be a "civil war between the rich and the poor," echoing some national MAS leaders at this time.[16] Doña Gladys, scorned as a "shepherdess" in Chapter 2, enthusiastically supported Evo, as did her four teenage daughters. There was a palpable sense during this time that many impoverished Sacabans were actively working to make indigeneity and campesino identity a source of pride rather than shame after centuries of discrimination. On New Year's Eve, 2006, I climbed onto a minibus in Sacaba headed to Cochabamba in the midst of a heavy rainstorm. The steamy air broadcast the smell of wet wool and of several drunken revelers, middle-aged men in rumpled jackets and trousers, who were passed out on the seats. The bus riders were quiet until two of the revelers roused themselves from their dozing and asserted several times in slurred words in a mix of Quechua and Spanish: "I am indigenous! I'm dark skinned [*noqa indígena kani, noqa moreno kani*]. Now is when! [*Ahora es cuando!*]" they also mumbled, repeating a MAS party slogan, before lapsing back into a silent stupor.

Many self-identified subalterns struggled to get by from day to day, like Doña Gladys. Many others, however, commanded a degree of wealth, and sometimes even education, comparable to Amanda and Marisol. It seemed that such activists' subaltern self-identification had developed in tandem with their burgeoning enthusiasm for the MAS principles of social and economic equality and for Evo as a model of upward mobility.

One of the prosperous people who supported MAS and also identified himself as subaltern was Don Félix Hernández, a successful trucker from Choro. Don Félix was the son of a medium-scale landowner, known colloquially as *juch'uy patrones* (little bosses) in the region. Such landowners had been as likely to side with the larger landowners in opposing land reform during the 1952 revolution as with campesinos. Don Félix's father cannily sided with campesinos during the Agrarian Reform and thus avoided expropriation of his land. Don Félix said cheerfully to me as he volunteered at the polls for MAS on the day of the 2005 presidential elections, "Now, no one can call anyone *indios*." The "people from the city" would be surprised if Evo were elected, he chuckled. Echoing Marlene, Don Félix continued, "They thought too highly of themselves [*mucho se han creído*]. And now there are a lot of professionals from the countryside, right?" He mentioned Doña Saturnina's family as an example. Don Félix thus drew connections between two trends that could lead to more equitable social relations in Bolivia: the election of a self-identified indigenous campesino and many rural residents' attainment of professional degrees. Ironically, Doña Saturnina's children were central figures in Don Félix's proud assessment of societal transformation toward equality even though they themselves could not bear to vote for "that Indian," Evo.

An elderly woman whose parents had also been medium-scale landowners before the Agrarian Reform and who was the only woman above the age of sixty in Choro who did not wear a *pollera* surprised me by her self-identification as a campesina when she affirmed, in October 2005, "He has to win! After a thousand years, there has to be a campesino president," and smiled broadly. Many people, including some wealthier than Doña Saturnina's family and as highly educated—teachers, agronomists—said matter-of-factly that they supported Evo "because he is a campesino, like us [*porque es campesino como nosotros*]." These more prosperous Sacaba MAS supporters—like MAS and social movement leaders, and Sacabans like Amanda, Deysi, and Marlene—depicted the Bolivian body politic as split into two opposed camps: urban/elite/non-Indian and rural/campesino/Indian. They placed themselves firmly in the latter, subaltern category. But MAS supporters actively debated the question: who else could count as subaltern?

Ironically, whereas Doña Saturnina's children were the targets of MAS activists' resentment for rejecting campesino and indigenous identities, some prosperous MAS activists who identified as subaltern provoked suspicion among other activists. They were accused of falsely claiming subalternity in a calculated ruse to benefit from the MAS party's rise, of not sharing their resources sufficiently, or acting socially superior in subtle ways despite their rhetoric of equality. The political benefits of assuming a subaltern identity had increased once Evo was elected, with his formal political project promising that the subaltern would be favored. Anyone with a modicum of prosperity or education who opted for the subaltern category within the rigid polarized dualism of elite and subaltern in the language of Bolivian political culture made them ripe for accusations—from poorer people and from those equal in wealth to them—that they were not poor, rural, campesino, or indigenous enough.

Doña Felisa, a leader of the municipal Sacaba women's agrarian union, was a lightning rod for these local debates. Doña Felisa wore a *pollera*, had only recently completed an adult education high school degree while in her forties, and spoke Spanish with a noticeable Quechua accent. Many MAS activists agreed with her self-presentation: she was "from the countryside," a *cholita*, and therefore legitimately subaltern. Doña Felisa employed the MAS party's definition of subaltern at a women's agrarian union seminar held in mid-June 2006 in Sacaba's sports stadium in advance of the upcoming Bolivian Constitutional Assembly. Doña Felisa contrasted "the wealthy" (*qhapaqkuna*) in Bolivia, who should be made to give up land, wealth, and political power in favor of "the poor" (*los pobres, gente humilde*). She specified explicitly, echoing several national MAS leaders' televised statements during that time, that "wealthy" did not mean someone who owned two Volvo tractor-trailer trucks, but rather only the superrich. The oligarch landowners in eastern Bolivia possessed hundreds of thousands of acres of land and were the objects of a new land reform that the MAS government was in process of writing, she reminded meeting attendees.

That Doña Felisa drew the subaltern class line to include owners of two Volvos tells us that class definitions in the regional space of Sacaba were shaped both by national MAS party rhetoric and the effects of the coca and cocaine booms. Given that even second-hand Volvo trucks cost tens of thousands of U.S. dollars and new ones hundreds of thousands, Doña Felisa was setting the bar well above the income of most Bolivians. The average per capita income in Bolivia in 2013 was $2,020 (World Bank 2013). But Bolivia's high rates of inequality meant that the majority of people earned less. Approximately 25 percent of Bolivians earned two dollars a day (Water and Sanitation Program 2006) and 37 percent lived below the poverty line of one U.S. dollar per day (Interamerican Development Bank 2008). Meanwhile, the average of the top fifth of Bolivians' income was just over US$8,000 annually. Thus, Doña Felisa was defining as wealthy only a tiny fraction of Bolivians.

The tactic of Doña Felisa and other MAS leaders to draw the subaltern boundary high—people she identified as *pobre, rural,* campesino, *indígena,* and *popular*—made intuitive political sense, allowing them to invite most Bolivians to participate in their political project. But her assertion that "*pobres*" constituted everyone else also downplayed the relative wealth, compared to the majority of Bolivians, of prosperous Sacabans who had benefited, directly or indirectly, from the coca and cocaine economy and who made up a core base of support for the MAS party in the region. Evo Morales himself was an upwardly mobile coca grower and still the head of coca growers' union while president.

Doña Felisa's own husband was a trucker and the couple owned a Volvo truck, marking Doña Felisa as a member of the community of affluent merchants and long-distance truckers as well as the community of campesinos who owned cows and planted agricultural land. Doña Felisa's always-tidy braids and immaculately clean *polleras* marked her as a political leader and as someone who had access to new clothes and clean water. Most non-professionals in Sacaba were not as assiduous in their daily grooming, having scarce access to water and little leisure time, or inhabiting a social world in which such grooming was not a priority.

The home that Doña Felisa built in 2009 was a very visible marker of middle-class distinction and upwardly mobile aspirations. Three stories tall and designed by an architect, unlike most rural homes, the house boasted decorative archways, multiple bathrooms, and enormous banks of windows that bathed the interior in light. The floors were covered in ceramic tile and linoleum contrasting with the cheaper polished cement of many provincial middle-class homes, and diverging most markedly from the dirt floors of many self-identified campesinos. Framed photos of Doña Felisa's various swearing-in ceremonies as a prominent agrarian union leader graced the walls. In short, her home gave off an air of much greater affluence and upward mobility than did Marisol's and Amanda's homes, despite their self-description as professionals and her self-description as an indigenous campesina. Doña Felisa's home even topped, in my view, the visible wealth of both Marlene's and Vilma's homes, which were above the median provincial spectrum of luxury.

Doña Felisa's raising of her children, furthermore, was similar to that of many Sacabans who aspired to join the middle class. Doña Felisa spoke Spanish to her children, a decision that many Sacabans told me they had chosen explicitly to allow their children upward mobility, and which differed from Doña Saturnina, who spoke to her children in Quechua, and from the MAS platform that promoted indigenous languages. Doña Felisa sent her daughter to a private and highly regarded teachers' college. Doña Felisa's granddaughter was baptized at one month old like affluent urban infants, and much earlier than most Choro babies, who were baptized at one year of age.[17] Even David, the most ambitious of Doña Saturnina's children, had not baptized his daughter until she was one year old. Thus, despite Doña Felisa's explicit declarations of subalternity and her adoption of key symbols of that identity, she asserted a middle-class identity in other ways. Doña Felisa in some respects was adhering to the MAS rhetoric, which said that someone who attained prosperity should still identify as indigenous and campesina. Like Marisol, the pharmacist, and Doña Saturnina's children, Doña Felisa's wealth and her family's educational status gave her options. And like them, some of Doña Felisa's unspoken and explicit expressions of identity clashed with the formal platform of the MAS party, even as it coincided in other ways.

In contrast to self-identified local professionals like Vilma, Amanda, and Marisol, who expressed anxiety over a potential loss of status and alternated between publicly identifying themselves as elite and as subaltern, Doña Felisa consistently described herself as subaltern: as a *chola, indígena,* and campesina. Through her clothing, language, education level, and national political affiliation, Doña Felisa emphatically did not assert middle-class distinction. Yet Doña Felisa asserted middle-class distinction in other ways: through consumption, by building herself a home that was fabulously luxurious by local standards, and through her immaculate grooming and impeccably clean new clothes. If consumption, including education, housing, hygiene, and clothing style, is an important preoccupation of middle classes (Liechty 2002; O'Dougherty 2002), Doña Felisa's decision to invest in the house and in her children's professional education constituted an unspoken declaration of middle-class status. While she did not express to me Amanda and Deysi's alternation between ideals of equality and ideals of superiority (and this may have been because I didn't know her as well as I knew them), Doña Felisa did subtly assert some of the same elements of middle-class superiority as they did.

These unspoken markers of upward mobility attracted the suspicion of other MAS activists. I constantly heard criticism of Doña Felisa as selfish in not sharing her newfound wealth. Some activists complained to me, for example, that Doña Felisa should have used her senator's salary for local community development—to build a community center or to furnish the local MAS party headquarters—instead of saving it for herself. When I saw her newly built home, enormous and ornate by local standards, I was certain that it would increase their disgruntlement. Core MAS activists' suspicions of her as politically suspect only grew after she openly allied herself in 2008 with a local right-wing politician, even while stoutly maintaining that her loyalty to the national MAS party had not wavered. In short, while Doña Felisa explicitly supported the national MAS party and attempted to assert a subaltern identity in keeping with the MAS platform, she was at times suspected by other MAS members as not being subaltern enough, once she began spending her wealth on personal and family consumption and shifted her local political alliances.

The relative affluence of many Sacaba coca growers strongly shaped the ideals and actions of many MAS activists like Doña Felisa, just as it did for Sacabans skeptical of or opposed to MAS. As I spent more time with these activists, it slowly became clear that some of MAS's explicit platform conflicted with its implicit platform. Many supporters read into the party platform, based on their participation in the coca boom, that a transformed Bolivia under the MAS would allow them to "get ahead" (*salir adelante, superarse*). The explicit injunction for collective action and the exhortation to be satisfied with moderate prosperity in order to redistribute wealth to the desperately poor (*buen vivir, sumaq qamaña*), conflicted with the party's implicit promises to help Bolivians achieve individual upward mobility. These Sacabans clearly aspired to professional status for their children in addition to the broader and more long-term collective goals of equality for their communities of class, race, and nation.[18] It seemed that Sacabans heard MAS leaders to be promising the opportunity to rise in the social hierarchy as an individual in addition to national prosperity, the redistribution of wealth within Bolivia, the assertion of ethnic and racial pride, and the transformation of Bolivia's subordinate economic status in the global economy.

The multiplicity of these expectations that many Bolivians hoped MAS and Evo would fulfill was made clear in one particularly intense conversation in August 2006. It was the day after Doña Felisa and several other local leaders had broken off from the Sacaba MAS party to form a small faction. The municipal MAS organization was in disarray, now split into three or four competing groups. Doña Felisa had opened a parallel MAS party office in Sacaba, just off the main plaza, and the small, bare, whitewashed room as yet held just one chair, so everyone had to stand. In this tense atmosphere, Doña Felisa and several friends eagerly welcomed my stopping by to chat. They reiterated their hopes for the national MAS party, it seemed to me, to distract themselves from the vexing local conflict.

With the electoral triumph of MAS, they argued fervently to me, they beheld the possibility of a total transformation. Doña Felisa and her friend Doña Susana, also *de pollera*, tried to make me understand the monumental changes they foresaw.

> *Doña Felisa:* We could manufacture airplanes: why couldn't we . . . ?
>     That thought is among the people now.
> *Doña Susana:* Now, we say to our children: "Now you, child, you
>     won't remain a donkey like us."
> *Doña Felisa:* In the past, no way! No one had these ideas. Now our
>     eyes have been opened.

In dreaming about manufacturing airplanes, Doña Felisa pointed to a promise by MAS leaders to return Bolivia to a state capitalist economy, an ideal first established during the 1952 revolution but rejected by governments since the 1985 free-market economic reforms. With the proceeds from increased taxes on natural gas exports, Evo had declared, his government would launch national high-tech industries in one of the world's least industrialized nations. The "we" in Doña Felisa's statement appeared to encompass an entire nation eagerly awaiting industrialization. "We" also seemed to refer specifically to indigenous and poor subalterns struggling for higher social status and wealth within Bolivia. When Doña Susana, Doña Felisa's agrarian leader friend, declared that she often told her children that they would no longer be "donkeys," referring to a common racist epithet, she seemed to be saying that all indigenous people could shake off racial exclusion by means of education (in aerospace engineering, for example) and reach for a goal of individual, or family-based upward mobility for children like her own and those of Doña Felisa's. In Doña Susana's statement, her children's hoped-for professional success was entirely compatible with the uplift of all of Bolivia's poor; she framed the goals of family upward mobility through greater wealth and social status as fully compatible with the the birth of national prosperity and prosperity for poor, indigenous people. Edgar and Deysi's father had similarly yearned for his children to escape the social humiliation he had suffered as an uneducated person; this was his explanation for why he worked so hard for them to become professionals. But his hope was overwhelmingly centered on the family and did not extend to uplift for all Bolivian subalterns.

If the promise of MAS for many Sacabans combined multiple, long-held aspirations for indigenous revival, national prosperity, and the arrival into middle-class (*profesional*) status of activists' families, this multiplicity of aspirations contributed to confusion because political conflicts were framed as struggles between elites and subalterns. Within the national frame of belonging that dominated MAS party rhetoric, activists like Doña Felisa could make clear-cut distinctions between a tiny superelite based in the agribusiness regions of eastern Bolivia and a subaltern majority. Within a municipal frame of belonging in the social world of Sacaba, however, Doña Felisa's aspirations for upward mobility in wealth, education, and consumption sparked accusations that she was elite, rather than subaltern.

These ambiguities of identification created difficulty for many Sacaban activists attempting to strategize their political projects and self-presentation within the municipality. Doña Felisa was not the only target of vituperative comments by other MAS activists questioning her subalternity. Sacaba MAS and agrarian union activists, including Doña Felisa herself, often attempted to identify political "traitors" by ferreting out hidden elites. On a grassy field during the lunch break of a Sacaba agrarian union congress I attended in May 2006, several local agrarian leaders worried aloud that wealthy people had infiltrated the party by falsely claiming to be subaltern. One local leader explained the problem to me in a mix of Spanish and Quechua, "Let's say that I'm a real, real [*neto, neto*] campesino and she [pointing to a leader sitting opposite him] is a real, real campesina." The woman leader, who wore a *pollera* and considered herself illiterate, leaned toward me, pointed to herself and said dramatically to make absolutely clear to me what being a campesina meant: "Let's say I don't know *any-thing!*" The man continued, pointing to me, "Let's say you are a millionaire businessman but you trick us [*engañawanchis*] by saying that you're a real campesino." Finishing each other's sentences, they complained heatedly that there were many more of these false campesinos than there had been before MAS had won control of the national government. People who did not care about, or even opposed, the MAS platform but simply wanted personal power were entering the movement. They also worried that hidden elites might deliberately infiltrate the movement in order to spy or sow dissension to weaken the MAS and push the party from power—a reasonable fear, since dictatorial governments had actively co-opted agrarian unions during the 1960s and 1970s. These MAS activists worried that if they failed to accurately distinguish between authentic and false subalterns, the "process of change," the political transformation and the equalization of power in Sacaba municipality and throughout Bolivia, could fail.

Such concerns among Sacaba MAS supporters about the authenticity of fellow supporters' subaltern status were deepened by tensions created by the Law of Popular Participation, as well as by the rise of the MAS party. LPP reformers had hoped that the law would ameliorate previously existing tensions between rural and urban Bolivians, from the Spanish colonial legal separation between the rural Republic of Indians and urban Republic of Spaniards to hostility between agrarian union members and townspeople during the 1950s. Campesino militias during the 1950s, composed of male residents of the countryside surrounding Sacaba, had regularly paraded through the provincial town, as they did throughout the Cochabamba valleys and many other areas of western and central Bolivia at the time. Brandishing hoes and Mauser rifles, they attempted to consolidate their new political authority relative to long-dominant *vecinos* (townspeople), as well as to dissuade any large landowners whose land had recently been confiscated from plotting to retake their property. Yet such agrarian movements had not stopped the net transfer of wealth from campesino farmers to urbanites, who benefitted from cheap food prices, government investment, and social prestige. LPP reformers hoped to reverse this long-standing mutual suspicion and political and economic inequality between rural and urban districts within regions, by fomenting "rural and urban development . . . in a harmonious fashion" (Molina and Arias 1996:35).

The Popular Participation Law sparked new tensions between rural and urban political blocs in Sacaba, however. This was because the law gave residents of formally rural areas the right for the first time to vote in municipal elections, and offered dramatically increased funding to municipalities. While the central government distributed funding on a per capita basis to each municipality, each municipal government could decide how to distribute those funds. Sacaba municipality was divided into ten districts, of which five were classified as rural and five as urban. Rural and urban political leaders debated heatedly whether or not the Popular Participation funding would be distributed according to need. This would allow rural districts to receive more funding, given their greater backlog of needs for roads, sewer systems, and other infrastructure. Urban leaders, however, insisted that Popular Participation funds be distributed within the municipal territory as they had been in the national territory: by population. Given that urban districts contained more people and hence more voters, their leaders' demands won over the municipal government. The national rise of the MAS party further increased these tensions in Sacaba as the MAS platform called for power to the rural and urban poor; this upset the previous balance of power resting on urban dominance within the municipality but neither bloc held a decisive advantage.

Yet while the MAS activists above described their attempts to distinguish between "real, real" subalterns and "millionaire businessmen," few of the superrich resided in Sacaba municipality. Most of these superwealthy resided in large cities like Cochabamba or on huge estates in Bolivia's eastern lowlands. The aspiring MAS leaders who faced suspicions of not being subaltern enough ranged from *vecina* lawyers like Vilma, to prosperous real estate agents residing in the urban sprawl like Don Álvaro, to self-identified campesina leaders like Doña Felisa. None of them was a millionaire. People I am terming Sacaba's provincial middle class could count as elites locally by virtue of their education, prosperity, or residence in an urban district, even as they could face discrimination themselves from city-based professionals and Bolivia's superrich. In short, the national scale of race and class differed from the municipal scale, but these scales became entangled in local political debates. While the national struggle did, indeed center on a duel between the superwealthy minority and a much poorer majority, within the political space of the municipality, identities and power relations were more ambiguous.

The Sacaba municipal agrarian union meetings were the site of many assertions of militancy and attempts to draw clear boundaries between the two opposed categories of elite urban and subaltern rural folk and to identify definitively which individual people belonged to which. A classic example of the difficulty of drawing these lines occurred at the 2006 annual Sacaba agrarian union congress, held in an outlying hamlet about half an hour from Sacaba Town. Inside the rural district administration building, filling twenty or so rows of wooden benches, sat several hundred men. Many of them wore the fedoras and worn, knitted pullover sweaters that served as symbols of male campesino attire in this region. The few women attendees wore *polleras*. The audience faced a row of community and municipal MAS officials who had just given a string of speeches in Quechua condemning a decade of municipal conflict.

Then the two MAS candidates for the upcoming Constitutional Assembly stepped forward to give stump speeches. In less than one month, elections would be held for delegates to the Assembly, in which the winners would rewrite the Bolivian constitution. Bolivian social movements had been clamoring for such an assembly during the previous fifteen years. The first local candidate, a trucker from another rural district of Sacaba, gave a speech in Quechua and received polite applause. The candidate for one of Sacaba's urban districts followed him at the microphone. Cristina Choque Espinoza, a young woman with dark skin and straight dark hair just past shoulder length, dressed in a T-shirt and jeans, introduced herself as a law student at the Cochabamba public university. Cristina spoke for a few minutes in Spanish notably unaccented by an indigenous language, in earnest tones entreating her audience that the success of the Constitutional Assembly could only be guaranteed "through mobilization and . . . the participation of all."

Catcalls began, as hecklers throughout the audience urged her to speak in Quechua. As the groundswell of irritated and impatient shouts grew louder, she faltered in her memorized speech, a helpless look on her face. "In Quechua, In Quechua!" Soon the entire room had erupted into outraged hoots and cries. After pausing for several moments, nonplussed, Cristina began to say in tentative Quechua that she was studying the language but did not yet speak it well. Following a few halting phrases, she lapsed back into her prepared speech in Spanish, a resigned look on her face. "The Constitutional Assembly is refounding the country," she said rapidly, "and it's now or never." After repeating a few more MAS party slogans, she hurriedly left the microphone. An agrarian union leader apologetically explained that Vilma, the local MAS official, had been a candidate, but had recently resigned. As a lawyer from Sacaba Town, Vilma had lacked popular support. She withdrew her candidacy shortly before the candidates' names were due at the electoral court and by law, at least one MAS candidate had to be a woman. The leader pleaded with the restive agrarian congress attendees to accept Cristina; if he hadn't put her name down on the ballot as an emergency measure, no MAS candidate would have run in Sacaba's urban district. The hoots dissolved into sporadic grumbles, leaving this issue to reemerge at later agrarian union meetings.

This episode was notable in demonstrating the militant concern of Sacaba agrarian union activists that MAS leaders be subaltern, in this case, that Cristina demonstrate her indigenous-campesina background by speaking Quechua. But why target Cristina? Her dark skin, hair, and eyes signaled that she was not a member of the superelite of Bolivia. Her last name, Choque, was well known to be an Aymara last name, as indigenous sounding as Evo Morales's second last name, Ayma. Her clothing and occupation were ambiguous: her blue jeans could have been worn by young women of any level of wealth in Sacaba; they did not signal subalternity as a *pollera* would, nor did they signal eliteness as a suit would have done. She was a law student, and most likely some audience members had children also in law school. On the other hand, Cristina was running to represent an urban district, and the audience seemed to assume that she had been raised there. Her Spanish was unaccented, in contrast to the indigenous accents of even Doña Saturnina's adult children in Choro, professionals and fully fluent in Spanish as they were. It may have been (though no one told me so explicitly) that Cristina's Aymara last name might have sparked some rivalry with the Quechua-speaking audience. Evo had transcended Aymara-Quechua political antagonism through longtime relationships with Quechua speakers while a coca growers' union leader, but Christina was young and unknown to this particular crowd.[19] In protesting Cristina's candidacy, the crowd was protesting someone who physically resembled their university student children. In the face of Cristina's presentation of a vaguely middling provincial identity, those who jeered were declaring that there was a firm line between subalterns and elites, between rural subalterns who spoke Quechua and elites, including Cristina, who spoke only Spanish. One of Cristina's supporters told me after the meeting that Cristina had grown up in the Chapare as the daughter of *cocaleros* and had been an ardent supporter of the MAS party since she was a child, but Sacabans unfortunately didn't know about her deep and long-lived commitment. One of many similar conflictive incidents in Sacaba, Cristina's candidacy sparked ongoing disagreement among MAS activists regarding her motives and her class and racial background.

The fervent request of a leader from a designated urban district to be recognized as a campesina, or at least valued as a daughter of one, marks a stark contrast with the vigorous attempts of people like Doña Saturnina's children to mark their distinction from campesinos. Both groups, because of their middling wealth and social status, had some choice about whether to identify as subaltern or elite. As part of their choice to ally with MAS, activists often identified themselves as subaltern. But they were stuck in a heated debate over which of the two camps they belonged to. Agrarian union leaders confronted the question of how they could maintain the radical promise of the MAS platform without excluding elite people as suspect. Meanwhile, MAS activists who were urban residents but identified themselves as having rural roots confronted the question of how they could convince other activists to accept their subaltern class and racial self-identification. Like Amanda and Deysi, these urban-resident or newly affluent MAS activists faced a binary logic of identity that did not acknowledge their middling wealth and social status and thus muddied the waters of local political analysis.

## Conclusion

Aspirations for upward mobility strongly shaped Sacabans' political sentiments and their debates about what the rise of Evo and the MAS party meant in 2005 and 2006. Yet these aspirations for middle-class status did not fit into the bifurcated identity categories that emerged from the long-standing national narrative of two Bolivias—one of superwealthy, white Bolivians, and one of impoverished, rural, campesino-indigenous Bolivians. The fact that Sacabans' markers of class and race were ambiguous and did not fit neatly into either of the two dominant categories meant that their political allegiances were often subject to dispute and contestation by other people.

People responded in heterogeneous ways to MAS during the honeymoon period of Evo's election and his first term of office, even when they enjoyed similar middling wealth and social background. Some of them asserted social superiority, like Amanda and Deysi, and opposed MAS; some identified as *profesionales* but asserted an ethic of social equality like Marlene; some asserted social superiority but supported MAS, like Vilma; finally, some Sacabans of middling wealth asserted a subaltern status and supported MAS, like Doña Felisa. Evo's attempt to interrupt Bolivia's tradition of elite rule elicited anxiety and shame for some Sacabans while sparking deep pride and triumph in others who shared a similar level of wealth and social status.

These patterns were not shared in all Bolivian provincial towns. In some regions, such as Santa Cruz in the east, local elites were the superwealthy of Bolivia, and they utterly dominated municipal politics. In such places, the social and economic divisions between elite and subalterns were enormous and undeniable (Postero 2007; Fabricant; Gustafson 2009). By contrast, in other municipalities, campesino farmers made up a large majority of the municipal population and were able to organize through agrarian unions to elect their own to municipal positions of power and successfully dominate local politics (Antezana 2003). Yet many provincial towns were like Sacaba: close to large cities, diverse in their demography, and containing a sizeable population of new middle classes.

MAS activists who identified as subaltern, like self-identified professionals, espoused middle-class dreams of individual and family-based upward mobility sparked by the promise of the coca boom. They also, however, presented the dream for family-based upward mobility as fully compatible with the dream to transform Bolivia's status into an industrial powerhouse, such as in the manufacture of airplanes, and with the dreams of uplift of all indigenous, rural, and working-class people. But what would happen if these goals were mutually exclusive, if one family's upward mobility meant the loss of resources to other people?

In the next two chapters, I exanine this question. I highlight the ways in which the ambiguity of middling identities and the rigidity of social categories contributed to political conflicts in Sacaba Municipality. In particular, these tensions emerged in local condemnation of and practices of clientelism—of favors exchanged between patrons and clients. Clientelism had, by 2005, become one of Bolivians' central complaints about politics and Sacabans participated actively in condemning clientelism. Complaints about clientelism expressed many people's frustrations with the ambiguity of identities in Sacaba, the incompatibility of the multiple dreams—individual, class and racial, and national—of upward mobility, and the pervasive perception that those who prospered politically were selfish and had usurped scarce resources or power.

# Condemning Clientelism

In early May 2006, the leaders of the Sacaba municipal branch of the MAS party called an emergency public meeting. Sacaba MAS leaders were outraged that the Sacaba City Council had recently forced the MAS mayor, Luis Orellana, to resign. City council members had charged Mayor Orellana with corruption and the failure to build *obras*—infrastructure projects such as bridges and schools. Orellana's ouster followed six years of political turmoil in Sacaba Municipality and the untimely downfall of four previous mayors following similar charges of corruption. At the public meeting, the MAS leaders hoped to galvanize support from rank-and-file supporters to plan a series of marches and road blockades to pressure the city council to reinstate Orellana.

Beginning in the early morning hours, the vacant lot in front of the Sacaba agrarian union headquarters gradually filled with the bustle of rural union leaders wearing shabby sweaters and MAS-affiliated municipal workers in bright blue polar fleece vests with the MAS emblem over the breast. They unfurled giant blue, black, and white MAS party flags, unloaded enormous sacks of potatoes and onions from the back of a pickup truck for the post-rally lunch, and as the morning wore on, attempted to corral a sparse, hesitant crowd to come closer to the stage set up in the cement soccer court under a galvanized metal roof. The audience included agrarian union members from rural districts of Sacaba, prosperous political operators from throughout the municipality, and some curious onlookers from the neighborhood. A truck playing MAS campaign songs from a megaphone circled the field, filling the air with the plaintive baritones of Bolivian folkloric music.

Dozens of agrarian union and MAS party leaders from throughout the Cochabamba region took the stage for the next four hours. Because Sacaba was a heartland of MAS support, many worried that conflicts here tarnished the image of the party throughout the country. They warned of "traitors" who were accusing Mayor Orellana of corruption simply because they wished a new mayor to enter office who would give them a job through clientelism (*clientelismo, peguismo*), as a patronage favor in exchange for their political support.

Then the regional president of the MAS party, Julio Salazar, took his turn at the microphone and gave a particularly impassioned appeal. He also argued that the corruption charges against the mayor were unsubstantiated—put forth by people acting in "self-interest" to remove the mayor from office to curry favor with a new mayor. "You all need to understand the philosophy of MAS and of Evo," he urged. "It is that we must make change inside each one of us. Each person must first change himself. In your heart, if there is selfishness [*egoismo*] and envy [*envidias*], this prevents unity." Political unity was necessary for Sacaba's economic development and to support the "process of profound change" led by Evo in Bolivia, he exclaimed fervently.

Several rally audience members independently explained to me that Salazar was arguing that Mayor Orellana's critics were selfish because they hoped to oust him to gain jobs under a new mayor, not because they really believed that he had pocketed public funds. Salazar was proposing that these selfish patronage seekers' envy reflected the greedy desire for a lucrative job inside the municipal government. Like several speakers that day, Salazar diagnosed clientelism, which he depicted as synonymous with envy and self-interest, as the cause of Sacaba's perpetual conflict. The chief obstacle to local and national transformation, in his formulation, was a moral failure that each individual needed to remedy through a process of reflection and self-improvement.[1]

In this chapter, I examine the widespread accusations and counteraccusations of clientelism in Sacaba and the ways in which middling race and class aspirations shaped these accusations. In all corners of Sacaba, people were accusing each other of clientelism and claiming that their antagonists were creating conflict that blocked the economic development of the municipality and the MAS party's promise of national transformation. Most politically active Sacabans faced accusations of clientelism by *somebody*. From my perspective, these condemnations signaled a widespread local concern that creating a radical shift toward social and economic equality in Bolivian society was more difficult than they had hoped during the previous decade of widespread protest against the prior political regime. Accusations of clientelism also, in my view, reflected some Sacabans' often-implicit concern that conflicting moralities were circulating in Bolivian society. Indeed, calls to transform the political culture of the nation by eliminating the envy and selfishness that many people believed to be the root of clientelism collided head-on with the also widespread moral imperative to become middle class. These competing imperatives—to eliminate clientelism and to attain middle-class status—were in conflict because clientelist favors constituted one of the few routes to finding a middle-class job in Sacaba, as in much of Bolivia. Acquiring a municipal government job in the city hall (*alcaldía*) or winning a political post as a MAS candidate was how many people became middle class or maintained a trajectory of upward mobility in Sacaba. Those jobs were scarce; acquiring employment necessarily meant that many other people did not receive the job. Unemployed persons then accused those with employment of defending their corrupt patron because he had offered them a job. The accusation of clientelism was thus a local currency, a ubiquitous moral language, in a highly competitive environment.

In the previous three chapters, I looked at the divergent ways that upwardly mobile Bolivians like Marisol, Amanda, Marlene, and Doña Felisa—people I am calling Sacaba's emergent middle class—reimagined their identities in the wake of the Popular Participation Law and the MAS party's rise to power. We have seen that the language of social hierarchy in the social world of Sacaba Municipality did not accurately describe the ways that people lived their race and class identities in the middle. Nor were the practical concerns, identities, and aspirations of the new middle classes acknowledged within the rhetoric of MAS or the Law of Popular Participation (LPP), which depicted the Bolivian nation through the framework of the national very real conflict between superwealthy, white elites and destitute, indigenous subalterns.

I am suggesting that middle classes complicated politics in Sacaba by presenting rhetorically unacceptable identities and aspirations, contributing to factionalism and the continual turnover of political leaders. Self-interest is impossible to expunge from human society, most particularly in an economy in which elected office and appointed jobs in municipal government offered some of the few routes to prosperity. The rise of MAS had intensified the concern among some members of this emergent middle class, like Amanda and Deysi, that their families, friends, and neighbors would view them as snobbish if they rejected the MAS party and its principles as an expression of their aspirations for upward mobility. Yet if those in the middle became MAS activists and successfully attained a job or political leadership position, they faced suspicion that they were claiming a campesino or indigenous subaltern status unfairly—they were elite wolves in campesino sheep's clothing or unfairly monopolizing local wealth, jobs, or political appointments. Mutual accusations of clientelism in the context of the MAS party's rise to power reflected concern about these conflicting imperatives in an environment of economic scarcity and of pervasive, deep anxiety around class and racial status.

I also show in this chapter that the lines between clientelism, liberal representative democracy, and radical grassroots democracy were in practice quite murky in Sacaba, despite the firm distinctions that many people drew in theory. The political currency of mutual accusations of clientelism, envy, and selfishness thus also reflects the multiplicity of frames of citizenship circulating in Bolivia in the early twenty-first century, frames that have emerged at different moments in Bolivian history. While the 1952 Bolivian revolutionary government had established clientelism as a formal model of governance, by the 1990s, indigenous and campesino movement leaders, MAS party leaders, and LPP reformers argued that clientelism posed a central obstacle to democracy. Their shared, vocal disgust echoed the frustration of Bolivians in many walks of life who argued that, since 1952, successive clientelist governments and political parties had served elite interests while failing to fulfill their promises of creating jobs and development.

Ironically, the long-running conflict for control of city hall in Sacaba and the widespread mutual accusations of clientelism that permeated the conflict were intensified by the heightened expectations for development, democracy, and equality established by both the LPP and the rise of the MAS party. The multiple mandates and sometimes overlapping practices of these various political frameworks—clientelism, liberal democracy, and grassroots democracy—presented dilemmas for Bolivians intent on considering themselves as morally upright and legitimate political actors. In practice, many Sacabans employed hybrid political practices, drawing elements in eclectic fashion from these multiple frameworks.[2]

Below, I narrate how the vehement denunciation of clientelism and common association of clientelism with envy and self-interest in Sacaba built on the LPP reformers' plans for liberal democracy, the national MAS party's promise to end corruption, and longstanding local concerns about inequality. I examine a central argument against clientelism in the scholarly literature and in Bolivian political culture, namely that it is an authoritarian form of politics that inevitably strengthens the hand of elites. I then look at how accusations of clientelism were nearly inescapable for politically active Sacabans not only because of the scarcity of jobs but also because the same action could be interpreted as conforming to the liberal democracy model of the LPP or the grassroots democracy platform of the MAS party. Denunciations of clientelism were fueled to a great degree by the ambiguities of race and class for middling Sacabans. Ultimately, I show, accusations of envy-as-clientelism revealed both the hope and anxiety that colored many Sacabans' efforts to simultaneously attain middle-class upward mobility and to align themselves with the MAS platform of equalization of wealth and indigenous pride.

## The Recent History of Anticlientelism
## in Bolivian Political Rhetoric

What accounts for the ubiquity of accusations of clientelism in Sacaba? To begin with, such accusations reflect frustrations among agrarian union and social movement leaders accumulated during the previous fifty years. The Bolivian National Revolutionary Movement (MNR), which took power in 1952 following the revolution, established clientelism as a political model. It built on much older feudal and colonial models of patronage between European elites and indigenous serfs. The MNR and later military governments of the 1960s and 1970s openly pledged that they would reward political support and votes with local leadership positions and funds for community development. During the 1960s, Bolivian agrarian union leaders allied themselves with these repressive governments in exchange for land reform and promises of community development. Rural residents in the Cochabamba valleys, including Sacaba, voted as a bloc for the MNR party. Local agrarian union leaders cultivated personal relationships with highly placed officials—often making the long journey by bus to La Paz to cement these ties—in an effort to attract funding for community irrigation reservoirs and schools.

Yet by the mid-1980s, most Bolivians, particularly members of urban labor unions and agrarian movements, openly condemned the clientelism of elite-run national political parties.[3] They argued that three decades of state promises for national development remained unfulfilled: most Bolivians remained poor. The free-market reforms of 1985 that increased joblessness and decreased government social services cemented this disillusionment. Agrarian union leaders came to the conclusion that clientelism, which they defined as politicians' buying votes with inconsequential gifts to voters, was the main mechanism through which Bolivia's racist super-wealthy had maintained their dominance (e.g., CSUTCB 1987; 1994). For example, a group of women campesina leaders argued in 1994: "We poor people [*pobres*] . . . have always served as ladders so that a few shrewd ones [*vivillos*] take advantage of the funds and resources of the government, and after promising us a thousand marvels, once elected, they forget about all of their offers and subject us to further suffering" (CSUTCB 1994:39). All political parties became widely seen as parasites—vehicles for selfish elites who promoted harsh free-market-policies while distributing insultingly small gifts such as *chicha*, noodles, and T-shirts in exchange for votes (e.g., Torihuano in Zuazo 2009:94; see also Shakow 2011).

Several parties emerged in the 1980s that continued clientelist practices while shifting their rhetoric by claiming to represent Bolivia's majority, which they defined as subaltern: *popular* (plebeian), indigenous, and poor. The parties, CONDEPA (Conciencia de Patria, Conscience of the Fatherland), emerging in the highlands, and UCS (Unidad Cívica Solidaridad, Civic Union of Solidarity) in Cochabamba, enjoyed a meteoric rise, helped by a national spike in television ownership (Mayorga 2002). Their charismatic leaders, Carlos Palenque and Max Fernández, respectively, presented themselves as working-class, self-made men of hardscrabble origins who had attained wealth through luck and hard work. In their platforms based almost entirely on building visible public works (*obras*) like sports coliseums and schools, and dispensing cash handouts to individual voters in personal crisis, they built on the populist clientelism of the MNR government and of subsequent 1960s dictator René Barrientos even as they claimed novelty as parties that served Bolivia's poor and indigenous instead of the country's tiny elite (see Lazar 2008). For several years, they effectively channeled Bolivians' outrage over their widespread suffering under free-market reforms from job losses, competition from cheap imports flooding in from other countries, and the government's removal of social services (Mayorga 2002). In essence, they implicitly claimed to replace a clientelism oriented around elite interests to a clientelism oriented around the interests of the Bolivian poor. The untimely deaths of both parties' leaders in the mid-1990s led to a decline in the parties' influence. These parties were not immune, despite their leaders' self-described "humble" (*humilde*) origins, to the criticisms of MAS and other social movement leaders that the gifts they gave voters were transitory and that their political practices resembled the clientelism of old, posing an obstacle to a true equalization of wealth and political power in Bolivia (e.g., Quispe in Zuazo:101; Bautista in Zuazo:144; MAS-IPSP 2008:92).

Elite Bolivian LPP reformers built on these criticisms of political party clientelism in 1994 by drawing on decentralization policies then in vogue among development policy makers around the world. They hoped to forge a path away from clientelism and toward liberal, representative democracy. Bolivian reformers argued that, if governance structures were changed, the inherently public-minded Bolivian civil society—consisting of all Bolivians minus political party leaders, government officials, and union leaders—would eliminate clientelism and the superelites' stranglehold over Bolivian society (Medina 1995; Molina and Arias 1996).[4] Their remedy for clientelism was to institute municipal elections (for the first time in some rural localities), provide new municipal funds for infrastructure projects, expand municipal (county) governments, and prescribe new and precise steps for local public planning and good governance.[5] Reformers also built on Bolivians' widespread disenchantment with political parties as channels for representation by promoting the notion that Bolivia's civil society would wield power outside of political parties and unions, through new municipal and community organizations (e.g., Molina Saucedo 1990; Medina 1995; Molina and Arias 1996).[6] Arguing that Bolivia's large indigenous population held a particular cultural genius for public-minded civic action, in contrast to selfish superelites, several LPP reformers argued that poor Bolivians would extinguish clientelism and self-interest from Bolivian public life and thus foster "the ancient [indigenous] utopia of solidarity and fraternity . . . from below, using a logic of . . . reciprocity (Medina 1995: 24; see also Molina and Arias 1996:25). Ironically, however, the LPP actually sparked the proliferation of clientelism and political conflicts in many of the hundreds of newly created municipalities, including Sacaba. Instead of just one central government in which to compete for elected positions, appointed jobs, and development funding, now there were 213 local arenas of cutthroat competition.[7]

From the moment that the MAS burst onto the national political stage in the late 1990s, party leaders channeled Bolivians' widespread discontent with clientelism, with traditional parties controlled by superelites, and with the significant limitations of the Popular Participation Law.[8] MAS leaders claimed to have founded the first political party that promoted a platform of political equality and redistribution of wealth in place of clientelism. National MAS leaders clearly diverged from LPP reformers' narrow definition of citizenship as a focus on local development to the exclusion of national policies. Yet they shared LPP reformers' denunciation of elite politicians as duping Bolivians with token, short-term gifts, which they scathingly termed "*fideitos*" (small packages of noodles).

National MAS leaders and other social movement leaders agreed with LPP decentralization policy makers and many social scientists that one of the chief problems of clientelism is that it creates strong, authoritarian patrons and a weak client populace (see Haugerud 1995; Brinkerhoff and Goldsmith 2002; Riley n.d.; World Bank 2000). In this shared critique, when poor or marginalized people ally themselves with a powerful patron in order to gain a concrete material good, the benefits accrue to the patron, who co-opts demands for widespread societal change with cheap gifts. Furthermore, clients benefit as individuals, rather than the nation as a whole. Leftist scholars, in particular, argue that class-based politics rather than clientelism is necessary to achieve the broad redistribution of wealth and power in highly unequal societies (e.g., Sandbrook 1972:104; Haugerud 1995).

Yet some scholars have shown that clientelism may also help clients create a more intimate political relationship that bridges the distance between voters and elected officials in a liberal democracy and hold politicians to their election promises (Lazar 2008:92; Auyero 2001). Furthermore, clients can sometimes win substantial gains, like jobs quotas and community development projects, from patronage relationships if they are already highly mobilized in unions and community organizations.[9]

Early in his first term in 2006, Evo attempted to show that he had broken the mold of the clientelistic and selfish political leader who cared solely about maintaining elite privilege. His indigenous origins and upbringing in poverty were central to this claim. He also pointed repeatedly to the MAS political platform that promised to redistribute wealth so that all Bolivians could "live well" (*sumaq kausay*) with dignity, though not opulence. Evo and other leaders summed up this transformation in the phrase "the process of change" (*el proceso de cambio*). He maintained that his own political practices and those of his government would mark a dramatic shift from clientelism. For example, Evo announced on taking office that his workday and that of his cabinet would begin at 5 A.M. In a further attempt to set himself apart from selfish clientelist politicians—who Bolivians believed to be wildly overpaid and "only seeking their paychecks"—Evo announced a 50 percent salary cut for himself and his ministers. These initial acts symbolizing the abolition of clientelism and affirming public interest earned him a fleeting and grudging respect from some Sacabans who were otherwise skeptical about his abilities or platform.

## Accusations of Clientelism in Sacaba

Despite widespread hope immediately following Evo's 2005 election that MAS would be entirely different from previous political parties, many Sacabans were already disillusioned about the municipal MAS party. As MAS had expanded in Sacaba Municipality since the late 1990s, local MAS leaders continued the practices of populist clientelistic parties such as the UCS and the MNR, focusing on building public works and distributing jobs to loyal supporters. Sacaba's conflictive political environment was exacerbated by uncertainty about the parties to which particular leaders owed allegiances. When the MAS party, claiming to represent rural agrarian unions, began to rise in power, a flood of people joined the party who had formerly belonged to other political parties like the MNR and the UCS. This soured some locals on the claim that MAS was wholly different in its aims and practices from previous parties. Some Sacabans described such party hoppers as self-interested and craven, "the same *chola* in a different *pollera* [*la misma chola pero con distinta pollera*]." Some new MAS leaders had reportedly claimed social superiority over campesinos and indigenous when they belonged to their previous parties, contributing to the widespread suspicion of their motives. The Sacaba MAS party as a whole and individuals associated with it spent much time warding off accusations that they were the same as politicians in older parties: self-interested, clientelistic, and simply seeking personal fortune rather than serving the public.

Disagreement about the class and racial identities of leaders and rank-and-file activists also played a significant role in these controversies over whether the MAS party had created a sharp break from previous parties' practices. While Evo's credentials as a person of poor, indigenous, campesino origins were credible and buoyed many Bolivians' hopes that he had broken with the status quo of elite dominance through clientelism, many

Sacaban political leaders could not claim such watertight subaltern origins. The national MAS discourse posited a societal clash between the super-wealthy and the utterly destitute, but as I have shown in previous chapters, the wealth and social status of many Sacabans, like those of Amanda and Doña Felisa, fell somewhere in the middle of national racial and class hierarchies. And even a modicum of wealth and political authority made leaders prey to accusations that they were out of step with the MAS pledge to lift up Bolivia's excluded poor and indigenous. At the very least, the relative prosperity of many MAS activists in Sacaba, from coca growers to lawyers to prosperous merchants, added a strong element of ambiguity to the motives and intentions of the party.

The national MAS leaders' argument that clientelism was more authoritarian than other forms of democracy was based on a model in which patrons give their small, individual, ephemeral gifts only at the moment of elections, while most decision making occurs in private, among elites. Sacaba MAS leaders and rank-and-file activists explained their formal commitment to consensus decision making by the rank and file (*base*) in open assemblies as an explicit rejection of authoritarian clientelism. Yet in my observation, neither leaders nor rank and file held the upper hand. Sacaba leaders did not exercise complete control over grassroots supporters when they gave out public works projects or jobs; nor did grassroots power flower under Sacaba's municipal MAS government. Instead, the authority of both the base and the leaders was characterized by fundamental tensions in the municipal and national MAS parties.

Some commentators in Bolivia have suggested that it is not only political parties' practice of granting small favors in exchange for votes that leads to authoritarianism in Bolivian politics. Instead, authoritarianism infuses many different institutions, including the agrarian unions. They have argued that the agrarian union structure, which borrowed elements from European Marxist and Trotskyist unions and which served as a model for some leaders in the MAS party, centralized authority in a manner similar to that of authoritarian clientelism, in which bosses make decisions for and distribute favors to clients (Rivera Cusicanqui 1990; Arias in Ayo 2004:37; Fabricant 2012; Regalsky 2010:39).

Others have countered that MAS leaders avoid clientelism by being more consultative than the leaders of most other Bolivian political parties (e.g., Gamarra 2003:291). National and Sacaba MAS leaders often argued that the party is infused with the democratic structure of *ayllus*—

indigenous Andean community governance systems. Two central features of *ayllus* are decision making by consensus in all-member assemblies, and leaders who rotate in office rather than run for election. This rotating leadership, in which all adult men (but not women) of a community serve for a fixed term is intended to both limit the power of individual leaders and distribute the burdens of leadership widely. While *ayllus* as a form of community organization had not been common in most of the Sacaba region in living memory, many Sacaba MAS activists expressed the principle of rotating leadership in their practices of electoral politics. A central feature of such rotation that most people accepted matter-of-factly was the common agreements for two or more local elected leaders to split a single political term. The principle of rotation of leadership was also evident in many Sacabans' frustrated exclamations that some local veteran MAS party leaders, such as Jaime, the MAS congressman, should step aside to "give someone else a turn."

National and Sacaba MAS leaders also claimed difference from authoritarian clientelist, elite political parties by advocating direct democracy through an assembly-based, consensual decision-making process in addition to elections. Leaders touted the party's hybrid union, indigenous, and social movement roots as evidence that decision-making processes, from the most local of levels to the national level, were subject to the approval of the rank and file, in contrast to the top-down management of traditional political parties. Indeed, MAS leaders faced more scrutiny from the rank and file than did other political parties (Gamarra 2003:298). MAS leaders had borrowed their rhetoric of consulting with the rank and file (*consultar con las bases*) from leaders of the social movements that supported MAS as an alternative to clientelism, including indigenist movements, the *cocaleros*, and CSUTCB national agrarian unions (e.g., CSUTCB 1994). When Cristina Choque, the local MAS candidate for Bolivia's Constitutional Assembly who had been booed at a Sacaba agrarian union convention in 2006 for not speaking Quechua (see Chapter 3), campaigned throughout Sacaba Municipality in 2006, she promised to "consult with the *bases* through constant meetings [*en reuniones constantes*]." Evo, too, proclaimed repeatedly during 2005 and 2006 that he would "lead by following" (*mandar obedeciendo*), a transnational indigenous movement catchphrase.[10] This rhetorical position of grassroots democratic decision making was intended to directly counter the image of the clientelist party leader who makes decisions in secret in favor of his elite interests and then doles out insignificant gifts and favors.

The MAS rhetoric promoting the rank and file's power to choose and remove leaders and control policy making also posited that individual leaders would be blocked if they attempted to pursue clientelistic self-interest, because agrarian union or community grassroots constituents would recognize leaders' illegitimate motivations and oppose them. Doña Felisa offered an example of this rhetoric when explaining that whenever candidates in regional and national agrarian union elections are too forceful in campaigning for leadership positions, "the rank and file would realize what is going on" (*bases cuenta qonku*) and say to themselves, "that candidate must have self-interest [*interés*]" and refuse to vote for them. In Doña Felisa's framing, the rank and file enact democracy by grouping around a committed leader. The surest way for leaders to lose the support of the rank and file was to demonstrate visible self-interest.

This attempt to perform public-mindedness to attract rank and file support could be seen in the most subtle, as well as the most explicit, levels of self-presentation and accusation of others. For example, would-be leaders used body language to deliberately display their commitment to the public interest. During the dozens of community and agrarian union meetings I attended throughout Sacaba, candidates nominated for office, who usually stood in a row facing the assembly as the group voted, nearly always maintained a look of intense distraction, eyes on the distant horizon or middle space, their faces resolutely slack. Such political habits clearly responded to the widespread belief that people visibly eager to win office were guided by "self-interest" (*interés personal*).

The verticality of chains of command within MAS was also tempered by the aura of fragility of leaders' power in Bolivia. Many Bolivians affirmed that Evo remained in power by the grace of highly mobilized movements that could topple him as they had toppled three prior presidents during the four years prior to his election. Similarly, when several MAS leaders, like Mayor Luis Orellana in 2006, were ousted following protests, marches, and road blockades, some of the rank and file argued that democratic-minded grassroots MAS supporters had successfully overcome the authoritarianism of selfish, clientelistic leaders.

Finally, and crucially, MAS leaders claimed that their party enacted grassroots power, rather than the authoritarian clientelism of all other Bolivian political parties, because leaders shared the subaltern status—indigenous race and campesino and working-class identity—of the majority of Bolivians.[11] While elites led other parties and tried to dupe subaltern followers with clientelistic favors, MAS's subaltern leadership meant that the party could avoid clientelism. Doña Felisa used this rhetoric when she explained her own success as a senator to me in 2006. Rank-and-file MAS activists had consistently supported her as a result of her tireless travel throughout Bolivia to its most remote rural areas to visit the country's most marginalized people. They recognized her energy and commitment as she organized educational and consciousness-raising seminars to foment indigenous and campesino pride as well as to promote policies like gas nationalization and an end to free markets. She told me that she successfully convinced the rank and file that she did not have "personal interest" based on her leadership qualities and policies of redistribution of wealth, rather than in exchange for patronage benefits. Unspoken, but intertwined in her self-presentation of legitimacy and public interest, was the implication that her native fluency in Quechua and her visible identity as a *cholita* in *pollera* and braids made her an appropriate racial and class representative for subaltern supporters.

Yet the middle-class aspirations and ambiguous racial and class status of many Sacabans, including Doña Felisa, also conflicted with MAS leaders' denunciations of clientelism that rested on the existence of a clearly identifiable elite oppressing a clearly identifiable subaltern constituency. Doña Felisa's architect-designed house and her relative prosperity, described in Chapter 3, complicated her self-identification as a poor, campesina, *cholita* and will be further explored in Chapter 5. The gap between Sacaba MAS leaders' self-identifications as subalterns and their middling wealth and social status in everyday life led many Sacabans to question whether MAS represented a break from other parties' authoritarian clientelism.

## Congressman Jaime: Archetype of Clientelism in Sacaba

If MAS activists attempted to prove their own subaltern credentials and public mindedness by accusing others of clientelism, authoritarianism, and elite identity, one man in particular served as a target. Accusations against MAS Congressman Jaime illustrate the tensions between grassroots democracy and authoritarianism within the MAS, and the ways in which middling racial and class status complicated political frameworks that depended on a binary of elite and subaltern. Jaime was widely seen in Sacaba as the archetype of a clientelist, power-hungry, "selfish" political operator. While there were many perspectives on the causes of the bitterly fought Sacaba conflicts, people from opposite sides often agreed that Jaime's clientelistic machinations were to blame for much of the conflict. By capturing the personal confidence of Evo, they argued, and defusing potential rivals by setting them against each other, Jaime had remained in congressional office too long—he should step down to allow someone else "to have a turn."

Stories abounded from both MAS activists and opposition party leaders about Jaime's strategy of divide and conquer, stirring up conflict to keep other leaders occupied in petty squabbles, and overriding local leaders' legitimate authority in the local party and agrarian union. Jaime figured prominently in Sacabans' everyday stories about their long-running political conflicts, which were filled with mutual accusations of clientelism, of envy, and of self-interestedness. In the sometimes-daily protests and road blockades to oust a mayor or city council member, in the yearly turnover of mayors and their administrations, in the schisms within the municipal MAS party that spawned up to four competing MAS factions on several occasions, many Sacabans pointed to the long arm of Jaime. Many Sacabans argued that, despite the formal support of Sacaba MAS leaders for the platform of anticlientelism and redistribution of wealth, MAS leaders repeatedly pursued clientelism. These selfish manipulations meant the continual postponement of local political cooperation that was necessary for the construction of public works such as new schools and paved roads that would signal that the Sacaba MAS party was enacting its platform of development and redistribution of wealth. Despite the MAS party's official goal of community development and redistribution of wealth, many critics argued, the Sacaba MAS—epitomized by Jaime—was firmly committed to clientelism.

Some further condemned Jaime as the original architect of clientelism in Sacaba. Doña Felisa and Don Álvaro each blamed Jaime for establishing the (classic) clientelist structure of political competition in Sacaba, by which each of the Sacaba MAS Municipal Council or mayoral candidates recruited their own *pegas*: groups of campaign volunteers who would support them financially, run their campaigns, and organize protests against their competitors. While Jaime was correct that *pegas* were effective at getting MAS members elected, once in office they had to return the clientelist favor by hiring their *pegas* in the municipal administration. Furthermore, *pegas* formed rival blocs that remained loyal to individual leaders rather than to the MAS party as a whole or its platform. Individual council members rallied their *pegas'* support when they were accused of corruption or when they wished to vote against a MAS platform principle. This fostered factionalism and constant, disruptive protests.

Many Sacaba leaders of the party and agrarian union also argued that Jaime was responsible for inviting into the Sacaba MAS former leaders of older elite-dominated parties associated with both a naked clientelism and neoliberal policies, such as the MIR and MNR. These party-hopping leaders secretly abhorred the MAS platform of redistribution of wealth and power to the poor and indigenous. I often heard rumors about Jaime's allies who were said to be deliberately plotting treachery for the MAS party and the Instrumento Político movement—hoping to discredit the party by promoting conflict and corruption so that locals would turn to other parties.

Jaime, as depicted by many Sacabans, including Doña Felisa, was thus a consummately self-interested and clientelistic leader. MAS leaders opposed to Jaime claimed that it was in response to his machinations that in 2003 they formed the local rival party, H. Obras. The party's platform was identical to that of the national MAS party, and its bylaws recognized the national MAS party leaders as their national representatives. The founders of H. Obras (among them Doña Felisa) hoped for a fresh start for Sacaba politics by providing a nonclientelistic space for public-minded leaders and the rank and file, who would exercise democracy in keeping with MAS principles. Unsurprisingly, however, Jaime's supporters and other MAS party stalwarts condemned H. Obras founders as self-interested, power-hungry, and clientelistic patronage seekers themselves.

Part of the cause of conflict over the meaning and effects of these political acts—of creating a *pegas* campaign system, of forming a local party to rival MAS—in my view, was the ambiguity of the class and race identity of the actors. If clientelism was commonly defined in political discourse as an elite person giving out insignificant gifts to a subaltern person, who counted as "elite" in Sacaba? As I showed in Chapter 2, a large swath of Sacaba residents, such as Doña Felisa, identified themselves alternately as both subaltern and elite according to provincial hierarchies, in both explicit and inexplicit ways. Congressman Jaime, the archetype of clientelism, was himself born into a rural community and a self-identified campesino family. Jaime's dark skin, thick thatch of black hair, and Quechua-accented Spanish pointed to these indigenous and campesino origins. Yet his beer belly suggested that he made his living at a more sedentary occupation than that of campesino farmers, who usually had flat stomachs from hard physical labor. He had risen from local agrarian union leader to lawyer, local MAS party leader, and congressman. In 2009, he would be elected Cochabamba's departmental governor (*prefecto*) on the MAS ticket. Though Jaime termed himself a campesino, his relative wealth, law degree, and longtime political leadership position meant that he did not fit cleanly in the polarized discursive categories of *pobre* and *rico*.[12] In Sacaban politics, he existed uneasily at both poles of elite and subaltern.

In part owing to this ambiguity, Jaime was perpetually accused of claiming an identity that did not belong to him. In a political context that required identification as a subaltern, Jaime faced accusation of being a secret elite, because he was reputed to have accumulated wealth in office from salaries and perhaps theft of public funds, and had stayed "too long" there. People who formed rival political factions, like Doña Felisa, justified their decision to break away by asserting that Jaime was, like many other leaders, falsely claiming to be subaltern.

Some people from longtime provincial elite (*vecino*) families who had a more tenuous connection to a campesino origin, such as the MAS ex-mayor Luis Orellana, also called themselves campesinos in some moments. Such identification as subaltern provoked suspicion and uncertainty from some followers. For example, in early 2006, before Orellana's forced resignation, Sacaba MAS party leaders often argued that the embattled Orellana was worthy of support in part because his family had been very poor. Only through his father's immense "sacrifice" as a destitute sand grinder had Orellana been able to study for a law degree and enter municipal politics. Yet other people in Sacaba countered that Orellana's father had been a wealthy member of the provincial elite, a medium-sized landowner in Sacaba before the 1953 Agrarian Reform, and that Orellana himself had become even wealthier by stealing public monies as a public official before becoming mayor. Still other people wondered in vexation which of Orellana's personal histories was true. As one agrarian woman leader exclaimed during a moment in 2006 when controversy surrounding Orellana's political legitimacy was at its height, "They say; they say; I don't believe anyone! [*ninku, ninku, ni pi creenichu*]." MAS leaders could be hiding Orellana's elite origins as a wealthy landowner to protect their patron in power, she lamented, but critics could also be unfairly slandering Orellana as wealthy in order to boost rival leaders. No language existed to mark Orellana as a middling sort or to distinguish between the subtle gradations of family wealth and status that marked social relations within Sacaba Municipality.[13]

Part of the problem, as mentioned above, was that social and economic hierarchies that shaped MAS party and agrarian union rhetoric differed on municipal and national scales. An interpretive impasse took hold when leaders' and supporters' class and race identifications were contested—was a particular political leader from a wealthy, urban family or a poor, campesino one?—and when few words existed to describe identities in the middle. When someone in Sacaba compared herself to the extreme wealth, whiteness, and power of Bolivia's national superelites, it was easy to claim to be a subaltern, indigenous campesina ranged against elite oppressors.

## The Overlapping of Practices Between Political Models

In part because of the ambiguity of class and racial identity, then, the labeling of a given act as clientelism was thus often contested in this environment of intense political competition. What one person called clientelism, another person termed the radical redistribution of wealth, the discovery of corruption, or the exchanges of everyday social life. For example, in July 2007, a former coca grower and MAS activist who worked in Sacaba city hall as a low-level accountant explained to me that he had joined MAS when it formed because Evo was the only leader who actively sought development opportunities (*caminaba*, literally "walked around") as much as President Barrientos, the military general and dictator who ruled Bolivia from 1964 to 1969. Barrientos had won the hearts of many people in the Cochabamba valleys with his many visits to the region, his speeches in his native Quechua, and patronage gifts of schools and irrigation systems to rural communities, including Choro. He had also brutally repressed miners and other industrial unions. This local MAS activist's equation of Evo with Barrientos spoke to the large area of overlap between the MAS rhetoric of grassroots democracy and preexisting models of patronage in many Sacabans' practical expectations of their political leaders. While national MAS leaders described Barrientos as a consummate clientelist leader and specifically contrasted his type of politicking with leaders like Evo who purportedly embodied a contrasting radical grassroots democracy, for everyday citizens the two models sometimes overlapped in the model of a vigorous leader who enacted development by whatever means necessary.

Neither national MAS leaders nor Sacaba leaders made a rhetorical distinction between ephemeral individual gifts like noodles, more significant individual favors such as employment offers for individuals, and substantial collective gifts like affirmative action plans and community development funding. Yet some people did seem to draw these distinctions between the ephemeral and the significant, the individual and the collective, in practice. This practical distinction emerged, for example, in an incident in early 2006, when Manfred, then newly elected right-wing state governor (*prefecto*) of Cochabamba, began the process of choosing a subprefect for Sacaba. Many people wanted the job, and Manfred requested that each of the rival candidates come to his office with their active supporters (*bases*). Manfred declared that the leader who could marshal the most supporters would win the post. MAS supporters complained that Manfred secretly favored Edwin, the candidate of the Sacaba local municipal opposition party, H. Obras.[14] Several H. Obras supporters I knew contended (somewhat disingenuously, since their candidate, an architect born and raised in Sacaba's provincial town, was a personal friend of Manfred) that this was a straightforward contest based on numbers of constituents to signal their democratic support. One such H. Obras supporter from Choro was Orlando, a frustrated member of Choro's emergent middle class, whose parents were considered to belong to the upper half of wealth and social status in Choro. For several years, Orlando had been working part-time as a taxi driver and trying to decide whether he should go back to the university to complete his engineering degree. Orlando was friends with Doña Saturnina's children and shared their support for the right-wing presidential candidate, Tuto. In private, Orlando told me with a sheepish half-smile that he was also motivated in supporting the H. Obras candidate, who was his personal friend, by his hope to get a *pega* (patronage job) from Manfred or from Edwin himself.

Some rank-and-file participants in the events surrounding the naming of the subprefect, by contrast, described their motivations straightforwardly and publicly as clientelism oriented toward community benefit rather than benefit for themselves as individuals. In early February, I accompanied a delegation of Choro leaders on a trip to show their support for the H. Obras subprefect candidate. Orlando drove us in his van to Manfred's Cochabamba campaign headquarters. When I stepped inside the van, a young Choro H. Obras activist returning from a stint growing coca in the Chapare explained earnestly and matter-of-factly, "We're going because if we do Edwin [the candidate] this favor, he will help us later. It's an exchange of favors [*intercambio de favores*]." A schoolteacher who placed herself in a different political camp, having voted enthusiastically for MAS, and who had no prior relationship to Manfred or the subprefect candidate, also told me simply that she was attending to carry out her duty as Choro's agrarian union secretary to marshal all possible resources for community development projects. By supporting Edwin, she hoped that Choreños would gain a sewer system or new high school building from the Cochabamba state public works budget, which Manfred controlled.

The matter-of-factness with which these two participants explained their motivations contrasts with Orlando's embarrassment when he told me privately that he was hoping for a *pega* for himself. It seemed to me that they voiced their motives in public and without Orlando's embarrassed smile because they were seeking collective, rather than private, gain. They had no fear of being accused of self-interest. This contrast suggests that in practice some Sacabans accepted collectivist motivations for clientelism as a practical necessity. This practical acceptance contrasted with the argument by MAS leaders such as Salazar that collective and individual motivations for clientelist favor seeking were equally selfish. From Salazar's perspective, any challenge to the power of the MAS was a problem; other Sacaba leaders who were unsuccessful in getting development funding also pointed out heatedly that one community's clientelistic gain of development funds meant the loss of those funds to another community. Nevertheless, people who could plausibly profess a collective interest appeared to have little concern that their friends or neighbors would see their actions as illegitimate or immoral.

This implicit distinction between attempts to capture collective rather than individual benefit helps explain why Sacabans sometimes disagreed on whether to label particular acts as clientelism or as the exercise of responsible community leadership and the justifiable attempt to redistribute wealth more equitably. The Choro schoolteacher went to Manfred's office in her capacity as a community agrarian union leader, doing her duty to attract development funds. This was one of many duties her fellow agrarian union members expected her to perform. And if Manfred were to shower Choro with development projects after they helped elect his friend as subprefect, who could say that this was not a redistribution of wealth from elites to subalterns, from urban neighborhoods that had for decades monopolized Cochabamba state development funds to a rural community that desperately needed vital infrastructure?

Sacabans also debated whether particular acts carried out by political leaders were substantial or insubstantial, and therefore clientelist or something else. I, too, found it difficult to form my own opinion regarding the significance or insignificance of the municipal government's actions in Sacaba in 2005 and 2006. A municipal government road crew patched what appeared to be the same pothole again and again between the towns of Chiñata and Catachilla over the course of several months. As I passed by daily on the bus, I could not help but wonder if this was the enactment of significant infrastructure or a paltry and ephemeral gift in exchange for local votes. As Sian Lazar found in highland El Alto, Bolivia, Sacabans also depended on the visible manifestation of public works (*obras*) to measure the honesty and dedication of their local government (see Lazar 2008). Yet Sacabans were often suspicious of officials' claims to have built these visible manifestations of development: shoddy workmanship meant that potable water tanks leaked, sewer pipes made out of cheap PVC often broke, and school buildings remained "under construction" for years.

The same act could, furthermore, be interpreted as clientelism or radical grassroots democracy led by subaltern political supporters (*bases*), depending on one's interpretation or the political faction to which one belonged. Don Félix Hernández, the MAS municipal official serving Choro's rural district and a sometime ally of Congressman Jaime, pointed obliquely to this overlap in recounting the origins of the schism between the Sacaba MAS and H. Obras in 2003. Oscar Angulo, the provincial elite lawyer who had many allies in the Sacaba branch of the agrarian union, had decided to topple Jaime as the head of the provincial MAS party so that he could become mayor. Word of Angulo's power seeking reached Evo Morales, who was then a senator, the president of the coca growers' union, and national leader of the MAS party. Evo called the rival leaders, Jaime and Angulo, in to a meeting and explained how he would decide whom to support. "Evo called them both. 'I'll go wherever the supporters [*bases*] are,' he tells everyone, and Jaime showed that he had more people and Angulo, few people . . . that's where the division started. . . . [Soon] there was a national MAS party convention held in Sacaba. Everything had been fine, but then all of a sudden Jaimistas [Jaime supporters] and Angulistas [Oscar Angulo supporters] appeared when there had been none before." Don Félix's narrative suggests an overlapping analysis that mobilizing behind leaders was both an expression of clientelism and of popular will in a grassroots, assembly-based democracy. On the one hand, he appears to support Evo's decision to compare the rivals' respective abilities to mobilize supporters as a method of bowing to the democratic will of the populace. On the other hand, in Don Félix's narrative, as a result of these leaders' competition with each other for local followers and for Evo's seal of approval, the local strength of the party had cracked and conflict had persisted ever since. Evo eventually expelled Oscar Angulo from the MAS party for sowing conflict; Angulo promptly formed H. Obras as a local opposition party.

Yet another cause of overlap between actions labeled democratic by some and clientelistic by others emerged because formally different types of institutions such as rural community councils (*sindicatos*), regional agrarian unions, and political parties shared similar organizational tactics. People were often members of all of these institutions at once. *Sindicatos*, for example, which were made up of every registered adult head of household in a campesino community, required residents to march in local parades, attend meetings and work parties, and contribute dues. Those who did not fulfill these duties risked fines or losing vital services. This structure had formed during the revolutionary agrarian organizing in the 1940s, following the examples of European industrial unions (Goodale 2009), and employed similar tactics as many urban and rural unions throughout Latin America (see Colloredo-Mansfield 2009). *Sindicato* leaders and many rank-and-file members believed that such coercion of individuals was necessary to maintain communal property such as irrigation ditches, to fund public projects, and to maintain a collective presence in municipal public life in order to remain eligible for development funds, whenever and from wherever they might come. When two Choro men were reluctant to spend the time to march in a Day of the Campesino parade on August 2, 2006, their neighbor rebuked them, "Do you drink potable water or not? Do you want to keep on receiving it? Then you have to march." In almost identical language, a Choro *sindicato* leader asked rhetorically, attempting to convince skeptical residents to appear for a rally in favor of Cochabamba's right-wing gubernatorial candidate Manfred, "Do you want public works?" If they supported Manfred during his election campaign, he would return the favor with public works in Choro once elected, the leader coaxed. When that Choro leader marched at one of Manfred's rallies with a banner proclaiming "*Choro presente!*" he was seen by some Choreños as doing his utmost as a good community leader to put Choro as a collectivity in line for public works from Manfred. Other Choreños, however, denounced him as selfishly currying favor in order to seek a job in Manfred's administration. The same act was identified as community-mindedness or as selfish clientelism, depending on the eye of—or faction of—the beholder.

The often fierce debates over who counted as elite or subaltern and who was pursuing clientelism over public-mindedness were fed, in some local analyses and in my own view, by the uncertain balance of power between Sacaba's rural and urban districts for development funding and political control (see also Chapter 3). Two-thirds of the municipal population, and hence of voters, resided in five officially designated urban districts, while the remaining one-third of the population lived in five rural districts. This rural one-third, while a minority, constituted a significant political bloc. With municipal funding allocated on a per capita basis, the more densely populated urban districts invariably received more funding. Meanwhile, rural district residents protested that they should receive more because of their backlog of long-ignored infrastructure needs. The rising national power of MAS from a base in Bolivia's agrarian unions gave weight to Sacaba's rural districts' demands without giving them a decisive edge. This inconclusive rural-urban conflict played out in power struggles between individual leaders as well. People identifying themselves as rural and poor had a formal advantage in reaching a leadership position in MAS, while at the same time, urban-identified middle-class professionals could potentially draw on the still-powerful authority that resulted from their relative wealth and social status in Bolivian society.

This competition for power and funding between rural and urban blocs nourished the disagreements over which acts should be labeled as clientelism. In one example of this disagreement, Don Félix, the low-level MAS official in Sacaba, explained to me in 2006 why some MAS members had withdrawn support for the embattled Sacaba MAS mayor Luis Orellana before his forced resignation that April. Don Félix recounted how Orellana had violated a written contract (*convenio*) he had signed the year before with the leaders of the Sacaba municipal agrarian union, most of whom were affiliated with the MAS party. In the *convenio*, agrarian union leaders had promised to vote for Orellana if Orellana would distribute at least 30 percent of municipal jobs to residents of Sacaba's rural districts once he took office. This jobs quota matched the 30 percent of Sacabans residing in rural districts according to the 2001 Bolivian census. Don Félix described the *convenio*—widely viewed as a type of legal document even though it went against the spirit and letter of the Popular Participation Law—as akin to an affirmative action policy. But agrarian union members realized that

Mayor Orellana had failed to honor his agreement during his year in office. Don Félix told me disgustedly, "He tricked us [*engañado*]." In the end Orellana hired only 17 percent rural employees. The exactness of Don Félix's figure suggests that Sacaba agrarian union leaders had pored carefully over the rolls of municipal employees and made precise and infuriated head counts. To make matters worse, those who had been hired from rural areas were "just drivers, night watchmen: the lowest of positions. That's where a campesino can work; nothing more," Don Félix exclaimed bitterly.

Don Félix was describing a practice—a jobs quota—whose meaning was locally contested: some in Sacaba would label these actions clientelism and others would label them social justice. Don Félix described this jobs quota as a measure for collective social justice, a source of jobs for rural folk who had long constituted an excluded, impoverished minority within the municipality, and an excluded majority in Bolivia. The quota thus promoted the spirit of the MAS promise to redistribute wealth. On the other hand, the existence of a jobs quota for loyal political supporters was derided as *pegas* by unemployed people and those unaffiliated with the agrarian union. A high-ranking, professionally educated Sacaba municipal planning official born and raised in the city of Cochabamba complained to me, for example, that the agrarian union's expectation of jobs in exchange for political support constituted clientelism. Like Manfred and Evo's practice of choosing local leaders based on a head count of their supporters, the meanings of many of these everyday repertoires of political action in Sacaba were fundamentally contested.[15]

## The Oven Debate

One episode in particular crystallized these debates over the defensibility of clientelism and over the relationship between authoritarianism and clientelism in the local MAS party. In a meeting in Choro in 2005, an NGO director and fervent national MAS supporter gave a lecture against clientelism to the members of a women's group receiving funding from his organization. In his diatribe and the women beneficiaries' responses, the ambiguities of Sacabans' class and race status came to the fore in an implicit disagreement over whether particular individuals were subaltern campesinos or prosperous middling folk. This NGO worker, like other Sacaba leaders and officials, condemned clientelism as an archaic political practice by combining the language of liberal democracy and the MAS party's language of grassroots democracy. In turn, he faced the accusation by his program beneficiaries that his very condemnation of them actually reflected the authoritarian practice of clientelism.

Don Carlos, a Bolivian agronomist from the capital, La Paz, had founded the small NGO Inti in Sacaba in 1999 together with his Danish wife, Doña Karin.[16] Inti's stated aims were to improve education and health in several towns in Sacaba Municipality, based on the principle of interculturality, a MAS watchword that meant mutual respect between the indigenous poor, mestizos, and European-descended elites. Don Carlos and Doña Karin had formed women's groups to provide income opportunities to women in several local communities, including Choro, by knitting and baking. The NGO directors also hoped, they told me, to promote a spirit of communal unity to promote development in each locality in which they worked and to teach women to become political leaders by making the group a chapter of the Bartolina Sisa Federation, a national women's agrarian union.[17] The Bartolinas had become an important national base of support for the MAS party. Don Carlos himself was a longtime supporter of the national MAS party, though he was critical of many Sacaba municipal MAS leaders.

Wealthier members of Inti's women's group who were members of what I have termed Choro's nonprofessional, emergent middle class—prosperous trucker families or high school graduates with regular income from low-level clerical jobs—made up about half the group. They appeared most interested in the group as a place to enjoy leisure time. They clearly relished having a space in which to catch up on community news, share personal experiences within a community of women, listen to workshops on domestic violence and child rearing, and learn knitting and baking as homemaking skills. They tended not to express interest in the Bartolinas' activities, likely because of their firm rejection of the MAS party and the open alliance of the Bartolinas with the party. These women, like Deysi and Amanda, also discussed with each other in racialized terms that Evo was not qualified to be president as an "Indian" and they believed he had not earned a high school degree. They professed these sentiments to each other out of Don Carlos's hearing, however.

Poorer women, on the other hand—single teenage mothers, landless day laborers, and coca growers with modest earnings—expressed most enthusiasm about the money-making opportunities, particularly the small sweater-knitting and bakery co-ops that the Inti directors were attempting to form. These were the members who expressed most support for MAS and tended to be most interested in attending the Bartolinas meetings in Cochabamba and other Bolivian cities.

Meanwhile, Don Carlos outranked all of the women. His title of agronomist-engineer (*ingeniero agrónomo*) gave him a high professional status in Bolivia, below only professionals who had attained their degrees in the United States, Europe, or wealthy Latin American countries such as Mexico and Argentina. His European wife gave him additional status, and his home contained signs of education and affluence such as books and computers, which most Choro homes lacked. He also had fairer skin and hair than most in Choro. Don Carlos considered himself to share impoverished roots with Choro residents, however. One of ten children from a poor urban La Paz neighborhood, Don Carlos often mentioned that he had grown up destitute and that he was one of only two siblings who had a college education.

At one weekly Thursday meeting in early December 2005, as the presidential campaign had reached a fever pitch, two of the more affluent group members made an excited announcement. They had secured a promise from the local campaign manager of Tuto Quiroga, the right-wing presidential candidate and principal opponent of Evo in the upcoming elections, to buy the women's group an oven. For several months of meetings, the women had been discussing their hope to buy an industrial-sized oven for cooking classes and to start a cooperatively owned bakery, but had come up short of the total cost. One of the women, Fernanda, a low-level secretary and one of two high school graduates in the group, said coaxingly they could receive Tuto's campaigners here, at the women's group headquarters, for a small celebration when they delivered the oven.

Ximena, the paid staff coordinator (*promotora*) of the women's group, suddenly looked anxious and said gently that Inti could not officially support any political party. Someone else asked aloud if anyone knew Don Carlos's political party, presumably to assess whether he might support their plan. Ximena answered that Don Carlos belonged to MAS. This would have been obvious to anyone who was active in formal politics from Don Carlos's distinctively agrarian union rhetoric, the posters of Evo and of social movement leaders that he had hung on the walls of the women's meeting room, and his decision to establish the women's group as a chapter of the Bartolinas in the first place. A woman responded, to widespread enthusiasm, that they could accept the oven and simply receive the campaigners in the health clinic nearby.

Ximena left to consult with Don Carlos and a few minutes later, Don Carlos, wearing his habitual faded green flannel shirt, burst into the room. A normally excitable man, he was practically quivering with intensity. He said sternly that he had heard from Ximena that the women were considering accepting an oven from Tuto's campaign. He then launched into an intense monologue in his rapid-fire mix of Spanish and self-taught Quechua that lasted at least twenty-five unbroken minutes—long even by his standards. We all had weary looks on our faces, but unlike during workshops on constitutional reform, all eyes remained riveted on him.

Don Carlos condemned clientelism, and particularly, clientelist ties to this particular right-wing candidate. He argued, first, that voting based on platform, rather than clientelist interest, was the most fundamental of citizens' rights and duties, and the only democratic right that Bolivians, given their unequal society, had the opportunity to exercise. He exclaimed that the moment in which we vote was the "only moment in which we are all worth the same [*todos valemos lo mismo*] when we are really brothers [*cuando sí, somos hermanos*]."

As Don Carlos launched into a tirade against Tuto, incredibly, his tone rose in intensity. "Don't forget," he shouted, "who took away our water." Tuto had championed water privatization in Cochabamba in 2000, which led to a spike in rates and was met with massive urban protest in the "water war" (*guerra del agua*). The water war launched the era of intense public protest and mobilization by social movements and the MAS that was still evident on the day of this meeting. "Who was president then?" he asked fiercely. One of the women who had proposed the oven scheme, a trucker's wife, recoiled as if attacked. The other proponent of the scheme, Fernanda, answered Don Carlos that the president had been Hugo Banzer, military dictator of Bolivia during most of the 1970s, responsible for an infamous massacre of campesino protesters in 1974, and elected again as president on a right-wing party platform in the late 1990s. Don Carlos continued, "And who was vice president?" Someone answered: "Tuto."

Don Carlos then placed Tuto in the historical bloc of the superelite, oppressive, white, and wealthy minority in Bolivia and defined the women and himself as members of the subaltern, oppressed, indigenous, and poor majority. He asked, "Who are the ones who have always been grinding us under their feet [*los que nos han pisoteado siempre*]?" Tuto had negotiated highly questionable deals with foreign companies in secret, selling Bolivia's chief export, natural gas, "behind the backs of everyone . . . gas at the price of a dead chicken." Don Carlos urged us to think hard about whether Tuto and his party were "our friends."

Don Carlos then denounced clientelistic vote buying in principle. Politicians "put a price on each vote." We all knew what they spent this money on, he prompted us, "Noodles [*fideitos*]." Fernanda took up Don Carlos's thread: "Noodles, T-shirts . . ."

Don Carlos also urged the women to think about the consequences if the women's organization supported the losing candidate; he enjoined them to be "very careful." Several women nodded suddenly, as if recalling the common Bolivian knowledge that siding with candidates who lost would exclude them from receiving benefits from the eventual winner— regardless of whether they had partisan sympathies and where those sympathies lay. Don Carlos said that this was why he tried to keep the NGO "neutral." He tapped his temple theatrically. "I know very well for whom I will vote," he said. But, if Inti officially supported a candidate, some Choreños would side with them and others against them and this would "create suspicion [*desconfianza*] in people."

Don Carlos then posed a series of rhetorical questions to argue that they should drop their commitment to leaders who did not represent them, and become leaders themselves. They could one day be elected Sacaba mayors or city council members and break the dominance of local elites (*vecinos*) from the town of Sacaba in municipal government. He declared, "I am lending a hand to Choro so that one day, you all can move forward alone [*Makita mañarini, sapaykichis ñaupaqman rinankicheqpaq*]." He left the meeting soon after, and the oven scheme was never broached publicly again. The women eventually bought a small oven—disappointingly small to several members—with a minor contribution from me and another Inti employee and with the proceeds of their small cooking business.

In this episode, Don Carlos echoed the MAS activists and allied social movement leaders who regularly condemned clientelism as an obstacle to the grassroots democratic platform of redistribution of wealth and indigenous power. He also echoed LPP reformers who condemned clientelism as an obstacle to individual liberal democracy. His condemnation of clientelism portrayed the majority of Bolivians, including himself, as subalterns who had been trampled (*pisoteado*) for centuries by an elite minority. His injunction to remedy inequality and injustice through elections rather than clientelistic favors reflected the dramatic shift in Bolivian political rhetoric away from that of the 1950s patronage state. Don Carlos portrayed the women's desire to get an oven from Tuto's campaign as an outmoded adherence to clientelism, a relic of the past that had no place during the MAS era of national platform-based politics. Furthermore, this was a dangerous obsolescence because it favored right-wing leaders such as Tuto at the expense of MAS and its promise of the equality.

Yet sympathetic though I was to his outrage at Tuto's elite interests, Don Carlos's tirade should also be seen as a classed act of domination. Tania Li notes a similar dynamic in Indonesia among professionally educated NGO workers critical of the Indonesian state, who saw their role as educating poor Indonesians in the proper definition of citizenship (Li 2007). NGO workers, for example, as part of their efforts to support the protests by impoverished rubber tree growers, took as their most urgent mandate to "instruc[t] people in the proper practice of politics" (Li 2007:176). Li highlights how Indonesian political activists supported the radical redistribution of wealth and power, like Don Carlos, yet simultaneously assumed authority as an intellectual vanguard to raise consciousness among the poor. Such a "will to empower" can perpetuate hierarchies of power, ironically, even when employed with the aim of dramatically transforming deeply unequal societies.

Don Carlos ignored the fact that several women in the group opposed MAS and Evo, and that this opposition was based on ideological principles and middle-class identification as much as on the practical concern of procuring an oven. Furthermore, he did not acknowledge that an oven was hardly as insignificant or ephemeral a gift as the "noodles" he derided.[18] In Don Carlos's frustration at what he apparently interpreted as the women's shortsighted material concerns, he disregarded their ideological commitments. Part of this clash in perspectives, however, reflected the multifaceted and ambiguous class and racial identifications of the women in favor of the oven scheme. Similarly to MAS leaders like Doña Felisa, who defined the *pobre* category as encompassing people who owned two Volvo trucks, Don Carlos portrayed Choro residents as homogeneously subaltern, and therefore, sharing common interests. While his characterization of the women through binary categories of identity is understandable—these labels were what he had available to him, and they reflected his hopes for MAS to prevail in attracting the majority of Bolivians to its political project—his tirade ignored the middle-class aspirations and identities of some of his NGO's would-be beneficiaries.

Furthermore, Don Carlos's accusation of clientelism was thrown back at him, in private. Fernanda, the secretary who introduced the oven scheme, discounted Don Carlos's claims to institutional impartiality, implying that his tirade was motivated by his own clientelist self-interest. When I asked Fernanda, whom I knew well, how she felt about the decision to reject the oven from Tuto, she replied plaintively that "it was not right" (*no era justo*) that Don Carlos had made that decision, "simply on behalf of his party . . . because he was for MAS." In asserting that Don Carlos was partisan, she was disputing his claim to adhere to disinterested democratic principles. Furthermore, she framed his actions as selfish, clientelist partisanship out of personal loyalty to a party, rather than as in the public interest. She contrasted her own motivations for seeking the oven as collective solidarity, saying, "Because . . . the oven wasn't just for me; it was for the whole group." Fernanda's comments echoed those of some Choreños who complained more broadly in other moments that Don Carlos benefitted disproportionately from his NGO's foreign finders. What Don Carlos explained as his own practice of radical democracy, Fernanda labeled a "selfish" clientelism; what Fernanda described as her own collective-mindedness, Don Carlos described as Fernanda's unthinking, short-sighted clientelism. Their debate reflected countless accusations and counteraccusations of clientelism occurring throughout Sacaba.

In addition, that none of the women openly discussed their opposition to the MAS party with Don Carlos also suggests that they feared threatening the flow of resources and opportunities from the NGO. His declaration that his aims as NGO director were to enable the women's group and the locality of Choro to become self-supporting in the future—that he and his wife hoped to "lend a hand" only temporarily—seemed to express his hope, voiced more explicitly to me in other conversations, that he would not fall into the classic patron-client pattern of power. Yet Don Carlos was nevertheless in the position of a patron. The privilege that allowed him to monopolize the attention of the entire group for at least twenty-five unbroken minutes demonstrated again the subordinate position of the women within this relationship of patronage. I suggest that this dynamic of accusation and counteraccusation of selfish clientelism was nearly inescapable in Sacaba—it was the framework through which people asserted their own legitimacy. Furthermore, the ill fit between binary categories of identity and middle-class aspirations added fuel to these countless political fires, large and small.

## The Political Life of Envy in Sacaba

Much of the condemnation of clientelism in Sacaba was expressed through accusations of envy (*envidia*), selfishness (*egoismo*), and synonymous words such as *miramiento* and *qhawanaku* ("mutual watching" in Spanish and Quechua, respectively). MAS regional leader Julio Salazar, introduced at the beginning of this chapter, repeated a local truism that the elimination of envy was a necessary first step in the elimination of clientelism. To create true democracy and development it was necessary to eliminate envy and then clientelism. This political transformation away from clientelism required a transformed morality, for Bolivians to be motivated by collectivist ideology and political platform rather than by envious, individual interest.

In Sacaba's political life, envy was a common answer to the vital question tormenting many locals: why, if both the Popular Participation Law and the rise of the MAS promised bountiful new resources, had development and a flourishing of grassroots democracy failed to ensue? As in the accusations of envy in personal life in Chapter 2—the woman who complained that her neighbors envied her because she had a well-paying job as a maid, the flower farmer who mistrusted the laborers who might stomp on her roses out of envy—Sacabans made the diagnosis of *envidia* in a wide variety of political conflicts. Common denominators in these frequent accusations of envy were rivalry, competition, mutual suspicion, mutual surveillance, and often, concern that other people were keeping harmful political secrets. People complained about envy in politics when recounting enmity between leaders competing for power, competition over scarce jobs, or a lack of mutual trust between members of an organization over whether all were contributing equal money and time.[19] An elderly Choro resident explained that the 1969 death in an airplane accident of General Barrientos, the populist Quechua-speaking military dictator, had resulted from the envy of his fellow officers; they sabotaged his airplane because they sought power themselves. When employees of a Cochabamba-based NGO remarked that some members of an NGO coalition resented other NGOs that neglected to pay their coalition dues, this was "envy" (*miramiento*). Often, the diagnosis of envy seemed to assert broadly that selfishness was always the root cause when people fought with each other, even when the particulars were unknown, as when an agrarian union leader complained, "I don't know what's going on exactly, but the leaders are envying each other [*dirigentes envidianakunku*] and they're not doing a good job."

Sacabans denounced envy from three common stances. First, like Salazar, they accused a group of people for causing needless conflict by envying each other and making unfounded accusations of corruption or ineptitude, and therefore causing harm to a political community—Bolivia, Sacaba Municipality, the national MAS party, or Choro. Second, they complained that a particular person or people envied the speaker, causing the speaker undeserved harm. Third, they protested that other people falsely accused the speaker of envy. As in the common narratives of envy-motivated witchcraft in Bolivia and elsewhere in the world, Sacabans argued that when a person envied another's well-being—whether of health, political appointment jobs, or political power—the envier caused harm in a hidden fashion (see Ferguson 1999; Ferme 1999; West 2005). Envy as a theory of politics conveyed that self-interest was illegitimate, and that self-interest and the failure to value group unity caused conflict. Sacabans' condemnations of envy as a principal obstacle to civic progress coincides with an older generation of anthropologists' analyses of envy, which anthropologists have since refuted.[20]

This local rhetorical opposition to envy-as-clientelism, however, did not account for the scarcity of elected offices, jobs, and development funds; all of these were certainly limited goods in Sacaba and unsurprisingly objects of fierce competition. Yet in addition to pointing out my own disagreement with the prevailing diagnosis in Sacaba of envy as a value that posed the central obstacle to political harmony and progress, I also want to emphasize the strategic quality of envy accusations in Sacaban politics. People who were politically active had to denounce others' envious clientelism in order to assert their own moral purity and therefore their political legitimacy. The accusation of envy-as-clientelism was one currency of political life.[21] These accusations can thus be seen as weapons in the political duels in Sacaba created by the political climate of scarce public funds, stiff competition for jobs, and a significant population in the middle whose wealth and social status did not fit the prevailing binary social categories of wealthy, white superelites and impoverished, indigenous subalterns. Activists and leaders defined themselves as publicly interested by gesturing to the LPP's principles of liberal democracy, MAS's eclectic grassroots democracy, or both; they had to denounce envy and clientelism.

A debate about the role of envy in the political career of El Chino, a veteran Sacaba MAS political leader and former mayor, illustrates one of the principal arguments in circulation about Sacaba's ongoing political conflicts: that envious individuals engaged in clientelism were sabotaging other people's political accomplishments in order to gain political power. This debate demonstrates how envy accusations sometimes signaled unspoken concerns that middle-class identities and aspirations were obstructing the longed-for liberal democracy promised by the Popular Participation Law and the grassroots democracy promised by the MAS party.

Don Álvaro, the provincial middle-class political operator, appeared in Chapter 3 violently demanding that El Chino allocate municipal funding for street paving in Don Álvaro's urban Sacaba neighborhood. Don Álvaro later told me that he had fought so heavy-handedly against El Chino in part because he was convinced that El Chino acted "out of envy" (*por envidia*)—the desire for power through clientelism—instead of an altruistic concern for Sacaba Municipality. El Chino's true motivation for denying Don Álvaro's neighborhood a loan for asphalt was the envious wish to prevent Chino's bitter political rival Oscar Angulo, then mayor of Sacaba, from building large, visible development projects. Chino hated Mayor Angulo for scheming successfully to impeach El Chino as mayor the year before. "With that asphalt, Oscar Angulo was going to grow politically . . . and he [El Chino] was going to stay small, because he had not built any public works [when he was mayor]," Don Álvaro assured me. Don Álvaro portrayed El Chino as motivated by self-interest and clientelism: a striver from a rural family who put his desire for political power and upward mobility above the well-being of the municipality. Don Álvaro implied that El Chino's quest for personal benefit was directly at odds with the LPP's liberal democratic prescriptions for good governance and with the MAS party's promise that its leaders would be public-minded and egalitarian.

El Chino, unsurprisingly, countered that he had repeatedly been the victim, rather than the perpetrator, of clientelism motivated by envy. When I asked El Chino in a 2006 interview to narrate his trajectory as a political leader, he immediately launched into an outraged tale of competitors' repeated dirty tricks motivated by their *envidia* of his success in politics. Despite these envious opponents, he said, he had risen from being elected campesino community council (*sindicato*) leader as a teenager to become a cofounder of the Instrumento Político (the movement that became the MAS party), Sacaba Municipal Council member, Sacaba mayor, and most recently, provincial representative to the Cochabamba state legislature. Along the way, he had earned a law degree.

The enormous mustard-yellow, three-story comprehensive public school in El Chino's hometown was the product of his leadership. The school elicited marveling admiration throughout Sacaba as well as resentment from places whose schools were not as new or as large. Chino's two-story home with its manicured front lawn (a decidedly urban, middle-class touch) shared its air of solidity with the gargantuan school he had built down the road. To my eyes, both buildings were deliberate elements of Chino's self-presentation as a prosperous upwardly mobile person who retained pride in rural roots and loyalty to the poor, rural folk of Sacaba.

In his autobiographical narrative, El Chino presented himself as a legitimate leader according to MAS' left-indigenist principles: a campesino who rose through the ranks of grassroots agrarian unions into elected politics and who maintained an allegiance to his rural hometown even after attaining a professional degree and political stature. He described himself as being "of campesino origin" (*de origen campesino*), affirming repeatedly that he had been born "in the rural sector" and that he planned to die and be buried in his home community of Chiñata. In direct, mirrored counterpoint to Don Álvaro, El Chino claimed that people accusing him of envy—including Oscar Angulo, who forced him to resign as mayor—only criticized him because they envied his trajectory of increasing political power.

Yet El Chino's personal narrative also drew on classically middle-class narratives of upward mobility through individual hard work, echoing the self-descriptions of people like Amanda, David, and Deysi as well as new middle classes elsewhere in the world (e.g., Cahn 2008; O'Dougherty 2002). For example, when explaining the sources of his success in politics and in achieving class mobility, he exclaimed that "One simply has to work hard [*Hay que trabajar, simplemente*]!" He had gotten to his current position by rising early, working tirelessly, and refraining from excessive alcohol, he said. He compared himself to envious fellow political leaders who failed to rise politically (*surgir*), because they drank too much or slept too late in the mornings.

In addition to defending himself against direct accusations of clientelist envy such as Don Álvaro's, El Chino implicitly argued here that the imperative to join the middle class and the imperative to be a publically interested leader did not conflict: his leadership yielded benefit for his constituents; as a benign by-product, he gained social, economic and political stature.

He used his origins ("I was born in the countryside!") to support his claim to be a morally upright and dedicated community and regional leader. El Chino used a similar argument in self-praise as Doña Saturnina's husband had in praising Evo's political ascent as a story of an individual who attained middle-class prosperity and social prestige as the result of hard work. El Chino was using a classic middle-class narrative of success and entrepreneurship. Furthermore, as this debate between Don Álvaro and El Chino makes clear, although Sacabans continually disputed which people were envious, envy-as-clientelism was a shared explanatory framework for conflicts. El Chino seems to be arguing that *any* successful political leader would be dogged by less successful leaders' envy; being the object of envy was a badge of pride as well as a source of endless trouble.

College-educated, middle-class Cochabamba area residents often feared that the region was particularly riddled with envy.[22] Several professionals living in Cochabamba City told me uneasily that theirs was reputed to be the most envious region of Bolivia. This concern also emerged in several jokes. One joke recounted by Celia, Doña Saturnina's youngest daughter, went: "In Italian, they call babies *bambinos*; in Cochabamba, they call them *envidiosos*." This was a play on *cochabambino*, meaning Cochabamba resident. Another common joke was about the crabs from various regions of Bolivia cooking in a pot, in which the Cochabambino crab will grab his companion who is about to crawl out to freedom and plunge him back into the boiling water to die.[23] An NGO director I knew echoed many development workers' laments when she despaired less jocularly that in Sacaba, "there is a lot of envy, a lot of rivalry. . . . They prefer that everyone be screwed [*jodidos*] rather than that anyone do well."[24]

## Conclusion

In this chapter, I have argued that accusations of clientelism in Sacaba expressed a locally perceived conflict between aspirations for grassroots democracy and middle-class upward mobility. Such accusations were a major trope in Bolivian political life that expressed anxiety about Bolivia's ability to transform into a prosperous society of social equality, as well as concerns about an ideological conflict between ethics of equality and ethics of social superiority. MAS leaders and rank and file used the moral language of clientelism accusations, particularly the condemnation of envy and self-interest. This moral reform, however, was an extremely difficult goal; the imperative to achieve upward mobility ran up against the imperative to avoid self-interest. Many politically active people were in a nearly impossible position, attempting to portray themselves as morally upright subaltern leaders committed to the uplift of the Bolivian indigenous, poor, and campesinos, and also as morally upright prosperous folk as the result of their own hard work and wise administration of their income. Many Sacabans whom I have termed an emergent middle class struggled within a political discourse that did not speak to their experience: a binary of rich versus poor and self-interest versus public interest.

One of the lessons we can learn from Sacabans' frustrations with envy and self-interest is that there is no way to eliminate self-interest from political life. Self-interest is a central human attribute, merely exacerbated in highly competitive and unequal environments. Furthermore, contrary to common understandings of clientelism as moral weakness in which an individual gives free reign to greed or selfishness, the practices that one person in Sacaba termed clientelism (*peguismo, clientelismo*) another termed radical democracy, altruistic efforts to secure a development project on behalf of the collective, or the necessary steps to secure a much-needed job. Accusations of envy and self-interest were thus inescapable for most people in Sacaba. The widespread aspiration and moral imperative to attain middle-class prosperity and social status bumped up against the practical reality that this was often achievable through clientelism. This fundamental quandary for anyone in a resource-poor setting suggests that we need to question the assumption that clientelism represents self-interested immorality.

Sacabans' disagreements over whether to label the same action as democratic or clientelistic also stemmed from the circulation of multiple political frameworks and notions of citizenship that originated in different moments of Bolivian history—clientelism, of the 1952 revolution, neoliberalism, the liberalism of the LPP, and the MAS platform of grassroots democracy. These frameworks inflected the multiple collectivities in which Sacaba's emergent middle class identified themselves: the nation of Bolivia, the region of Cochabamba, the municipality of Sacaba, and the rural or urban district of the municipality, as well as even smaller-scale family loyalties and aspirations. In clientelism, ideals were at times framed as collective or, more covertly, as individual; classical liberalism emphasizes individual autonomy; the LPP's liberalism emphasized a narrow form of collective citizenship on the scale of bounded communities and municipalities; MAS party rhetoric framed collectivism on the scale of the nation and posited indigenous and impoverished Bolivians as a collectivity.[25] Sacabans disagreed about what counted as a collectivity and who counted as an individual, however. Don Félix lauded a municipal affirmative action for rural Sacaba residents as an instance of grassroots democracy; unemployed persons denounced people with municipal jobs as selfish, clientelist *pegas*. Don Carlos chastised his NGO's beneficiaries as defining their collectivity too narrowly when they planned to receive the gift of an oven from a right-wing politician instead of viewing themselves as part of the national collective of oppressed, indigenous poor; Fernanda chastised Don Carlos as acting selfishly to provide clientelistic support for the Sacaba MAS party when he said no to the oven.

Sacabans' conflicting interpretations of political acts drew on a shared local theory about envy as the apotheosis of individualist selfishness. Their local theories, in turn, drew on foreign and Bolivian theories that people could and should naturally pursue the public interest and squelch self-interest in political life. Salazar and policy makers in international development circles, along with many Sacabans, attempted to distinguish between self-interested acts and acts in the public interest and to eliminate selfishness. I suggest that in some political contexts it is difficult for anyone—whether engaged as observers or participants—to distinguish whether a person is motivated by individual or collective interests; often, we are motivated by both.[26] In the next chapter, I turn to the ways in which women MAS activists attempted to portray themselves as public-minded subalterns adhering to the MAS platform even as they faced an onslaught of accusations of being elite, self-interested seekers of clientelism.

# Laments of Betrayal

Many people in Sacaba, like national policy makers, argued that clientelism, liberal democracy, and grassroots indigenist democracy were utterly opposed to one another. Yet these distinctions often broke down in practice. What one person condemned as *peguismo*, the giving and receiving of patronage jobs through clientelism, another person defended as affirmative action or the hiring of a qualified person who deserved it. Furthermore, Sacabans' arguments that a stark opposition existed between subalterns and elites in theory was confounded in practice by middling identities and levels of wealth, as when Doña Felisa portrayed her own newfound prosperity as representative of the future prosperity of the Bolivian nation under MAS. In this chapter I look more closely at the fierce competition for jobs, sparked by economic scarcity and middle-class aspirations, which in the early 2000s formed the backdrop to widespread condemnations of clientelism. Many Sacabans narrated bitter stories of being unjustly overlooked or excluded from appointments through political parties—an exceedingly common genre of stories that I have termed laments of betrayal. I focus on the laments of women, as they were often excluded from positions of power.

Political models are profoundly moral. Transparency, civil society, and "process of change" were linked, morally inflected watchwords through which many Sacabans explicitly framed their hopes that they were witnessing the birth of a new, more just political era following Evo's election. Meanwhile, discussions of clientelism, envy, self-interest, and *peguismo* framed their fears that Bolivia might remain unjust, impoverished, and unequal. Yet moral justifications for clientelism such as loyalty, reciprocity, and individual striving toward prosperity, were also esteemed values in

Sacaba. With the following examples, I illustrate the ways that rank-and-file members and midlevel leaders in Sacaba attempted to wrestle with these multiple political and moral ideals, which sometimes they portrayed as overlapping and sometimes as conflicting.

While some people completely rejected the notion that parties could act for legitimate purposes, moreover, many Sacabans were eager to believe that MAS was unique—a new party that worked for the redistribution of resources and power. Activists were often faced with frustrations and uncertainty. The primary source of anxiety for many activists I knew was that their new party, formed to erase inequality and exclusion, was moving away from its social movement roots by continuing older patterns of exclusion on the basis of gender, rural identity, class, and race. They diagnosed the problem as stemming largely from the recent influx of elites. National MAS party leaders argued their party was driven by the principles of the grassroots movement that spawned it. But some Sacaba MAS activists and sympathizers attempted to conceptually separate the movement principles from the MAS party in order to create room to criticize the party while leaving its ideals intact. They were often frustrated in maintaining these distinctions in practice.

## The Sacaba Bartolinas Try to Pick a Candidate for the Constitutional Assembly

The leaders of the Sacaba branch of the Bartolinas Federation, the national women's agrarian union, called a meeting several days after the forced resignation of the Sacaba mayor Luis Orellana in early May 2006. They hoped to elect a woman as a MAS candidate to run in the July national elections of delegates to the Bolivian Constitutional Assembly. The Constitutional Assembly was the year-long congress of representatives elected through existing political parties and charged with rewriting the Bolivian Constitution. While indigenous groups had urgently demanded the assembly since the early 1990s in hopes of launching a land reform and other measures to lessen Bolivia's gross economic and social equality, at this moment many MAS supporters feared that it was being co-opted by right-wing groups. From 9:30 in the morning until noon, about twenty-five women stood in the rutted cobblestone street in front of the Sacaba agrarian union headquarters, eating oranges as they talked. We sidled in and out of the sunlight, trying alternately to escape the intense heat and cold shadows in which we could almost see our breath. Many of the women wore *polleras* and braids;

some young women wore the knit leggings or form-fitting, boot-cut jeans that marked them as newly lower-middle-class residents of Sacaba and surrounding towns. The rank and file clustered around the smaller group of leaders who railed against Sacaba's political conflicts. They were trying to decide whether the poor attendance—a common complaint given general burnout following the many emergency meetings called during that municipal political crisis—should prevent them from holding a vote to choose the Sacaba MAS Constitutional Assembly candidate.

Two leaders with ambiguous middling identities played a large role in the meeting: Doña Felisa and Doña Patricia. Doña Felisa usually exuded an air of calm control, but today her face held a look of weariness and frustration. She explained to the assembled members that Vilma, the lawyer and former Sacaba MAS municipal official, had been the Sacaba MAS candidate for the upcoming Constitutional Assembly elections. But the previous Monday, Vilma had publicly resigned her candidacy in response to complaints by agrarian union activists, including Doña Felisa, that as a lawyer and member of the provincial town elite, Vilma was not "with the social movements" that made up the core constituency of the MAS. Vilma was too elite (urban and professional) to be a legitimate leader, and furthermore, she hadn't spent enough time and effort supporting the agrarian union or the Bartolinas to prove her commitment to the MAS platform. Because Vilma had been the only female candidate in the district, and Bolivian law required each party to list at least one woman candidate from each district, the Sacaba MAS party leaders had offered Doña Felisa the chance for the Bartolinas to pick another woman candidate.

Doña Felisa and other leaders lamented to the assembled women that the Sacaba MAS party leaders had excluded the agrarian unions, including the Bartolinas, when picking Vilma to be the original candidate. This was a collective complaint on behalf of all Sacabans who considered themselves campesinos, particularly women. This decision had been made, Doña Felisa said, not from grassroots consensus in assemblies of all the rank and file, as national MAS leaders promised, but rather, through a secret agreement forged by Jaime, the local MAS congressman. One of the Bartolinas' leaders mused that they needed to rectify the original mistake by finding an unambiguously subaltern candidate: "We want someone as Constitutional Assembly delegate from the rural counties, not the urban districts of Sacaba." Only a rural woman could truly understand and represent their interests. "But," she continued, as if casting about for ideas, "we don't want to make enemies of the urban Sacaba groups, either, because if they don't like our candidate, they will vote for other parties." Doña Felisa took up this thread, calculating out loud that if the urban MAS activists of Sacaba insisted on an urban candidate, the women present today could accept that, but only if she were clearly "of the line . . . of the Instrumento Político," the social movement that had spawned the MAS party. Her voice rising passionately, Doña Felisa continued that any candidate had to understand their collective "suffering" as rural women. The Bartolinas' secretary, a schoolteacher from a prosperous rural family, agreed darkly that there was a clear danger that an urban candidate, once elected, could become a "traitor" to Instrumento Político principles. The meeting's leaders thus asserted that they experienced discrimination based on several intersecting lines of inequality—class and race defined by rural origin, and gender—even within the Sacaba MAS party itself.

Another leader of the Bartolinas, Doña Mirtha, then warned about hidden allegiances and self-interest among municipal government officials. She declared that the new municipal government bureaucrats recently appointed by the new mayor, Walter Terán, were secretly anti-MAS, secretly elite, and secretly acting to further their own self-interest. She exclaimed in a tone of dismay that these bureaucrats had worked under a previous H. Obras mayor and been proven to be "corrupt"—fired for stealing public funds. As Doña Mirtha called out a few names of bureaucrats and their new positions, there were repeated, soft, alarmed "Ohhhs" from the other women present, who had remained mostly silent up to that moment. They clearly took this as evidence the new mayor, while nominally a member of MAS, was secretly plotting to jump parties and bring H. Obras, MAS's local rival party, back into municipal government. Doña Mirtha then listed the names of rural community leaders who, she said scathingly, had accepted cash payments from H. Obras to stop protesting when MAS mayor Luis Orellana was ousted and Walter Terán entered office. This litany elicited more gasps from the rank-and-file members.

At this moment, Doña Patricia, a slender, fortyish woman wearing black jeans and a bright orange and red sweater in an abstract pattern, moved to the center of the circle. Her dark hair was gathered behind her head in a barrette and a single braid hung down her back, accentuating her high cheekbones. The combination of avant-garde clothes, dark skin, and long hair marked her as a new middle-class intellectual; her Spanish unaccented by Quechua suggested an urban upbringing. Doña Patricia introduced herself as a founder of the national MAS party and gave a brief history of the party as if to assert her credibility. She warned the group in dramatic tones that they were fooling themselves if they believed that a rural woman would stand a chance against an urban woman in the election for Constitutional Assembly delegates. She said impatiently and briskly in Quechua that she wanted to alert everyone to the high barriers they faced in running their own candidate for the Constitutional Assembly. The MAS party "didn't emerge in the urban districts," she called out. Several people agreed, chiming in that it had emerged in the countryside. She exclaimed that, if they examined the list of other MAS candidates in Sacaba, however, they would see that the candidates were no different from the elite, untrustworthy candidates for other local parties: "lawyers: dirty, filthy people! [*abogados: gente cochina, sucia*]." She was reiterating the point made by previous leaders in the meeting that all the available politicians were morally bankrupt and the Sacaba MAS party leaders were no different than leaders of the other parties. "Lawyers" symbolized this moral bankruptcy because of their elite status, it seemed, rather than, as in the United States, a view that the profession itself is untrustworthy. The new leaders of elite backgrounds had "infiltrated" the Sacaba MAS, where they perpetuated a virulent form of racism, she continued. She had heard one politician exclaim a few years ago, for example, that MAS was made up of "dirty Indians" (*Indios cochinos*), but he nevertheless joined MAS last year when he saw the party gaining power.

After lamenting the multiple forms of subordination the Bartolinas women faced collectively on the basis of class, race, gender, and rural origin, Doña Patricia then exclaimed in frustration. "Truly, we don't have other alternatives" besides the MAS, even though male MAS leaders betrayed campesino and indigenous Sacabans, particularly women. "How we women have been used!" (*manejadas*) by male MAS leaders. She drew a parallel between women's exclusion from the Sacaba municipal MAS leadership and the Sacaba agrarian union's exclusion from decision-making authority with the municipality. "That's how filthy men are," she concluded.

Several of the meeting attendees then tried to propose a woman MAS candidate who could combine their need for someone who was well connected and experienced as a political leader, and who held impeccable rural credentials and ties to the Instrumento Político movement. A woman from the Choro Bartolinas group who wore a *pollera* and rarely spoke in regional meetings stepped forward and quietly nominated Doña Felisa as the Constitutional Assembly candidate. Doña Felisa had long been a regional and national leader, she explained, and Doña Felisa "works in the countryside." Doña Felisa's experience, her rural origins, and her status as a former senator and cofounder of the Instrumento Político and MAS party made her allegiances irrefutable. Several other women agreed that Doña Felisa would be an ideal candidate because she "knows the laws." One of them asked rhetorically: "Why do we need a lawyer? We will support Doña Felisa," she affirmed, "because she has a strong voice [*pay vozniyoq*]."

Doña Felisa, meanwhile, stood with the intensely distracted expression typical of people nominated for Sacaba leadership positions in unions, visibly exuding disinterest. The Bartolinas secretary, the Choro schoolteacher, broke in anxiously that a proper election needed to be conducted by "secret vote," rather than as an assembly. Doña Felisa broke out of her faraway, anxious expression and said hastily, "Thank you for your support. But . . . I am not campaigning, *compañeras* [comrades]." She said that she had hoped that they could choose among three or four candidates today. Echoing her comments to me at other moments that leaders had a responsibility to remain disinterested, she explained to the group that if she went forward as a candidate now as the meeting-goers were urging, people could later say about her that "she wanted to go," that she was pursuing self-interest.

Doña Patricia of the bright orange and red sweater then stepped forward again to urge the women against their plan to choose a rurally affiliated candidate like Doña Felisa. Her look of intense impatience had increased. She asked rhetorically, "What is it that decides whether a candidate will get elected?" A few rank-and-file attendees replied softly, "We do," as if repeating something learned by rote about the power of voters in democracy. Doña Patricia corrected quickly: "Those who decide are the ones in the urban districts (*eje urbano*) of Sacaba" because those neighborhoods were more densely populated, and therefore contained more voters. A candidate had to be "educated" (*yachaq*) to be appealing to those urbanites. "If we put Doña Felisa as candidate, she would be like a flower vase [*florero*] on the ballot," she declared vehemently—merely an adornment, and not a viable candidate. Other parties would surely win.

The meeting dissolved into a chorus of laments. Another leader broke in with a warning about the corruptibility of politicians: national MAS congressmen were "allowing themselves to be bought [by right-wing interests] to change their votes" at that very moment in the nation's capital (*rantichikunku a la hora de votación*). The Bartolinas could not permit the Constitutional

Assembly to be corrupted by vote buying the way the Congress had been, several women argued fervently. One leader said in a worried tone that the assembly presented the last chance for making fundamental changes in Bolivia, that it was the culmination of decades of work and sacrifice. She reiterated a familiar litany of the recent rhetoric of the MAS party and the Instrumento Político: that the Bartolinas and national agrarian union had fought for years, through protests, hungers strikes, road blockades, and arduous multiweek marches through mountain passes to the Bolivian capital to demand a Constitutional Assembly. Once the assembly began, she added anxiously, they would not be able to use their past tactics of disruptive protest, because now, for the first time, their party held power. Another woman chimed in dispiritedly, as if collapsing the growing despair into one central argument about gender inequality, that the male Sacaba politicians would never pay attention to the concerns of women.

Attendees had already begun to leave quietly when it became clear that no election was forthcoming. The meeting's three most prominent leaders, Doña Mirtha, Doña Felisa, and Doña Patricia, all of whom were accused by some people in Sacaba as not being subaltern enough, began walking slowly from the union headquarters down the street to the highway. They regaled each other with specific examples of male political leaders in Sacaba who had "let themselves be bought" in exchange for making false allegations of corruption against Mayor Orellana or for allowing self-interested elite leaders into the Sacaba MAS party. All these male leaders were thus "wallowing in garbage [*q'opa*]." After one brief silence, Doña Felisa exclaimed forlornly, "How sad!" and sighed. She burst out, in an angry complaint against the murkiness of leaders' allegiances, that she wanted to ask the new Sacaba mayor, Walter Terán—mimicking a challenging tone—"are you working for MAS or for the MNR?" The MNR, the oldest Bolivian political party then active in politics and Terán's former political party, symbolized clientelism in its purest form. After complaining that some people suspected even her of disloyalty to MAS, Doña Patricia exclaimed, merging self-blame as a Bolivian with a condemnation of the gossips who challenged her loyalty to the movement, "I'm tired. This country can just go to hell [*Este pais, que se vaya a la mierda*]."[1] We reached the dust and wind of the highway. A stream of minibuses barreled by en route from Sacaba's rural districts to the city of Cochabamba. Doña Patricia and Doña Felisa exclaimed to each other bitterly, shaking their heads in disgust that so many men in the Sacaba MAS party "let themselves be bought with one cask of *chicha*!"

These women's concerns spoke in part to the many challenges involved in transforming a subaltern, grassroots protest movement into a political party and government in power. Their complaints illustrate how social movement activists puzzled over how to include elites to make the MAS party grow while at the same time maintaining vigilance over those elites' allegiances. And yet each of the women leaders at times defended herself against local accusations that she was also too elite. At the meeting, leaders of the Sacaba Bartolinas attempted to walk a fine line between supporting political parties as vehicles for societal transformation, condemning the practices of particular party leaders as self-interested and clientelistic, and declaring themselves to be legitimate leaders because they avoided self-interest and held subaltern identities. The Bartolinas' leaders attempted this in part by juxtaposing those who they recognized as bearing allegiance to the Instrumento Político with those who they suspected of joining the MAS party out of desire for power or to steal public funds. Doña Felisa's vehement assertion that she did not want to go to the Constitutional Assembly, despite the bitter disappointment she expressed to me in other moments about having been pushed aside from leadership positions in the MAS, illustrates the ambiguous and thorny path for leaders who must continually affirm their lack of self-interest even as they held or aspired to leadership positions.

Furthermore, Bartolinas members lamented collective betrayals stemming from marginalization through multiple categories of political exclusion. As women, they were concerned that sexist male political leaders excluded them on the basis of gender from important leadership positions and from decision making about the direction of the Sacaba MAS party. The women also lamented their exclusion as people who had helped found the Instrumento Político movement, precursor to the MAS party, and who had initially entered politics through the movement. They felt cast aside by leaders who had entered politics through earlier parties long discredited as incorrigibly clientelistic and elite dominated. Finally, as self-identified subaltern, rural, and indigenous people, they lamented exclusion on grounds of race and class by urban-affiliated, wealthier, and more highly educated people who did not identify themselves as strongly as indigenous. The Bartolinas members aired concerns that many Sacaba MAS politicians were closet racists who hid their contempt for the radical redistribution of power called for in the national MAS platform.

For Doña Felisa and Doña Patricia, their own subaltern class, race, and gender were central claims of legitimacy, through which they compared themselves favorably to competing leaders. Doña Felisa's and Doña Patricia's subaltern status substantiated their self-presentation as public minded, just as they condemned other leaders' elite status as evidence of those leaders' moral turpitude. They attempted to define clear boundaries between their own allegiances and origins—poor, illiterate, rural, campesina, *pollera*-wearing, Quechua-speaking, and experienced in suffering—and elites defined as rich, educated (*yachaq*), professional, and urban. Yet in practice, these Bartolinas leaders' class and racial status was not fixed; such distinctions were in fact contentious and inconsistent in practice. For example, meeting attendees condemned the power plays of Congressman Jaime as typical of elite domination, though Jaime was from an indisputably rural community and became the butt of jokes by his opponents that he was unsophisticated and uneducated, despite his law degree, when he was elected prefect of Cochabamba Department several years later. Doña Felisa herself was described by some eager meeting goers as an ideal representative because she was a rare woman who was both politically experienced and indisputably rural. Yet Doña Felisa faced accusations by MAS activists from other political factions of refusing to share her senator's income for community projects within the municipality. Eventually this income took visible shape in her enormous new urban-style home. Bartolinas meeting goers, in their condemnation of the MAS's infiltration by "traitors," were mapping the local categories of race and class identification onto the available binary oppositions between elite and subaltern in Bolivian political speech. In practice, some of the Bartolinas' leaders themselves, like the male leaders they criticized, were at times labeled as elite (*ricachona*), as well as selfish and clientelistic. Doña Felisa and Doña Nancy were, like their political opponents, suspected by some people of pursuing self-interest in seeking leadership positions out of desire for money and power, and therefore of straying from Instrumento Político ideals of social equality and redistribution of wealth. The requirement to be utterly collective-minded was quite difficult to enact and portray convincingly in practice.

## Laments of Unknowability: Transparency and Leaders' Hearts

The laments of collective betrayal at the Bartolinas' meeting also included a deep frustration about the unknowability of fellow political actors' identities, motivations, and actions. Laments of unknowability in Sacaba should be understood within the context of the national political culture and trans-national currents of good governance theories. When MAS regional president, Julio Salazar, urged leaders to give up envy and self-interest (and therefore, clientelism), he portrayed envy and the desire for clientelism as located in Sacabans' hearts, indicating both that people held these values secretly and that these values sustained a strong emotional attachment. Complaints about sentiments and allegiances hidden in other people's hearts were very common in Sacaba and reflected the widespread concerns among party activists about the success of MAS in attracting elites and other new members beyond its original base of social movement activists. At the same agrarian union meeting in which Salazar exhorted against envy, MAS leader after leader came to the microphone to argue that the worst enemies of the Sacaba MAS party were those who presented themselves as MAS, but "in their hearts" belonged to H. Obras or to other discredited political parties.[2]

Political leaders' regular practice of leaving one political party to join a new one was partly responsible for this widespread suspicion about hidden allegiances. This practice was compounded by the sheer number of political parties that offered similar platforms or practices. Not only did more than a half-dozen parties compete seriously at the national level in 2006, but additional municipal and regional parties had mushroomed since the Law of Popular Participation (LPP) passed in 1994.

This concern about leaders' hearts went beyond rural-affiliated activists. In early 2006 (before the meeting described above to choose candidates for the Constitutional Assembly) I dropped by Vilma's house. Vilma wanted me to inform her about a particularly contentious agrarian union meeting in which union members accused several MAS city council members of committing "treason" by supporting Walter Terán, then a city council member with questionable MAS party loyalties, to replace MAS mayor Luis Orellana. Vilma showed sudden interest when I told her that one of the named "traitors," Councilwoman Norah González, had skipped the meeting. Vilma said confidently: "Norah says that she is MAS, but in her heart of hearts, she still belongs to the MNR [*en su corazoncito, sigue siendo del MNR*]."

The emphasis on sentiments hidden in hearts points to the speakers' concern that MAS was just like other parties, while also holding out hope that MAS was different. This fear stemmed from the fact that it was only through political parties that people could hold formal political power—

win elections and govern a country—yet the institution of political parties was largely discredited in Bolivia. If a person wanted to believe that MAS was fundamentally different from other parties because its leaders were committed to the public good, he or she had to assert that a few bad apples' moral failure of self-interest caused problems, rather than a systemic defect of the party itself.

In addition, if many Bolivians hoped that MAS would be controlled by poor people to reverse centuries of extreme inequality and institutionalized racism, the notion that it had been secretly infiltrated by self-interested power seekers—people from elite backgrounds who held racist views—was extremely painful. This wrenching fear could warrant the notion that these unscrupulous elites held such racist convictions in the core of their beings. As Doña Patricia lamented in the Bartolinas meeting, many new, elite MAS activists were "barely repressing their hate for us [as indigenous and poor people]" and had entered the party merely in order to take advantage of its recent success.

The condemnation of hidden sentiments and allegiances in leaders' hearts also resonated with the rhetoric of transparency that became common in Bolivia following the neoliberal reforms of the 1980s and 1990s, particularly after the launching of the LPP. Calls for transparency (*transparencia*) in municipal governance were on the lips of all college-educated people in Sacaba in 2005 and 2006. This language of transparency had been employed by reformers in Bolivia as well as by international anticorruption institutions over the previous two decades, such as Transparency International and the World Bank. Many Sacabans called for transparency by mayors and other leaders, while simultaneously expressing suspicion of leaders' claims to be adhering to the principle of transparency (see Hetherington 2011:153).

The expectation that Sacaba's politics and governance could become transparent heightened the suspicion that MAS leaders, just like other party's leaders, might be pocketing public funds. Don Félix Hernández, the MAS leader who lived in Choro, recounted in frustration how the first six mayors' administrations following the passing of the LPP bilked Choro and other communities of their money by listing greatly inflated prices for construction materials, such as plastic piping for potable water systems. He described how they had come slowly to this realization: "There will always be nosy people [*curiosos*] who go to check out how much [PVC plastic tubing costs] per square meter. Everyone knows where the hardware stores are; before, they didn't. So they tolerated everything and thought that things were as they had been before [the Popular Participation began]. And for those six terms, they fooled us at their pleasure [*mamado a su manera*]; they tricked [*engañado*] us." Don Félix's language of "trickery" echoes many Sacaba observers' use of the term "transparency" in complaining that Mayor Orellana (and his predecessor and his successor) was pocketing or otherwise misusing funds.

The Sacaba ex-mayor El Chino, who was himself ousted on charges of corruption, also expressed a yearning for transparency in Sacaba. During an interview with me in 2006, he argued that it would take a superhero. Referring to a parody superhero in a Mexican sitcom that many Bolivians watched avidly, *El Chapulín Colorado* (The Red Grasshopper), El Chino argued: "I don't think there could ever be a Chapulín Colorado who would say, 'Stop!'" to the thieving and dawdling on *obras* in Sacaba municipal government since the Law of Popular Participation began. This was because the root problem was an intractable immorality: municipal workers in Sacaba seemed to be incorrigibly "drunk . . . with self-interest." Maybe, El Chino said wistfully, someone new could enter who would promote "transparent management [*manejo transparente*]," but he doubted that such a heroic person existed.

Whether phrased as "transparency" to reveal corruption or as the revelation of the self-interest residing in other people's hearts, this condemnation of secrecy reflects Sacabans' rarely fulfilled desire for certainty. Harry West and Todd Sanders (2003) have described how the deep yearning for transparency throughout much of the world during the past few decades has been prompted by the unfulfilled expectations created by institutions that claim to promote good governance. West and Sanders argue that the rhetoric of transparency has sparked widespread suspicion that leaders have concocted vast webs of hidden agreements to concentrate wealth and power on a global scale. This is because the very institutions that tout the need for transparency around the world, such as the World Bank and the World Trade Organization, have simultaneously promoted secrecy and the concentration of wealth. Popular fears of hidden agreements—conspiracies —by powerful leaders are a very reasonable response, the authors argue. West and Sanders argue that the neoliberal promise of transparency is in fact impossible to carry out.

The concern in Sacaba about what was hidden in leader's hearts and the neoliberal rhetoric of transparency were connected, in two ways. First, the rhetoric of transparency embedded in the LPP in Bolivia was coupled with the promise that civil society could be a realm of discussion and action aimed at the public good, separate from and more powerful than the political arena of selfishness, partisan politics, and the corrupt state (compare to Hetherington 2011). Second, the LPP had presented an unfulfilled promise that the reform's creation of community organizations, prescribed steps for development planning, and laws to punish public officials who stole public funds would eliminate corruption and elite rule. Many MAS activists—local leaders as well as the rank and file—expressed a sense of betrayal at the hands of municipal MAS leaders whom they suspected of hidden elite allegiances, secret ties to long-discredited traditional political parties, power hungriness, and secret theft of public money.

In even more concrete ways, some Sacabans suggested transparency's impossibility when they argued that one political faction's claims to have enacted transparency was actually evidence of their corruption and self-interestedness (see also Hetherington 2011). Doña Patricia, who made the comment at the Bartolinas' meeting that Doña Felisa's Constitutional Assembly candidacy would be as useful as a "flower vase," offered me a measured defense of the ousted MAS mayor Luis Orellana in a 2006 interview by explaining that the documentary evidence of his corruption was itself murky and uncertain. She described a public meeting in which Orellana's opponents had shown dubious "proof" (*pruebas*) of his having stolen municipal funds: "Look, this Orellana is no saint . . . but I will tell you that I wouldn't wish on anyone what they have done to him . . . because they have made him appear like the *most vile thief*. I don't know if he is or isn't [guilty of the corruption charges]. But at the very least, you back it up with documentation, with documents, not with any old piece of paper. That day, I saw them grabbing any piece of paper and saying, 'Here are the documents!'" Doña Patricia thus argued that claims to transparency had been bent in the service of H. Obras party members' clientelist interests, even as she affirmed her faith that transparency was possible to attain—with the right kind of documents.

## Betrayed Reciprocity and Conflicting Political Frameworks

Thus far, I have described Sacabans' arguments in which they decried self-interest (*interés personal*) as a moral wrong while positioning themselves as utterly disinterested, collective minded, and oriented toward the MAS party platform, the Instrumento Político. In other moments, however, some people subtly suggested the difficulties of asserting a sharp line between private and public interest, for example, confronting their own joblessness or failure to attain a hoped-for leadership position. Their claims of disinterestedness and allegiance to the platform were accompanied by claiming other types of moral virtue, such as prosperity as a sign of hard work, or loyalty to a political party, to family, to patrons, or to clients. Some Sacabans also affirmed their need to earn a living in the midst of Bolivia's double-digit unemployment. Two women activists' laments of betrayal demonstrate the ways in which Sacabans affirmed elements of multiple political frameworks and the ways in which middle-class aspirations intertwined with a subaltern class and racial status. Their experiences also bring home how MAS activists' stated goals of becoming new, altruistic political subjects clashed with the vital concern about joblessness.

### Doña Nely: Betrayed Client

Like many Sacabans, Doña Nely, a moderately prosperous market vendor, suggested that she struggled to maintain her sense of herself as a morally upright person by avoiding clientelism while using political frameworks she viewed as competing—clientelist, radical democratic, and liberal democratic—to analyze her own and other Sacabans' political actions.

Doña Nely was a highly visible figure among Sacaba municipal MAS activists. A robust woman with a powerful laugh, her hair was so long that her braid hung past her waist. She had been a butcher in the Sacaba municipal slaughterhouse until being fired when Mayor Orellana left office in April 2006 and the new mayor fired all of Orellana's clients and hired his own. Since Orellana's ouster, she had worked tirelessly (and unsuccessfully) to reinstate him by helping to organize protests of the new mayor, Walter Terán. I often saw her at MAS events—shouting abuse in Quechua at Terán's municipal bureaucrats in agrarian union meetings, hauling enormous bags of potatoes to feed attendees at local MAS rallies, listening intently to other women leaders' political woes at post-meeting *chicha*-drinking gatherings. One day, she darted across the potholed street in front of her stall in the Sacaba market and invited me, with a friendly call through a bus window, to visit her. At her kiosk, she told me proudly, laughing, that Evo

*Figure 5.* Doll dressed up in a *pollera* in the MAS party colors, 2006.
Photo by the author.

often called her his "*Sinchi guerrera*," his "strong warrior woman," when they caught glimpses of each other at MAS rallies. "Hey, my *guerrera!*" he would call out to her with a pleased smile, over the crowd. "Warrior" seemed an apt description, given the severity I had witnessed when she confronted people she claimed were betraying the Sacaba MAS party.

Doña Nely appeared to inhabit the lower end of the middle stratum of wealth and social status in Sacaba. In 2006, she spent several days a week at her hardware parts kiosk in the Sacaba market, across the street from a seller of school supplies and next door to a yogurt stand. Owning her own stall provided her with a more secure income than was available to many of the market sellers who rented space or squatted on sidewalks, and her self-assurance seemed to reflect this modicum of prosperity. Her middling status was reinforced by her adult son's high school degree and by her self-identification: she was not a cholita and regularly wore pantsuits. Her social stature was enhanced by her many godchildren—being a godmother was expensive—who often stopped by to visit. On the other hand, she had little disposable income, had left school after third grade, and spoke Spanish with a strong Quechua accent, albeit fluently.

Doña Nely told me how Evo and the MAS party had first inspired her to hope that Bolivia could be radically transformed: "We see that he is from the countryside, like us: indigenous. He didn't buy our consciences with noodles or money; he bought our consciences with his wisdom, his humility, with all that they have done to him since he was a boy. . . . That's why we have supported him without any self-interest [*interés*]. He never gave out one cent, Señora Miriam . . . he never even bought us a glass of soda. . . . Many times, by contrast, other parties have bought people's consciences." With this, Doña Nely echoed many Sacabans' chief excitement about MAS: that it was completely different from previous political parties, particularly because its leaders abhorred clientelism. She expressed the well-developed condemnation of clientelism uttered by Don Carlos, at the women's meeting in Choro. Noodles were potent symbols of vote buying. Doña Nely asserted that Evo was not only committed to the platform, but that he deliberately attempted to discourage self-interest among his followers.

Doña Nely also, however, made an oblique criticism that suggested to me that she saw conflicts between the political frameworks that she tried to adhere to. When I asked what she thought of Evo's administration, several months into his term, she said that she was thrilled that Evo had won. He was doing "beautiful things, marvels [*lindas cosas, maravilla*]," she exclaimed. But, she added wistfully, she wished that some time Evo would send emissaries undercover to walk around the market in Sacaba. I expected her to say that she hoped that these spies would take the pulse of the nation and gauge how Bolivians viewed Evo's policies and report back to him. But then she explained that she hoped that these spies would casually ask Sacabans whether or not the locals who had campaigned hard for MAS and Evo were employed. They should ask after loyal MAS supporters, "How were they now? Did they have jobs?" Doña Nely explained that Evo would be very disappointed if he found out that loyal party members, such as she, had not been given a job in the new municipal government controlled by nominal MAS members who were widely suspected as fronts for H. Obras. She continued, with a hint of bitterness: "I always said that if he became president, I would be content. But . . . right now, Evo is thinking that I have a good job, when actually, I don't have any job; they have pushed me aside."

I was astounded at first to hear her expectation that her particular problem of employment should be a personal preoccupation of the nation's president, until I realized that Doña Nely, like many Sacabans, held multiple expectations of the state at once. She wanted the state to redeem party politics through morally upright leaders and who would end clientelism, to bring prosperity to subaltern groups in which she included herself, and to act as a generous political patron to particularly loyal followers.

Doña Nely's yearning for a patronage job could be glossed as envy and clientelism by the regional MAS party president, Salazar. Yet the fact is that few Bolivians held well-paying jobs. And so it became clear to me during my research that many people, like Doña Nely, actively sought jobs through the MAS party, even as they asserted firmly that clientelism should be abolished, and condemned other people for seeking personal relations of reciprocity with political leaders. Doña Nely applauded Evo as breaking from the mold of political leaders motivated by patronage, and at the same time, she saw him as her patron. Her sense that her unemployment represented a betrayal by Evo rivaled her hope of being part of a movement toward societal transformation. She was obliquely arguing that, in the patron-client relationship of reciprocity in which she was engaged with the president, he had failed his obligations. Like Doña Felisa, Doña Nely argued for multiple ideals: hopes for a new kind of political party, for national economic renewal, for indigenous power and the collective prosperity of a long-excluded majority, *and* for individual upward mobility.

As in the conversation in Chapter 3, when Doña Felisa and her friend thrilled to the prospect of their children designing airplanes, Doña Nely's account portrayed her own particular prosperity or upward mobility as synonymous with the uplift of subaltern Bolivians as a bloc. This came through in her description of how she was drawn to Evo as a model of individual upward mobility, of one who had ascended to political power despite poor origins. Doña Nely rapturously recounted to me that Evo had declared to his small audience at the first MAS meeting that she had attended, "I am a poor person: poor I was born, [but] I will be someone in this life [*voy a ser alguien en la vida*]; you will remember me." The affirmation *voy a ser alguien en la vida* was a common refrain in Sacaba to describe one's aspirations for upward class mobility by becoming a *profesional*. Doña Nely, like Deysi and Amanda's father, appeared to connect Evo's self-declared identity as indigenous, rural, and poor to herself, as a model to emulate in seeking a middle-class life. Doña Nely often spoke yearningly of how she would have had an easier life with more education. She told me confidingly that some MAS leaders had actually offered her a job on several occasions performing office work, but she had declined them because she was afraid she wouldn't be able to speak Spanish fluently enough or would have to confess that she did not know how to use a computer.

That Doña Nely could express hurt at not being given a municipal government job also reveals another important value in Sacaba's political culture—that of loyalty to a party. She, like many other Sacabans, asserted unselfconsciously that volunteering for a political party established a relationship of reciprocity that should be rewarded with jobs. She compared herself favorably to current municipal workers who were disloyal. Arguing that all the municipal workers under the new mayor were "professionals, MIR, MNR [older parties]: they just want to get their paychecks," she implied that their lack of loyalty to the MAS platform and their elite (*profesional*) status would impede their effectiveness as municipal workers. And by extension, these twin faults would impede the goal of achieving municipal development. Doña Nely and her son recounted, by contrast, their own loyalty to Evo and the MAS party as inseparable from their more subaltern identity and their commitment to the platform. Doña Nely, they argued, was a harder worker and more loyal than the new municipal employees who had pushed her out. "We have suffered a lot so that politics [i.e., MAS] could grow [*Hemos sufrido harto para que crezca la política*]" in Sacaba, she declared. She recounted marching with other MAS activists for hundreds of kilometers from Cochabamba to La Paz during the Gas War demanding nationalization in 2003, and sitting through endless MAS meetings during the previous ten years with only Yupi (Bolivian Kool-Aid) for sustenance. "I sewed hats, flags, as if I were a candidate myself, to attract people [to the party], to say: 'This is what Evo is about!'" She and her son, as "heartfelt Masistas [*Masistas de corazón*]" bought the cloth themselves. Meanwhile, she said disdainfully, those who worked on campaigns for other parties, such as the MNR and MIR, received the cloth for free from their parties to sew the campaign flags. Further material evidence of her party loyalty to the MAS was a small plastic doll perched on a dusty, empty water cooler in front of dangling chains of shiny gear shafts and stacks of foot pedals. The blonde, blue-eyed doll wore a dozen layers of acrylic, flouncy *pollera* skirts, crocheted by Doña Nely's goddaughter, in the MAS colors of deep blue, white, and black.

Loyalty of grassroots party activists should be repaid; this was how parties were supposed to work. At the same time, she hoped that MAS would work differently. While she and almost everyone else derided clientelism, they also reframed the moral calculus when they asserted that loyalty was an important virtue. Doña Nely, like most Sacabans I knew, only occasionally indicated that these multiple framings of morality seemed contradictory and that she faced an internal struggle over how to be a morally upright person. Affirming vehemently that she was not a *busca pega*, a party patronage job seeker, she insisted to me that she would continue her loyalty to Evo and the party despite her joblessness. She would have reported to Evo the nepotism and corruption of the new municipal government under Walter Terán, she told me, but for her fear people would say that she was seeking a *pega*.

> *Doña Nely:* H. Obras is screwing us over [*perjudicawanchis*] in city hall here in Sacaba. Right now in the slaughterhouse, I have a lot of proofs [of corruption] that I could take up to Evo. But I don't want to go to him, Doña Miriam.
> *Miriam:* Why not?
> *Doña Nely:* Well, they could say about me, "She is just a *busca pega*."

Doña Nely clear feared that, given her vocal arguments that people who accused her ally of corruption were simply trying to get jobs for themselves, if she accused anyone of corruption, she would draw similar attacks of being a greedy job seeker. Drawing these moral distinctions between herself—deservingly poor, public minded, loyal—and the feckless *profesionales* from traditional parties—elite, self-interested, disloyal—appeared to be her way of reconciling the potentially conflicting moral mandates between stamping out clientelism on the one hand and loyalty to a party and patron on the other hand. Doña Nely also contrasted herself with Congressman Jaime, who she said had committed "treachery" by shifting his allegiances to the new mayor Terán only in order "to get *pegas* [*pegasrayku*]."

In addition to values of loyalty and reciprocity and the desire for a job, Doña Nely also suggested that she saw in her personal friendship with Evo the enactment of the social equality his party promised (see also Lazar 2008). Part of her wistfulness about Evo's ignorance of her current jobless state stemmed, it also seemed, from having lost their former intimacy. Once he was elected president, he no longer visited Sacaba or went out for a beer with Sacaba MAS supporters. Several Sacabans similarly told me mournfully that they never saw him anymore. Having been a coca growers' union leader for a long time, working his way up in the hierarchy, Evo came to personally know many Sacaba-based people who had now or in the past worked in the Chapare. As one of the first urban starting grounds for MAS, dozens of people told me they had attended the many meetings that Evo had organized and attended to launch the party there.

The distinction made by Narendra Subramanian (1999) between trivial and long-lasting gifts in clientelist relationships, described in the previous chapter, also helps explain Doña Nely's theory about how MAS ought to function. Subramanian's depiction of authoritarian clientelism describes the mode of older Bolivian parties that gained power by distributing insignificant material goods (such as noodles or a bottle of Coke) in a short-term relationship of exchange for votes. Doña Nely condemned such practices with her scathing disgust for gifts of "noodles." And yet she did argue for a model of patron-client reciprocity, in that her loyalty and "sacrifice" for Evo and the party should be returned in the form of a job. This exemplifies Subramanian's model of "populist clientelism" in that it is a relationship of longer-term, significant exchange between leader and followers, a relationship that engaged Doña Nely as a highly mobilized supporter.

Another illustration of how Doña Nely connected an ethic of patron-client reciprocity between party leader and particular constituents, such as herself, as inseparable from a platform that promised to redistribute wealth throughout the nation, came through in her complaints about Doña Felisa. Doña Nely declared scathingly that Doña Felisa's election to the Senate had only been possible because of the labor of Doña Nely and other grassroots Sacaba MAS party activists. The two women were from the same hometown, and this hometown constituency had contributed funds and significant time to Doña Felisa's campaign. Residents of candidates' home communities expected their campaign work to be repaid in community development projects once their candidate was elected. And yet, Doña Nely declared disgustedly, Doña Felisa had not reciprocated with largesse to the Sacaba MAS party or to their hometown. Not a soccer field, Doña Nely declared with emphasis, not a health clinic, not a single computer, not a chair for the Sacaba MAS headquarters.[3] Here Doña Nely implicitly distinguished between her expectation of a gift of development largesse for a community or institution, on the one hand, and on the other hand, the "buying of consciences" through insignificant handouts to individual supporters.

Doña Nely's portrayal of Doña Felisa as a political parasite because she did not deliver material benefits locally is directly at odds with Doña Felisa's own statements to me that her role as senator was to strengthen the platform of the party rather than distribute development funding. Doña Felisa argued that while in Congress, she had focused her energies on making sure that the congressional representatives of the Instrumento Político movement stuck to its platform, which later become the platform of the MAS party. She described herself repeatedly pleading with them to not let themselves be bought off (*rantichikuy*) by the opposition. She detailed a heroic effort on her part to encourage them to keep presenting bills, prior to Evo's election, even knowing that their legislation would be shot down because they were in a minority. In counterpoint to Doña Nely, Doña Felisa described her proper role as working to further the movement and party platform, rather than reciprocating material benefits directly to her constituents, loyal as they may have been.

### Doña Patricia: Betraying as Patron and Betrayed as Client

Doña Patricia, the woman who wore the orange and red sweater at the Bartolinas' meeting, echoed many of Doña Nely's implicit arguments about the difficulties that MAS activists faced. Doña Patricia's account of her political and personal trajectory in June 2006 conveys how challenging it was in practice for Sacaba's middle class to portray themselves as consistently abiding by the multiple moral mandates of Bolivian society: loyalty, reciprocity, upward mobility, indigenist grassroots democracy, and anticlientelism. Like Doña Nely, Doña Patricia held an ambiguous, middling identity that combined elements of the subaltern and elite categories that MAS activists needed to describe—because of very real conflicts between the superelite and MAS's political base—as opposed. In contrast to Doña Nely, however, whose contribution to MAS as a staunch member of the rank and file meant sewing party flags and cooking for rallies, Doña Patricia described herself as a leader. Doña Patricia was therefore in a position of potential patron as well as potential client.

When Doña Patricia described her class and racial background at the Bartolinas' meeting, she aligned herself with campesina and indigenous subalterns. Some elements of this self-identification came through when she recounted her personal history to me later. She was from a poor mining family, she said, that had migrated to the city of Cochabamba during a period of decline of the mines. Her parents had instilled in her the miners' famously radical critique of Bolivian elites. Her parents also cultivated an

understanding of herself as ethnically indigenous and economically and politically aligned with the working (*popular*) class. This subaltern allegiance
echoed several other economically struggling professionals I knew who
resided in the city of Cochabamba and who were also the children of miners.

Yet according to the prevailing models of class and race within Sacaba
municipality, Doña Patricia's lifestyle and aspirations also placed her in a
class position superior to the poorer and more rural Sacaba residents. In
2006, Doña Patricia lived in an urban district of Sacaba, on a newly paved
street in a neighborhood populated by many professionals, conveniently
close to the bustling highway that linked Sacaba to Cochabamba. She had
studied for a university degree in psychology for a time but switched to
becoming a veterinary assistant because her family couldn't afford for her
to study for a lengthy degree. With obvious satisfaction, she showed me
how each of the shelves that lined the walls of her study held books on a
different discipline: psychology, sociology, history, biology. Indeed, this was
a startlingly large book collection for even the wealthiest families I had
observed in Cochabamba, supporting her self-presentation as an intellectual of modest means who aspired to upward mobility through education.
Doña Patricia seemed to consider herself as precariously situated in the
middle class. Her home, with its polished cement floor rather than expensive tile, walls of books, computer, and flower-filled garden, reminded me
of the homes of several other middle-class Bolivian families I knew who felt
their lifestyles to be fragile and the product of much hard labor. Such a
self-positioning in her daily life did not align neatly with the rigid rhetorical
categories of elite and subaltern in Sacaba.

The ambiguity of Doña Patricia's middling class position also came
through in her narrative of her quest during the previous five years to win
an elected municipal post through the MAS party. Whether such a quest
for leadership represented a selfish desire for material prosperity or a self-
sacrificing desire to carry out service to the public was in the eye of her
beholders. Certainly, Doña Patricia presented her desire for elected office
as one of self-sacrifice, public service, and radical dreams to transform the
country. She narrated her political journey as one of the intellectual authors
of the national MAS and Instrumento Político platform. She, like Doña
Felisa, told me detailed stories of having traveled throughout Bolivia during
the 1990s, teaching a message of indigenous consciousness and pride, anti-
neoliberalism, and redistribution of wealth, as part of her efforts to attract
followers for the nascent MAS party.

Doña Patricia had then been betrayed (*traicionada*), she told me. She had a falling out with the Sacaba MAS congressman Jaime in 2003. She claimed that he created false rumors that she had turned against the platform of the Instrumento Político and therefore, against the principles of the MAS party. His attacks on her followed his pattern, she said, of disarming challengers to his leadership in order to remain a congressman and head of the Sacaba MAS party. She admitted that she had, in fact, helped form H. Obras, the Sacaba municipal opposition party to MAS, but did so because she had become disgusted with Jaime's poor treatment of her and other veteran Instrumento Político leaders. She was also aghast at Jaime's allowing elite long-time members of discredited parties, such as the MNR and UCS, into leadership positions of the Sacaba MAS party. She argued vehemently to me that her aim had been to create a new political organization separate from all political parties, in order to "demonstrate to Evo" that Jaime had lost the support of Sacabans who followed "the line" of the Instrumento Político movement. But, she declared dispiritedly, her move to create H. Obras as this institution walled off from the influence of parties, and in which she would be a leader, was widely misunderstood as being an expression of self-interest and a rejection of Evo, the national MAS party, and the Instrumento Político movement.

Her coconspirators in the new party, H. Obras, then lost whatever moral authority they had possessed by pursuing nakedly self-interested efforts to win spots on the Sacaba City Council. She was betrayed again, she said, when a cofounder of H. Obras party, Oscar Angulo, pushed her aside as a city council candidate to make room for the very MNR leaders whose entry into the Sacaba MAS party she had tried to protest by forming the new party. These racist elites were infiltrating both the MAS and H. Obras in Sacaba because they "didn't want to let go of the baby bottle [*soltar la mamadera*]": they couldn't stand to lose the flow of wealth and power they had enjoyed when they belonged to elite parties that were losing ground to the MAS. Their unsavory reputations had weakened the popular appeal of H. Obras, just as they had weakened the Sacaba MAS under Congressman Jaime's leadership. Thus, H. Obras' potential as a viable rival party to Sacaba MAS, one that still followed the principles of the Instrumento Político, was shattered. And what was worse, these self-interested elite leaders managed to tarnish Doña Patricia's own local reputation as an honest leader by accusing her, baselessly, of pocketing public funds and of being power hungry.

When Doña Patricia contrasted her own motivations and methods with the motivations and methods of Oscar Angulo, her new rival, she accused him of clientelism and asserted that she avoided and abhorred clientelism by clinging to grassroots democracy. Oscar Angulo was "a leader built on a base of money that he [distributed to attract followers] . . . this is not a natural leadership like a leader born in the grassroots [*nacido en las bases*] who [earns leadership] without paying a cent." This portrayal of a legitimate leader echoed Doña Nely's argument that Evo never paid any of his followers "one cent." Of herself, Doña Patricia explained that Oscar's "betrayal hurt me very, very much . . . not for myself, not because I am hungry to be in the spaces of power. No. [It hurt because of] all those comrades who followed me, who . . . believed in me."

Doña Patricia asserted that the moral failure of both the Sacaba MAS and H. Obras leaders had destroyed her hopes of ever redeeming Sacaba politics, and shaken her confidence that MAS as a national party could escape the pitfalls of traditional political parties' elite dominance and self-interest. She told me dispiritedly, "That is politics, the distorted politics [*politiquería*] of the traditional parties; nothing has changed. Those of us who believed in an honest politics, in a true politics of change, we still haven't seen this change. And we are out here, on the sidelines, isolated, watching to see what will happen."

Even more disheartening, she argued, the Instrumento Político movement, her last refuge as an institution based on pure ideals separate from the self-interest of political parties, was also losing its purity. At the regional headquarters of the Instrumento Político in downtown Cochabamba, she had recently begun to find herself uncomfortable in her bohemian, somewhat shabby clothes amid a new crop of elite, urban leaders who wore suits, makeup, and high heels. What had begun as a subaltern movement in which she felt she shared other members' class and racial background had become dominated by people more elite—and potentially self-interested—than herself. It was good that MAS was growing, she remarked wistfully. She was pleased. But these meeting goers were benefiting as political candidates throughout the region while she and other MAS founders who had performed all the work of creating the Instrumento Político and the MAS party were left without work or the chance to influence the party locally. "There are people jumping into the car after it was already moving. And we were the ones who have been pushing the car, and now that it's moving, we're still the ones pushing," she said. Doña Patricia revealed how her middle class position contributed to her woes as a political leader. People with more wealth, like her rival Oscar Angulo and the slick new members of the movement in Cochabamba City, could gain office by distributing their money and asserting their social authority as local elites. Other Sacabans with clearer ties to the countryside and campesino status could win support as subalterns. She, who considered herself subaltern, could not negotiate these binaries in practice.

Thus far in her account, we can see that Doña Patricia argued that the transformation of Bolivian society toward equality and redistribution of wealth could best happen if she held public office. She echoed Doña Nely's lament of having supported leaders without receiving reciprocity, in this case, the opportunity to become a political candidate for a party likely to win. But, holding a higher class status through her education and being higher up in the municipal party leadership than Doña Nely, Doña Patricia also lamented that she had been unable to fulfill her own responsibilities as a patron who bestows favors. Other leaders' betrayals of her—Jaime of MAS and Oscar Angulo of H. Obras—had ricocheted down to unfairly harm those who had supported *her* campaign for city council. Each city council candidate formed a group of supporters to help fund and work on their campaigns, who, like Doña Nely, then expected patronage jobs. Her pain at disappointing people below her in the political hierarchy comes through when Doña Patricia recounted how she occasionally ran into members of her former campaign team. The young men and women on her team berated her for having dropped out of the race when she lost the crucial support of Oscar Angulo. They thought she had given up too easily, denying them the possibility of jobs as her clients. "The time that I really cried was at the end-of-campaign party," she explained. The members of her campaign team had criticized her, " 'You should be up there [on the candidate's dais]. You didn't think about us: you have abandoned us, you betrayed us [*traicionado*].' It was such a bitter experience," she told me, "of such dirty betrayal, so disgusting [*asquerosa*] . . . and not just for me but also for my comrades who right now are working," she paused forlornly, "in odd jobs."

Like Doña Nely and Doña Felisa, Doña Patricia conveyed multiple goals that were emblematic of Sacaba's political culture and the experiences of its new middle class. She hoped to further the MAS platform's "process of change," attain a leadership position for herself, and create jobs for her clients. In her portrayal of her campaign team's laments, Doña Patricia made clear that she felt responsible for their well-being. She betrayed them by killing their hopes to enter the middle class. Doña Patricia's sense of responsibility for her supporters was a moral imperative, even as her opponents, like Congressman Jaime and Oscar Angulo, condemned her as an immoral clientelist and presumably, derided her supporters as *pegas*. She adamantly maintained that she was motivated not by self-interest but rather by loyalty to particular individuals and by the ideals of the Instrumento Político to achieve the equalization of wealth and power in Sacaba. She conveyed anguish at both being betrayed and betraying others through circumstances beyond her control.

## Conclusion

In this chapter I have traced some of the moral and practical dilemmas party leaders and the rank and file have confronted in the wake of the public denunciation of clientelism by both Law of Popular Participation reformers and by MAS leaders since the 1990s. I have highlighted laments of betrayal as a genre of political speech, because they were so common and because they bring to light the contradictory moral requirements many Sacabans encountered. Doña Patricia's litany of disappointments at being edged out of leadership positions and Doña Nely's laments at losing a lower-level job as a client suggest that they were adhering to multiple political frameworks, including clientelist expectations of reciprocity and ideals of leftist-indigenist grassroots democracy. Such laments illustrate how frameworks of political philosophy that were formally in conflict—liberal representative democracy, clientelism, and grassroots democracy—in practice formed a set of overlapping principles and repertoires for action. In public discussions, such as at the Bartolinas' women's meeting, many Sacabans portrayed these frameworks as clearly distinguishable from each other and from clientelism as an easily identified evil. Yet in laments of betrayal, reflecting the messiness of everyday life, Sacabans suggested that these frameworks involved similar practices and that individual people experienced multiple and sometimes conflicting moral imperatives. The ideal of a pure political life in a new society of prosperity for all, free of clientelism, clashed with the need to get a job, to support others who needed jobs, and the moral imperative to attain or maintain a middle-class lifestyle.

MAS supporters in Sacaba attempted to remain hopeful that their party's leaders, unlike leaders of older parties, were genuinely working toward national transformation based on the ideological platform of the Instrumento Político. The fear that Sacaba MAS politicians engaged in the same underhanded, hidden practices and allegiances as those of other parties was at the center of narratives of collective and individual betrayal such as those of Doña Felisa, Doña Patricia, and Doña Nely. Yet those leaders' experiences, in which middling aspirations and the MAS platform of redistributing wealth were tightly intertwined, point to the practical difficulties of avoiding the moral pitfalls that they denounced in others. Their statements also point to the challenges faced by leaders who must represent the racial, class, and often gender interests of constituents in an environment of ambiguous and shifting identities. Doña Felisa in particular faced the wrath of Doña Nely and other activists for gaining prosperity without reciprocating with concrete items for local community development projects.

The MAS platform of radical democracy and the notion of civil society embodied in the LPP both present utopian visions of societal change. Such depictions of society as a struggle between the virtuous and the venal are necessary for political mobilization, but usually impossible to carry out in everyday life. Just as the liberal concept of civil society is flawed in its assumption that society is divided between a fundamentally altruistic public and selfish politicians, we should question the common assumption among MAS leaders that clientelism represents a radical disjuncture from both liberal and direct forms of democracy. Self-interest is often in the eye of the beholder; it is subject to contestation. Rather than reform based on a model of abrupt moral change, I suggest that MAS leaders would do well to acknowledge the economic and other structural constraints on both leaders and followers. The multiplicity of political frameworks in circulation and ambiguous identities as subalterns and as an upwardly mobile middle class pulled Sacabans in different directions as they struggled to consider themselves morally upright people. In the next chapter, I trace in the ways in which these struggles to define middling groups, legitimate political practices, and the morally upright course of action came to a head in one more important arena of Bolivian political culture: debates over the meaning of community.

# Middle Classes and Debates over the Definition of Community

October 3, 2005, was a bright, chilly, spring morning. In the Rural Planning Office on the second floor of Sacaba's city hall, several men and women were entering data into Excel spreadsheets. The high ceilings and battered, ornate ironwork on the office doors betrayed the age of the building, circa 1880. Inside, across from me at a scuffed table, sat Don Carlos and Lucho, his enthusiastic agronomist friend and employee. Completing the group was Diego, a high-ranking municipal planning official who lived in an expensive gated high-rise condo building in Cochabamba City. Diego's chain-smoked cigarettes filled the office with a soft haze.

For the previous two hours, we had been staring at a laptop computer, reviewing Choro's list of project requests as part of Sacaba's Annual Plan, fruit of the state-mandated participatory planning process that Don Carlos spearheaded in Choro. Don Carlos had followed the guidelines of the 1994 Popular Participation Law (LPP), within which Choro was officially designated as a rural peasant community (*comunidad campesina*). The Choro wish list included money to buy a plot of land for a new high school, cement to pave several irrigation canals, and tubing to expand Choro's drinking water system.

The ongoing failure of Choreños to engage in the collective action necessary to capture the funding from the LPP quickly emerged as a chief concern in the meeting. Don Carlos remarked to Diego that, as elected agrarian union (*sindicato*) president and codirector of Inti, the NGO, he was trying to build social capital (*capital social*) in Choro, but it was very difficult. He and community members were intensely frustrated because

Choreños were failing to organize collectively to access the LPP's significant new resources for development projects. Collective action as a community was essential, development workers knew from experience: residents had to agree on which projects to prioritize from their LPP funds; sustain pressure on lackadaisical municipal officials—protesting in the street, when necessary—to disburse funds and draw up project blueprints; and collect the money from each household to make up the inevitable shortfall of government funding for each project. They needed to mobilize in work parties to build the irrigation canals and health clinic they wanted and to meet often to decide on their priorities and budget. Choreños failed to carry out these collective actions and therefore missed out on immense funding opportunities.

Even the municipal government's simplest and most essential offers of assistance slipped through Choreños' fingers, said Don Carlos. When the Sacaba government announced that it would vaccinate cows against foot-and-mouth disease, for example, there was no organizational structure in Choro to take advantage of the offer, because this required leaders and the rank and file to express interest and set up a system to collect the cows to receive their shots. Choreños had received only occasional bags of cement and a few adobe classrooms for their ancient and decrepit elementary school in the ten years since the passage of the LPP, hailed by former Bolivian president Gonzalo Sánchez de Lozada as "the most important redistribution of political and economic power in the republic since the 1952 Revolution" (Sánchez de Lozada in Molina and Arias 1996:30). Don Carlos and Lucho spent several more moments lamenting that social division in Choro impeded this collective action and therefore blocked development in Choro.

Diego remarked offhandedly that only an "organized civil society" (*sociedad civil organizada*) could effectively launch development. He was echoing the terminology of the designers of the Popular Participation Law (e.g., Finot 1990:87; Molina and Arias 1996:26) and continued regretfully that this was a problem throughout the municipality of Sacaba, subverting LPP planners' intentions. Don Carlos's face lit up and he asked Diego to repeat himself. He cried out with a jubilant smile, "organized civil society!" and wrote it down with a flourish in his date book. He exclaimed, beaming, that what Diego had just called "organized civil society," he and Lucho had been calling "social capital," but Diego's phrase captured his notion more precisely. The three men lamented for a few more moments that most

Bolivians, Choreños and other Sacabans among them, did not organize collectively to reap the enormous potential resources that the LPP provided as an institutional framework and source of funding. Then, with a collective sigh, the three men returned to their triage of the Choro wish list on Lucho's laptop.

This chapter traces debates in Sacaba over how to define the meaning of communities in the context of rising middle-class aspirations and dynamically shifting state development policies, particularly in light of the 1994 LPP and Evo Morales's 2005 election. This meeting in the Sacaba city hall in 2005 was one of many moments in which professional development workers, community leaders, or rank-and-file residents attempted to define Bolivians' collective responsibilities as citizens. Where the preceding chapters have traced the effects of middling aspirations upon Sacaba municipal politics, in this chapter I examine how these middling groups shaped local political debate and conflict over the meanings of community—another vital arena of Bolivian political life.

Don Carlos and the other development workers in the city hall meeting advocated a hybrid of two models of community in this quite typical conversation among Sacaba's development professionals. On the one hand, their borrowing of the phrase "organized civil society" from LPP reformers alluded to the Popular Participation Law's characterization of Bolivia's rural communities. LPP *comunidades campesinas* were marked by firm geographic boundaries that contained residents who naturally shared campesino identity and common goals and aspirations. Communities were tasked with collectively carrying out local development, defined as public works such as schools and health clinics. By defining community in this locally-oriented way, LPP reformers had explicitly hoped to squelch the national power of Bolivia's agrarian union federation, the Confederación Sindical Unica de Trabajadores Campesinos de Bolivia (CSUTCB), which was a central base of support for Evo and the MAS party. LPP reformers rejected the CSUTCB's political aims of directly shaping national economic policy through public protest (e.g., Molina Saucedo 1990:65–80; Medina 1995:22).

Don Carlos and the other two men were also enthusiastic supporters of the CSTUCB, of the national MAS party platform, and of Evo. MAS leaders, like LPP reformers, defined rural communities as populated by indigenous campesinos, but in direct contrast to LPP reformers, they also defined communities as agrarian unions (*sindicatos agrarios*). These unions, rather than geographically bounded and narrowly focused on building infrastructure, were linked together in a strong network to constitute the national CSTUCB agrarian union federation as a political force (e.g., Zuazo 2009:50).[1] In their conversation, these Sacaba development professionals framed their aims through models of community promoted by both the LPP and the MAS party.

Yet neither the LPP's organized civil society nor the MAS party's *sindicatos agrarios* explicitly acknowledged many Bolivians' middle-class aspirations and lifestyles that fell outside of the definition of a campesino community, or Bolivians' regular migration and periodic absence from particular rural localities. In other moments, development professionals advocated an additional, third model, that of an indigenous community in which residents would use indigenous culture as an inspiration to carry out collective actions—a model that held even less resonance for most Choro residents (compare to Fabricant 2012).

As will be explored in more detail below, Choreños created multiple kinds of communities over the course of the twentieth century as they pursued their middle-class aspirations. In some historical moments, Choreños followed formally constituted or state-sponsored models of community, such as agrarian unions during the 1940s and 1950s, when it helped them achieve their aims of upward mobility.[2] When those models did not align with their middle-class aspirations, however, they pursued alternate forms of collectivity. Deysi, Doña Saturnina, Bald César, and other new middle-class Choro residents participated actively in communities beyond the official boundaries of Choro—in teachers' unions, political parties, coca growers' unions, and in personal networks of friends, godparents, and family whose members traveled often between Sacaba and the Chapare. Other Choreños were part of national networks of truckers, sawmill business owners, Cochabamba metropolitan bus and taxi drivers' unions, and large regional irrigation associations. Given their greater wealth than the poorer people living next door to them, there was little uniformity in the dreams of Choreños for economic development.

Owing to their institutional position as development workers, Lucho, Don Carlos, and Diego expressed a professional and personal responsibility to fulfill both the LPP's and the MAS party's promises of local development. This burning goal led them to accept the definition of rural community as a bounded, "organized civil society" of campesinos and to place responsibility for an enormous amount of effort and coordination upon residents. They knew in practice that a huge gap lay between many actual Choreños' identities and this organized civil society. Yet they struggled mightily to use moral suasion and consciousness-raising to try to convince Choreños to change their outlook in the hopes that this would then change their behavior.

Despite ongoing frustrations with disunity, Choreños began construction on several long-awaited public works projects in 2006. These included a community center, a public park, a sewer system, and a new public high school. Don Carlos attributed Choro residents' newly discovered solidarity and community-mindedness to the flowering of Choro's organized civil society. Yet, as we will see, these triumphs owed at least as much to the harnessing of clientelist relationships, motivated in part by several Choreños' desires for upward mobility through their acquisition of *pegas* (patronage jobs).

## Multiple Models of Community in Bolivia

Throughout the Third World, people living in rural areas have often borne a greater burden for building and maintaining their own basic infrastructure than have residents of urban areas and the First World. Participatory development policies that emerged around the world in the 1990s, including Bolivia's Popular Participation Law, continued the assumption that rural communities should be responsible for development. Participatory development provided increased opportunities (primarily funding) and challenges. One of these challenges was a definition of community as harmonious, geographically bounded, solidarity. This narrow model of community persists in transnational development policy making despite scholars' extensive criticism. These scholars working in the field of critical studies of development have shown that the model of bounded community responsible for development is itself to blame for ubiquitous complaints about failures of community organization (Agrawal and Gibson 2001:19; Peters 2004; Ribot 1999; Mosse 1999; Cooke and Kothari 2001). The role of communities in development changes historically according to new class and cultural aspirations of their inhabitants and to new political conditions.[3] Certainly, the definition of community as organized civil society was only one model circulating in Bolivia.

The community dynamics in the Cochabamba region, in which Sacaba is located, were particularly at odds with geographically bounded descriptions of Bolivian community proffered by LPP policy makers in the 1990s (e.g., Medina 1995; Molina and Arias 1996). For a variety of reasons, Cochabambans have historically emphasized the pursuit of family-based upward mobility. From the moment of colonial occupation, rural Cochabambans successfully avoided Spanish colonial taxes and forced labor by moving to other communities or cities; the implications of this were as far-reaching for Cochabamba community dynamics as for race and class identities (see Chapter 1). Cochabamba valley community leaders always retained a more tenuous authority over their residents than leaders in highland communities; community-based efforts were subject to the political and economic needs of the moment rather than grounded in the long-standing authority of leaders.

When, in the late nineteenth century, Cochabamba valley serfs (*colonos, pongos*) began challenging the dominance of large landowning elites by buying up small plots of agricultural land and becoming free farmers (*piqueros*), they already had experience migrating regularly to urban markets and to other areas of Bolivia. Communities' geographic boundaries blended into each other and overlapped. By the early twentieth century, rural residents were organized for multiple types of actions in various configurations, from servitude to large landowners to membership in multiple irrigation associations to participation in saint-worship fraternities.

As Doña Saturnina recalled her early childhood in the 1940s, the majority of families in Choro owned their own small plots of land, like her parents, and "just lived" (*kakullaq kanku*). They were not subject to the rules of an overarching local political organization based upon territorial boundaries.[4] Then, in the late 1940s, rural Cochabambans formed agrarian unions (*sindicatos*) to take possession of land from large landowners and to push the government for suffrage, education, and agrarian reform. Many Choro residents downplayed differences in wealth and racial identification among themselves, claiming a shared identity as campesinos to join together in common political cause for land reform. Aided in forming their *sindicato* by industrial labor organizers trained in European union strategies, union members played up their commonalities by contrasting themselves to the bourgeois landowners they hoped to oust.

Yet, at the same time as Choreños sought a shared self-identification as campesinos to help their political organizing for land reform, many saw this campesino identity as a means to upward mobility rather than an end in itself. In the 1940s, agriculture appeared to be the best way to launch children on a path to middle-class status. Most elderly Choreños remembered the 1950s and early 1960s following the Agrarian Reform as a time of relative economic plentitude filled with promise for future prosperity, newfound freedom from the domination of large landowners, and strong *sindicato* organization.[5]

Following the 1952 Revolution, the MNR government leaders contributed only minimally toward Choreños' and other Cochabambans' dreams of upward mobility. The MNR sought to institute its own clientelist model of community in which it co-opted community *sindicatos* as voting blocs. The MNR then distributed sporadic development aid from the United States' anticommunist Alliance for Progress aid program and also sent campesino militias to repress radical miners and other dissidents elsewhere in the country (Gordillo 2000; Dandler 1975). When MNR officials reneged on promises to build schools and health clinics that many people saw as vital to becoming middle class, Choreños often had band together to build their own schools and other infrastructure. Dictator General Barrientos further co-opted community *sindicatos* during the late 1960s, appointing his own local agrarian bosses in rural areas while continuing the pattern of sporadic funding for infrastructure.

When, in 1985, the Bolivian government adopted orthodox free-market reforms, community building was absent from government attention. Nine years later, however, government LPP reformers followed global trends in development policy to put local communities back at the center of their development model (Cooke and Kothari 2001). They redefined communities as responsible for development, with democracy in place of a central clientelistic government that doled out projects on an ad hoc basis in exchange for political support. LPP reformers continued previous governments' institutional dependence upon rural community self-government—*sindicatos*—but renamed them Territorial Base Organizations (Organizaciones Territoriales de Base, OTBs) to define rural communities as everyone living in a particular geographic space. Communities, in this view, consisted of residents who stayed put in one locality and focused single-mindedly on building infrastructure.

The LPP architects who defined rural community policy tended to discount middle-class aspirations in arguing that indigenous culture and campesino identity provided a shared framework for harmonious collective action (see especially Medina 1995; Molina and Arias 1996). They characterized rural Bolivians as oriented toward a collective livelihood as subsistence peasants and argued that their communally and agriculturally oriented culture would provide a template for them to carry out development projects under the LPP. They based their depictions of Andean communal culture largely on ethnological studies of the highland region of La Paz (e.g., Carter and Albó 1988). They posited that there was a cultural core of rural communities that remained unchanged by the large shifts in rural Bolivian life over the previous half century: mass migration within and outside the country, the formation of agrarian unions, the explosive growth of cities, and the coca economy's booms and busts.[6] Their stance of social critique of the status quo, combined with a notion of indigeneity as a static and mystical connection to nature and harmonious communal life, reflected the influence of Bolivian elites' philosophy of indigenism (*indigenismo*) dating back to the early twentieth century (e.g., Diez de Medina 1950; Botelho Gosalvez 1982 [1945]; for critiques, see Starn 1991; Albro 2000).

Following Evo's election in 2005, his administration has continued to downplay middle-class aspirations by explicitly defining rural communities as composed of campesinos who share indigenous identity, albeit with some differences from the LPP reformers. The Morales administration shifted the emphasis of the Bolivian government's economic policy from the LPP's local focus to a nationally oriented focus on gas nationalization, land reform, and an end to political leaders' corruption (MAS-IPSP 2010; Postero 2007). Some MAS leaders also argued for a nuanced view of rural communities as multiclass and sometimes conflict ridden.[7] Furthermore, the coca growers' unions were a central support base for the MAS party and these unions contained diverse and highly mobile inhabitants. Yet the government has most often depicted rural communities as bound by indigenous collective ideals that do not include middle-class aspirations, in keeping with its explicit depiction of Bolivia as composed of superelites and subalterns discussed in previous chapters.[8] In fact, the Morales administration has increasingly employed romantic rhetoric of rural communities as embodying a static, harmonious, and subsistence-oriented indigenous culture over the course of two terms as it has sought to divert Bolivians from their concerns that the government had not fulfilled its promises of redistribution of wealth and prosperity (see Fabricant 2012).

In sum, at each recent historical juncture, new definitions of rural community have entered circulation in Bolivia from state leaders, but few leaders have acknowledged local inequalities of wealth, the aspirations of middle classes, or Cochabamba's flexible community practices. During the time of my research in the late twentieth and the early twenty-first centuries, Sacaba residents and development workers held up hybrid ideals of community. They drew in eclectic fashion upon elites' romantic ideas of harmonious and timeless indigenous communities from the early twentieth century, agrarian *sindicatos* with their rigid rules and centralized leadership, the MNR government's clientelist models of community, the LPP's model of OTB residents in a bounded locality working single-mindedly to construct infrastructure, and the MAS's hybrid model of *sindicato* and national agrarian unions bound by shared subaltern campesino and indigenous identities and worldviews.

## Complaints About Community Failure from Development Workers

Development workers like Don Carlos, Lucho, and Diego wove together these diverse threads in their notion of an organized civil society in 2005 and 2006. Their theory of community action, like the rhetorical rejection of clientelism (see Chapter 4), captured the imagination of some of Choro's residents but ignored many of their middle-class aspirations. A pervasive, frustrated narrative from development workers held that Choreños had failed as a campesino community to enact community solidarity owing to self-interest, apathy, or a failure of union or indigenous consciousness. Lucho, Don Carlos's agronomist friend and employee, argued that Choreños had experienced a failure of morals and consciousness because they lacked "union discipline" (*disciplina sindical*). When I asked Lucho how his work in Choro compared to work he had done in Colomi, a market town located further away from Cochabamba City than Choro, he said immediately, "There, they have better discipline." He continued,

> [Here in Choro] you can't even be doing a workshop for two hours without people starting to look around [i.e., wanting to leave]. [This] has been the desperation of Don Carlos: when he calls a meeting, only two or three guys show up. [In the meetings, we want to promote] reflection. . . . If the leader [calls the meeting] at midnight, you have to go, because only in this way are we going to be able to internalize [*interiorizar*] our rights, be able to make demands [*exigir*]. But unfortunately, these communities that are much closer to the urban areas, like Choro, are the ones that have the least collective interests. They are individualists . . .

> I have worked a long time with that other project that I told
> you about, on the border of Cochabamba department and La Paz,
> Inquisivi Province. . . . We had to travel almost a day to get there,
> but it was satisfying [*daba gusto*] because when we did a workshop
> we would find 100 people waiting for us. . . . But, [it must be that
> here] the people are thinking more about their individual interests
> and not about collective issues. One of [Inti's] objectives is to . . .
> not allow people to think individually.

Lucho articulated here the commonly accepted notion that values are about "thinking," that is, about consciousness. Lucho complained about individualism as an obstacle to collective action and hoped to promote instead a consciousness of a shared campesino identity, shared responsibility for development, and communal action. His framing of the problem as one of lack of "union discipline" pointed to the rigid organizational rules of the regional and national agrarian union, the CSUTCB. Indeed, regional and national CSUTCB congresses remained notoriously strict. Following guidelines inherited from European industrial unions in the 1930s, for example, Sacaba agrarian union congress delegates were often locked into meeting halls overnight. "Union police" wore ersatz badges and carried sticks to enforce, only partly jokingly, the rule that delegates should stay up all night to deliberate over union rules and public stances on government policies.

Lucho supported the national MAS party, its platform of redistribution of wealth, and its promise of national transformation. He often expressed intense frustration that Choreños and other rural residents were not receiving the redistribution of wealth within Sacaba municipality that they deserved, given the poverty of rural areas relative to urban ones. But he believed that his goals were stymied by Choreños' passivity, their "I-don't-care-ism" (*nomeimportismo*), in addition to their individualist values. This prevented them from organizing marches to pressure municipal officials for their funds and from organizing effective collective work parties to construct community buildings like a high school. Lucho decried a process of cultural and moral degeneration, owing largely to increasing proximity to the city of Cochabamba. Lucho also portrayed the failure to act collectively as a *sindicato* as first and foremost a problem of mistaken individual (middle-class) identity instead of a true (campesino) identity. These development workers, including Don Carlos and Lucho, born and raised as provincial elite *vecinos* in other valley towns or raised in Bolivia's cities, thus argued that solidarity was an inherent feature of Bolivian indigenous and rural culture but that it was disintegrating in Choro.

Don Carlos likewise downplayed the legitimacy of middle-class aspirations and vowed repeatedly to squelch individualism in favor of a shared indigenous and campesino identity. As a cofounder of the party, he closely echoed national MAS leaders' ideals of both indigenous community and *sindicato*-oriented models of community. He and his wife, Doña Karin, peppered nearly every public speech and private conversation in 2005 and 2006 with an exhortation for communal unity, using the 1940s agrarian union rallying cry, "We need to be like one person [*uj runa jinalla kananchis tiyan*]." They also often promoted indigenous identity among Choro residents, harnessed to the message about communal unity and condemning individualism. For example, a Peruvian film they showed at the Inti offices in 2006, entitled "The Two Forms of Knowledge" (*Iskay Yachay, Los Dos Saberes*), depicted residents of a highland town near Cuzco, Peru, arguing for the need to overcome a recent "loss of values" (*pérdida de valores*) by promoting indigenous culture among their children.

Don Carlos marshaled every resource at his disposal—from his own church sermons and those by the local priest, to indigenist films, to agrarian union rules—to convey his message about the need for a reformed, "unified" consciousness that could support the collective action that he yearned for. He criticized Choreños' racism, complaining about Choreños' insulting each other with racist epithets, as well as class prejudice, as when they accused each other of being poor out of laziness. He also worried aloud, often, about their self-interest and "envy" (*envidia, qhawanaku*).

A local Catholic priest whom Don Carlos urged Choreños repeatedly to heed argued similarly during Mass in 2006 that Choreños should adopt an ethic of class and racial unity. When people acquired money, he preached, they should not buy expensive cars or clothes, or seek to acquire many godchildren (a source of prestige), but should share what they possessed with poorer people in Choro. This was a common thread of antimaterialism promoted by Bolivian clergy, even as it went directly counter to many Choreños' most cherished ambitions of upward mobility. The priest's depiction of self-interest as the purchase of expensive consumer items appeared to frame selfishness as being synonymous with middle-class identity and aspirations and posited that these aspirations were the root cause of failures of community solidarity. Where MAS leaders and other political activists denounced self-interest as dangerous for Sacaba's municipal political life and for the national "process of change" (see Chapters 4 and 5), development workers like Don Carlos, Lucho, and the local priest worried that self-interest was the central problem inhibiting community life.

Don Carlos also rebuked particular Choreños whom he deemed to be motivated by individualist clientelism rather than Choro's collective development. I described in Chapter 4, in the oven incident, how fiercely Don Carlos condemned efforts of Choreños to align with right-wing parties. He uttered similar condemnations in expressing frustrations about community. In particular, Don Carlos often sparred with Torrico (a pseudonym, no relation to Celima Torrico), a prosperous, middle-class farmer who was reputed to be an incorrigible *busca pega* and who often urged Choreños to attend political rallies to support politicians in order to get patronage support for public works in Choro. Many Choro residents were annoyed by Torrico's exhortations to support his successive patrons—who changed as soon as a new mayor or state governor entered office—or at least saw them as laughably transparent attempts to raise his own economic and social stature. Torrico particularly enraged Don Carlos. Don Carlos, his wife, and other development agents often lamented that Torrico's brand of clientelism "divided" Choro into smaller fragments of its natural territory, stymying development.

## Middle-Class Ideals of Community and Complaints About Individualism

Most Choro residents certainly agreed in theory with elements of development workers' critique of disunity and their frustration with the failure to capture LPP funding. Choro residents also used an ideal of agrarian union solidarity (though not of indigenous cultural purity) as a model of community against which they measured themselves and found themselves or their neighbors wanting. Yet their daily practices and aspirations also created other forms of community that were not recognized in these models. Many of these practices of community were based around middle-class aspirations that, since the 1950s, began to conflict with models based upon a campesino collectivity with uniform interests. In addition to seeking upward mobility through nonagricultural work, which ran counter to the agrarian union's traditional role as a manager of agricultural land, middle-class residents tended to prioritize community infrastructure less than did impoverished residents. The school and health clinic that were vital for poor Choreños were less urgent goals for wealthier people, since they could afford to pay more for these services in Sacaba and Cochabamba and sometimes preferred those urban services, anyway, as being of higher quality and higher prestige. These divergent needs and aspirations conflicted with ideals of community based on the premise that Choreños were all campesinos with shared interests and objectives.

When I first arrived in Choro in 1995, I was struck immediately by how often and how bitterly residents of all levels of wealth and education lamented lack of unity (*unidad*) in Choro. This was one year after the passage, with much fanfare, of the LPP, and people often remarked disgustedly that in the year since the law was passed they had not been able to capture any of the thousands of dollars that the Sacaba municipal government owed them. For example, in 1995, an NGO hydrologist giving a group of Choreños a tour of a huge regional irrigation network in a nearby Cochabamba town enjoined them to "*aprovechar*" (take advantage of) the Popular Participation money to similarly expand Choro's irrigation system. Several Choro *sindicato* leaders replied disgustedly that the LPP money was slipping through their fingers because "we are not well organized" (*no estamos bien organizados*). Residents' complaints of lack of community unity was the central thread running through my field notes of the dozens of Choro *sindicato* meetings I attended between 1995 and 2009.

The concern about lack of collective unity had intensified in the 1990s, not only because of pressure to collectively take advantage of the LPP money, but also because of the decline of the coca and cocaine economies in the wake of the drug war, the widespread unemployment that had deepened since free-market reforms in 1985, and the intensifying drought. Many families that had moved to the Chapare in the 1970s and 1980s to grow coca were, by 1998, spending more time hustling work in Choro; new families from the Chapare were also swelling Choro's population.

Many rank-and-file members of Choro's *sindicato* agreed with development workers in principle that community was defined as the *sindicato* and that the obstacle to successful capture of LPP funding was residents' "self-interest." In May 1995, I waited for several hours for a *sindicato* meeting to begin with a group of Choro men alongside the highway outside the health clinic, where the meeting was supposed to be held. As the hours wore on, they grumbled that even the leaders were terribly late. "We aren't well organized around here," they chimed in together in outrage. Usually, no more than half of the members came to meetings. One man added with a disgusted snort, "But when people have a [personal] interest, they come to meetings—even the cats come." A year later, this very man, now the *sindicato* treasurer, was the target of ire when he missed several Choro meetings while attending his other *sindicato*'s meeting in the Chapare.

Many Choro residents of all social classes, like the development workers, thus denounced self-interest and envy as sinful values that were at the root of Choreños' inability to work collectively to enact development projects. When parents of the Choro school parent association failed to contribute personal funds to pay the electricity bill for their children's school, and the school consequently went unlit for several weeks, Amanda and her mother shook their heads and criticized the parents' *envidia*. A middle-aged Choro woman exclaimed more matter-of-factly, "of course there is envy [*qhawanaku*] in the *sindicato*! People say that the leaders are eating up the members' dues."

Many people in Choro likewise shared NGOs' and other officials' narrative of a decline in collective action through the *sindicato* between the era of 1940s agrarian union organizing and the present. Doña Saturnina, like other elderly Choreños, often smiled wistfully and said she missed the sound of the ram's horn that leaders used during the 1940s, 1950s, and 1960s to call people to meetings. At the time of the Agrarian Reform, upon hearing the ram's horn, "people would fly [*runas phawaq kanku*]" to the meeting, she reminisced. She, like many Choreños of all levels of wealth, attributed this difference to a decline in morality. "People were much more responsible then [*más cumplidos eran siempre*]" was a perpetual refrain. Choreños often praised their community leaders from that time as "strict" (enforcing on-time attendance at meetings with floggings, for example) and nearly always contrasted this strictness with leaders' "disorganization" in the present.

To be sure, nostalgic accounts of unity by Choro residents, like those of development workers, ignored deep class divides of that time.[9] Some Choreños alluded to these class conflicts when narrating their own or their parents' and grandparents' hard labor and determination during the decades prior to the Agrarian Reform to become *piqueros*, independent small-holding farmers, rather than serfs (*pongos, colonos*). *Piqueros* who managed to save money and buy small plots of land escaped the social and economic oppression of debt-servitude to large landowners. A rural high school teacher in his fifties told me how his mother told him often and emphatically, "I bought our land with my sweat, child [*Hump'iywan jallp'ata rantini, wawitay*]!" Buying land helped *piqueros* attain a middling class and racial status, become the masters of their own time, and reap the entire profit of their labor (Dandler 1975; Gordillo 2000). Not everyone was able to achieve this leap in class and racial status, however, and many Choreños remained poor prior to and after the 1953 Agrarian Reform. Choreños of varying levels of wealth in recent times told me stories of intense suffering when, as serfs, wealthier piqueros would not marry them or treat them as social equals.

Most people, then—rank-and-file Choreños, community leaders, and development workers—argued explicitly that values could make or break development and community feeling. If their recalcitrant neighbors could only overcome their self-interested individualism and instead pursue an ethic of collective solidarity through the *sindicato* they could finally carry out development projects.

Occasionally, however, people in Choro explicitly or implicitly proposed alternate definitions of community that acknowledged middle-class aspirations without condemning them as morally bankrupt. One of these alternate definitions acknowledged that the *sindicato* leaders' authority in the 1950s and 1960s had rested on material resources—fertile and irrigated agricultural land—that were less available in 2006 and less able to support upward mobility. For example, an elderly man who served as the first *sindicato* president in 1953 remarked to me in 2006 that Choreños had joined the *sindicato* in droves during its early years in part to gain title to hillside land formerly owned by large landowners that was amply fed by rainfall but no irrigation water. 1950s dirigentes were the authorities who redistributed this land from large landowners expelled during the Agrarian Reform. If people did not "fly" at that time to meetings when dirigentes blew the ram's horn, they would have lost their access to this newly available, fertile, land. The ensuing drought since the 1960s had made this land nearly worthless and certainly not a basis for launching an attempt to join the middle class.

*Sindicato* leaders' narratives of the more recent past also pointed to material, rather than moral, explanations for the decline of *sindicato* authority. It was during the late 1960s, when Choreños began to seek upward mobility by moving to the tropics in order to escape drought and small plot sizes, that community leaders began having difficulty in rallying residents to work on collective infrastructure projects. The mid-1980s, when Choro had been reportedly empty because the vast majority of residents were in the Chapare growing coca or working in cocaine production, became an even more difficult period for collective action through the *sindicato*. Leaders who had been in office at that time recounted to me their despair when they couldn't muster even a dozen residents to show up for *sindicato* meetings or to conduct the most uncontroversial and urgent of collective tasks, such as cleaning irrigation ditches or painting the school. By the late 1990s, enough people had returned to Choro from the Chapare, at least part-time, to turn out for basic work parties to clear weeds from the irrigation canals or the cemetery, but leaders could not mobilize people the way they had in the 1950s.

Agricultural land was worth less to many people simply because farming became less and less viable as a means to upward mobility. This change reflected both the increased availability of alternative ways to earn a living through commerce or a profession and the decline of small-scale agriculture throughout Bolivia. In a bare economic calculus, many people agreed that "farming no longer pays [*la agricultura ya no rinde como antes*]". Choro experienced a sequence repeated in countless rural localities in the Third World: drought, erosion, decline in soil fertility, the shrinking size of plots as they were divided among successive generations, and decline of the terms of trade for small farmers, known as the "scissors squeeze" (Prudencio Böhrt 1991). Between 1953 and 2006, the price that small-scale farmers received from cash crops such as potatoes, onions, and corn dropped, while the cost of purchased necessities like cooking oil, pasta, toothpaste, school supplies, and fertilizers rose. Amanda and Deysi were outraged when their mother, Doña Saturnina, bought a small plot of farmland when she came into a sum of money in 2005. They exclaimed exasperatedly to her, to each other, and to me that their mother was making a poor investment since any fool knew that "farming doesn't pay any more!" Doña Saturnina, raised during the 1940s when all people who aspired to upward mobility single-mindedly bought farmland, was dismayed.

In 2005 and 2006, instead of dedicating themselves full-time to farming in Choro as they had in the mid-twentieth century, people commuted back and forth between coca growing in the Chapare and a variety of jobs in or near Choro. Only those who owned the greatest amount of irrigated agricultural land or who were destitute day laborers worked full-time in agriculture in Choro. Disgust about disunity also expressed many people's deep disappointment of having lost their access to another material resource—several regional irrigation canal systems—despite having contributed dues and labor to the required work parties during construction. The frustration of several drawn out but fruitless lawsuits against the irrigation canal association leaders, who were based in neighboring localities at higher altitudes and who had had been reportedly been aided by the infamous Congressman Jaime, was also reflected in the perennial exclamation, "We are so disorganized [*Estamos tan desorganizados*]!"[10]

Middle-class residents like Bald César and Deysi shared the pervasive moral complaint about disunity, even as their interests diverged from those of less wealthy people. When I asked middle-class Choreños, some of whom did not regularly attend *sindicato* meetings, which issue was most pressing for them, they often replied immediately "there is no unity [*unidad*] in my community." Ironically, they pointed to other people's failure to attend *sindicato* meeting attendance as the reason for not attending meetings themselves.

But I suggest that a major reason they did not attend meetings or participate fully in efforts to acquire funding for infrastructure from the LPP and other funding sources was that they could afford to give up on the *sindicato* and pursue their own goals without the framework of a collective organization. Not only did they not work in agriculture, they did not need infrastructure desperately. Poorer Choreños like Don Felipe and Doña Gladys depended upon the *sindicato* to ensure that they had basic services like water hookups, a good local school that did not require expensive bus fare to attend, and good quality, inexpensive health care at the public health clinic. They needed wealthier people to contribute money, as well as time and energy, to building those projects in Choro; they couldn't sustain the monetary contributions or significant workload from their own meager resources. Wealthier people like Doña Saturnina and Bald César, by contrast, often preferred to buy higher quality health care and education in Sacaba or Cochabamba and saw less need to commit their money, time, and labor to projects that would primarily benefit poorer people. The children of the wealthy Bald César went to a Cochabamba orthodontist to get expensive braces when they were adolescents and did not need the poorly equipped, state-subsidized dentist in Choro. They did hope for Choro to achieve progress by becoming more densely populated, but this was a less central yearning than for poor people, who depended infinitely more on a decent school and health clinic in Choro.

## Other Models of Middle-Class Community

All of these discussions by both Choreños and development workers about failure and absence defined the term "community" (*comunidad*) primarily as the geographically bounded village and its inhabitants consisting of the *sindicato* or the registered community (OTB) created by the Law of Popular Participation. These ubiquitous complaints of failure bound up in these particular definitions of community beg the question of how people *did* enact community in the context of their deeply held aspirations for upward mobility. In fact, much of Choreños' everyday social and economic life involved other configurations of relatedness that I would term "community." The bonds of godparenthood (fictive kinship, *compadrazgo*), as well as bonds of family, friendship, and neighborliness, drew people to Choro from the Chapare and further afield for weddings, funerals, and baptisms; celebrations in the Chapare similarly drew people from Choro. For any large gathering, dozens of women—goddaughters, godmothers, aunts, nieces, daughters-in-law, sisters, grandmothers, granddaughters, cousins, and friends—pitched in for days to help prepare huge vats of *chicha*. They plucked chickens, peeled mountains of carrots and potatoes, and chopped chili peppers, onions, and tomatoes. A small army of women, and sometimes men, served hundreds of guests plates heaped high with roast chicken or fried guinea pig on a bed of potatoes with a side of salad. They kept busy throughout weddings and baptisms pressuring guests, on behalf of the hosts, to drink and dance continuously. They accompanied the dead and bereaved all night at wakes, bathed in the purple light of rented electric crosses. Such outpourings of energy required extensive social networks and excellent organizational skills.

Choreños also created new communities in their migrations even as migration challenged the exercise of community *sindicato* authority geographically based in Choro. As the desire to attain middle-class status inspired many Choreños to migrate to the Chapare and further east, they created dozens of new communities when they claimed tropical land as agricultural colonists.[11] Doña Saturnina, for example, helped found a new settlement, Choro Colony, with members of her extended family and strangers from throughout Sacaba municipality in the late 1970s. After months of attending organizational meetings, prospective colonists each signed an agreement to occupy a tract of forested land with collective responsibility for building roads and other infrastructure. Doña Saturnina developed bonds with her new Chapare neighbors as they traded supplies in this frontier region or huddled together for comfort when confronting unfamiliar jungle animals such as pumas and poisonous snakes. Choreños also organized militias, together with fellow colonists, to defend this land from wealthy landowners who contested their claim to the land.

Many Choreños also joined regional and national coca growers' unions, beginning in the 1980s, in the creation of another important form of community distinct from the geographically bounded community of Choro. The *cocalero* movement has been one of Bolivia's most well-organized movements (Pinto Ocampo 2004), yet one built firmly on the middle-class aspirations of its members. *Cocaleros* repeatedly demonstrated their militancy and tight organization through protesting the drug war and supporting the MAS party beginning in the 1990s. Ironically, then, during their periodic absenteeism and halfhearted presence in Choro, which caused endless frustration for those based firmly in Choro, including Don Carlos, many Choreños were participating in other communities, including Bolivia's most tightly organized and militant movements. In the coca growers' unions, the pursuit of a valuable commodity (coca) and the need for organized protests formed the glue of their organizational strength, while in Choro by 2006, there were fewer shared material goals that bound middle-class and aspiring middle-class people together in a common purpose with poorer people.

Members of the emergent middle class did hold a version of the dream for collective progress centered on the trappings of urban modernity. Though they rarely committed backbreaking labor to projects such as an irrigation canal, preferring to pay someone else to work in their place or simply not taking part, they did talk about the proposed new high school project in a tone of awe and lamented Choro's lack of a town plaza or market as a missing symbol of modernity. On the day in which the Sacaba mayor Walter Terán visited Choro to announce that he would fund the new high school, for example, Deysi remarked with an embarrassed giggle, "It makes me ashamed that Terán sees that my town doesn't even have a plaza [*Me da verguenza que vea que mi pueblo no tiene plaza.*]." And yet this dream for collective modernity, because it was less vital for them in their personal lives, was easy for them to denigrate when it did not measure up to the urban standard they held from their familiarity with towns like Sacaba or cities like Cochabamba. When, eventually, in 2009, Choro leaders secured funding for a much-needed sewer system and began the laborious processes of installing it, Amanda scoffed that the components were cheap and broke easily, and that such a faulty sewer was nothing to be pleased about. And following the end of my fieldwork in 2009, whenever I talked on the phone with Amanda and asked her to recount news of Choro, she responded invariably in an impatient tone, "My town hasn't progressed at all! [*Mi pueblo no ha progresado nada!*]." Don Carlos and some of Choro's poorer residents, like Doña Gladys, were delighted, meanwhile, with the construction of the sewer system, the new high school, and a community center.

Finally, I suggest that one more meaning of community in Choro was a stage for the drama of upward mobility and the attainment of middle-class status. When Doña Saturnina's children declared proudly that they were the only family in Choro of "*puro profesionales,*" their achievement sparkled in part because of the rarity of Choreños who shared this achievement. When their neighbor across the street saw her son graduate with an MBA and find a job with the government of a nearby municipality, she could broadcast her news as a distinct triumph. Their accomplishments were not as notable in the provincial town of Sacaba or the city of Cochabamba, filled with professionals. If the daily interactions between neighbors make up an important part of the experience of face-to-face community, the pain and glory of inequality for these middle-class Choreños was a salient part of their experience of community.

I am suggesting, then, that multiple definitions of community in circulation were competing with each other in 2006. Some of these models of community had been promoted by the Bolivian state at various moments in history, while others were forged by people as a practical response to economic pressures and the desire to become middle class. Although the requirements of the LPP, and to a lesser extent, the rhetoric of the MAS government, called for a geographically bounded community whose object was to unite along shared goals to build infrastructure, Choreños enacted other ideals of collectivity in practice. In some ways, migration and middle-class aspirations drew people apart, making Choro a conglomeration of people living in proximity but pursuing very different goals, experiencing differing lifestyles and traveling constantly to other locations. In other ways, however, people formed alternate forms of collectivity.

## Community and the Politics of a Fruitful Political Opening

Until this point, I have focused on the frustration of development workers and Choreños with their inability to enact the ideal of a campesino "civil society," defined in Sacaba as community collaboration for public works and agriculture within rigid geographic boundaries. Beginning in 2006, however, the Choro *sindicato* began or completed several public insfrastructure projects that many residents had yearned for since the promulgation of the Popular Participation Law in 1994.[12] The Sacaba municipal government finally constructed an enormous galvanized roof over the cement soccer court, after months of Choreños' requests, and remodeled Choro's small health clinic. *Sindicato* members built the first floor of a planned three-story community center (*sede sindical*). Most significantly in the local commentary, Choro leaders procured US$100,000 from the Sacaba municipal government to buy a plot of prime, centrally located land to build a new high school. These projects represented by a wide margin the largest amount that Choro residents had garnered from the Popular Participation funds to date.

What accounted for this unexpected miracle? I often saw Don Carlos beaming during the month of August 2006 when several of these projects came to fruition. Don Carlos exclaimed many times excitedly, in public and private, that "a great unity" (*uj jatun unidad*) among Choreños had taken root and paved the way for these achievements. He cited a collective work party in July 2006 as changing his own diagnosis of the obstacles to collective action and development. Rather than Choreños' moral failing of selfish individualism, as he had formerly thought, he told me that he had realized that communal unity required talented leaders who could channel what he now saw as abundant appetite on the part of Choreños for public works and collective action. "The problem is not Choro [rank-and-file residents]," he affirmed then and several years later. "The problem is leadership."

Even after his epiphany, however, Don Carlos continued to express frustration with "lack of unity" because of the perpetual movement of people out of Choro for work. "There is only development if the people love their locality [*lugar*]," he reflected in 2009 while lamenting the "double residency" of many Choreños who commuted to other regions of the country. He explained that he wanted to transform the *sindicato*'s authority from land based, as it had been since the 1950s, to authority over "development in general." He envisioned a collective organized around the construction and management of public works projects such as the sewer and school.

From my vantage point and in the perception of many Choro residents, these new *obras* were at least as much the product of Don Carlos's unique advantages as a community leader and a few Choro residents' pursuit of clientelism as they were about Choreños' values of community harmony.[13] Don Carlos's status was unusual. He was a rare elected rural community leader who held a professional degree (as an agronomist) and had been raised in an urban family. His professional title and self-confidence greatly increased the leverage of Choreños in their negotiations with municipal employees that year. I witnessed the deference with which municipal officials treated Don Carlos during planning meetings at Sacaba city hall, as his academic credentials sometimes helped him outrank those officials. Furthermore, his position as a paid consultant for several international development organizations freed him up to treat the Choro *sindicato*'s business as his salaried work rather than the demanding volunteering of time and energy it was for other community leaders. Don Carlos's extra income allowed him unusual freedom to travel daily to Sacaba to pressure the municipal employees and officials to speed up their work on Choro projects. Some Choreños credited Don Carlos with single-handedly procuring the new infrastructure projects in 2006.

In addition, a unique political moment helped speed up the flow of development funding from municipal and regional governments to Choro. Evo's then-recent election as president seemed, according to Don Carlos and other community leaders, to increase the clout of Sacaba's rural districts that year. At least as critically, Choro leaders including Don Carlos took advantage of a particular fruitful opening (*coyuntura*) in the municipal balance of power. The fragility of Sacaba mayor Terán's authority—his desperation for political support—permitted Choro leaders to leverage their power as clients with unusual success. Terán, who had taken power in April 2006 after the ouster of Orellana, was still embattled. Rumors had continued to circulate that protesters and behind-the-scenes deals might succeed in ousting Terán and reinstating Orellana or another mayor who held more credible ties to the MAS party. Evo had unilaterally expelled Terán from the MAS after Orellana's allies had complained that Terán seemed likely to switch parties to H. Obras.

Finally, the middle-class aspirations of several individual Choreños also played a crucial role in the sudden showering of *obras* from the municipal government to Choro. In Choro, the word on the street had been that one of the more widely disliked community leaders, Torrico, had been actively scheming to secure a patronage job with the new mayor Terán. Torrico was the longtime community leader whom Don Carlos and many other Choreños suspected to be a self-seeking *busca pegas*, a man they argued often put communal interests far behind his personal desires for a well-paying public sector job. Torrico had lost his job as a MAS client in the municipal government in 2004, when he had placed his support behind the losing H. Obras party during a municipal election. He had since then appeared to be casting around actively for a patronage job. For example, during the gubernatorial election campaign for Cochabamba in November 2005, Torrico led a small contingent of Choreños on a campaign march for the right-wing prefect, Manfred, through the downtown streets of Sacaba holding a long, home-made banner—the only banner in the rather sparse crowd—that stated, "*Choro presente!*" (see Chapter 4). Many people thought that he was simply seeking a job in Manfred's administration.

During May and June 2006, Torrico finally succeeded in wrangling a job for himself as a Sacaba "agricultural advisor" of the embattled Mayor Terán. This was roughly equivalent to an agricultural extension agent. Torrico could be seen often at the Sacaba city hall and at Choro community meetings, announcing the availability of free onion or eucalyptus seedlings from the municipal government, in fulfillment of his semiofficial duties. He worked tirelessly to keep Terán in office and tried to galvanize Choreños' support by urging the mayor to fund Choro's long-deferred Popular Participation projects, such as the new high school. Eventually, as a result of both Torrico's insistence and the pleadings of other Choro leaders, including Don Carlos, Terán agreed.

These machinations—individual Choreños' striving for middle-class status through patronage jobs, Don Carlos's personal pleadings to the municipal government, Mayor Terán's desperation for political support—came to fruition on a crisp winter day in 2006, when Terán came to deliver the $100,000 check to Choro's leaders. The Day of the Campesino, August 2, was a national holiday for rural districts, commemorating the 1953 launching of Bolivia's Agrarian Reform. Don Carlos and Inti organized a parade and celebration. Under a brilliant blue sky, several hundred marchers set off from the decrepit elementary school. Schoolchildren were dressed in suits and white taffeta dresses and thigh-high boots, the girls' hair sprayed into elaborate curls and puffs. They played xylophones in the shapes of lyres. After marching down a rutted dirt road with its ancient-looking adobe houses, the marchers passed onto the Cochabamba-Santa Cruz highway fringed with the two-story stucco homes of coca growers. As they dodged enormous Volvo tractor-trailers, marchers speculated about

*Figure 6.* Truckers and festival dancers shared the highway, 2006. Photo by the author

whether Mayor Terán would really appear to deliver the $100,000 for the school; many were skeptical.

Then, miraculously, he was there. People lined up in the school's soccer court for the hour-long signing ceremony. The mayor stood with his retinue on the outdoor stage in front of several brightly colored pink and red and blue cloths with which Choro leaders had decorated the wall. He held up the $100,000 check, drawing out the drama of the occasion. Don Carlos led the assembled people in cheering "Long Live Sacaba; Long Live Choro!" Several Choro *sindicato* leaders, including Don Carlos, embraced the mayor on the stage amid clouds of white confetti.

Don Carlos in his speech of thanks exclaimed that this momentous occasion was the product of Choreños' newfound "unity." Yet, in the days following Terán's check delivery, Don Carlos also remarked bemusedly that it seemed as if Torrico's clientelistic self-interest—motivated by his ceaseless desire for upward class mobility—and Choreños' collective interests for development projects had aligned in a rare instance of harmony.

*Figure 7.* The principal was bursting with excitement in 2009 to show me the long-awaited first step in construction of the new high school: the foundation. Photo by the author.


## Conclusion

Middle-class aspirations have deeply shaped collective life in Sacaba. In this chapter, I have argued that the meanings of community for people as they live their lives are dynamic, changing over time in response to their aspirations for middle-class mobility and to changed political and economic conditions. Sacaba development workers, because of their yearning to fulfill their professional goals, often promoted a narrow definition of community, framed as "civil society," that combined the ideal of the agrarian union *sindicato* with the ideal of the bounded community based upon the 1994 Law of Popular Participation and the renewal of Andean indigenous culture. Choro residents also often compared themselves to the ideal of the *sindicato* and pronounced each other immoral. As frustration built among development workers and residents at the slow pace of public works construction in Sacaba, they often blamed this glacial pace on a lack of strong collective action among residents. They pinned this failure of collective action upon self-interest as a failure of morality and consciousness.

The notion that community feeling had declined owing to culture loss and self-interest, and that such loss was greater closer to urban areas, made intuitive sense. After all, as Lucho, the NGO agronomist, noted above, some communities farther from the city than Choro demonstrated a higher degree of collective action on infrastructure projects, more residents showed up for meetings, remained the entire way through, and overall, were generally more visibly "unified [*unidos*]." Similarly, if Choro residents carried out collective action during the 1953 Agrarian Reform, but did so less in recent times, it was possible that the encroaching city had brought new, individualist, values.

Yet this definition of community depended upon a geographically bounded collectivity composed of campesinos and did not take into account the middle-class aspirations of many rural residents. The nostalgic memory of a golden age of communal unity held by many people in Choro was in reality a very specific, quite recent period: after the Agrarian Reform when land was valuable for agriculture and therefore, for upward mobility, but before drought, land shortage, and declining terms of trade made agriculture a doubtful investment. Once agriculture in Choro was no longer able to support most residents' aspirations for upward mobility, Choreños scattered to multiple places and entered a variety of new occupations to pursue their dreams of prosperity. Aspirations among middling folk led people away from the declining economy of small-scale agriculture in Choro in favor of professions or trades, or spurred them to commute between multiple locations as merchants, students, or farmers. Persistent inequality meant that wealthier people had less vital interest in contributing labor and money to local infrastructure projects.

At the same time, middling Choreños created new forms of community. As they migrated in pursuit of income to support middle-class upward mobility, they created new collectivities as members of coca growers' unions and as coresidents of new communities in the tropics, even as they continued to build networks of godparenthood and informal mutual assistance based in Choro. While Choreños' middle-class identities and aspirations interrupted the official narratives of community as constituted by a shared campesino identity and aspirations for a future in small-scale agriculture, they pursued other collective aims and practices. Development policy and political leaders' rhetoric would do well to acknowledge these actually existing forms of collectivity, just as they would do well to acknowledge middle-class aspirations in the critiques of clientelism explored earlier in this book. I suggest that we acknowledge the middle-class aspirations of rural folk and the fact that self-interest is a central facet of public life.

# Conclusion

I was leaving Doña Patricia's house in the urban corridor of Sacaba in May 2006. We had been speaking for three hours, during which she had offered tale after tale of political double-dealing, the selfishness of other political activists, and the betrayal of her hopes to become a Sacaba city council member. Her faith in the Sacaba MAS party—or any political party—as an agent of radical transformation had been deeply shaken. But as she accompanied me through her flower garden and bid me goodbye in the hot, late afternoon sun, Doña Patricia worried out loud that her focus on all that was "dirty" (*sucio*) about Bolivian politics would give U.S. audiences the wrong impression of Bolivia. "What I have told you puts Bolivia in a very bad light! There is much that is beautiful about this moment in Bolivia, too. Next time, let's talk about that." And yet, we didn't. The next time we met, her narrative quickly returned to her disappointment and bitterness about Sacaba's political conflicts.

Similarly, this book, by focusing on many middling Bolivians' disappointments, has perhaps given short shrift to the wonder and hope that many Bolivians felt during the rise of MAS and Evo's political honeymoon in 2005 and 2006. There is no doubt that Bolivian society has changed since 2006, from economic policies to legal rights, to the daily experience of citizenship. The Morales government quintupled taxes on foreign corporate profits on the sales of its largest exported resource, natural gas, and has channeled this into funding for prenatal care, education, and public works projects. A new constitution, passed in 2009, recognizes indigenous community law and affirms the right of the state to redistribute agricultural land more equitably. New laws against racism have formed the basis for civil lawsuits over everyday racial discrimination—a change that would have been unthinkable two decades ago.

Yet most Bolivians today remain deeply frustrated at what they see as the continuation of high unemployment and little fruit from the shift in faces at the head of state (see, for example, Fabricant 2012; Goodale and Postero 2013). Like reformers and revolutionaries from Egypt to South Africa, many middle-class Sacabans had hoped to begin afresh, to launch a new era, to refound the country, and they have been terribly disappointed. In 2009, for every Sacaban who believed deeply in aims of the new government, another middling Sacaban expressed disillusionment at the still-high unemployment rate, or felt threatened by the challenge to her local social dominance. Where Don Carlos remained in awe of the Morales government's purchase of an ambulance for all rural municipalities, Vilma complained that Evo had become "haughty" (*soberbio*), and feared that Evo's ministers were just as corrupt as those of previous governments.

Indeed, as this book goes to press, the MAS government is embattled. Right-wing newspaper editorials pronounce that only the coca growers remain of his once-broad alliance with indigenous movements, miners' and industrial unions, and urban middle classes.[1] The traditional protest season around May 1, International Workers' Day, saw hundreds of marches, road blockades, and hunger strikes in 2012 (Ledebur 2012a), a dramatic increase over previous years of the Morales administration. As Katherine Ledebur notes, despite raises in the minimum wage, increased development funds to municipal governments, and endless cultural promotion of indigeneity, the enormous expectations many Bolivians had of Morales have been exceedingly difficult to fulfill. Ledebur argues that the present government's autocratic rhetorical style, inherited from prior governments, has contributed to diminishing trust on the part of many former supporters. She highlights in particular that Evo often accuses his critics of selfishness:

> The government has made some significant concessions—such as . . . raising the minimum wage to 1000 Bs. (about $140 USD), expanding maternity and paternity benefits, suspending the supreme decree for the doctors, budgeting money for the victims of dictatorship—but these measures generally do not occur as a result of agreements with protestors or social movements or dialogue. As a result, protesting groups feel marginalized because this top-down leadership goes against the Morales discourse on the key role of

unions and social movements. Since the administration frequently dismisses demands or characterizes them as "selfish," and tends to pass unpredictable measures, some protesting groups mistrust its motives and fear that concession will be temporary in an effort to demobilize protest. (Ledebur 2012a)

Many protesters and skeptics thus continue to complain about the poverty, inequality, nepotism, theft of public funds by government leaders, and dismal levels of unemployment that they had hoped would evaporate upon Evo's rise to power. They also complain that the radical grassroots democratic participation they had hoped for is lacking. Meanwhile, when Evo has been pressured by these multiple constituencies to spend more money than the government has in its coffers, he has retorted with accusations. As in Sacaba municipal politics and Choro community politics, Evo and other national officials have lashed out at critics with the accusation that they are simply self-interested *busca pegas*.[2]

## The Influence of New Middle Classes on Bolivian Politics

As I have shown throughout this book, some of the widespread disillusionment with MAS and Evo stems from the particular aspirations, anxieties, and ideals of new Bolivian middle classes. Leaders of the MAS had to portray Bolivian society as a struggle between superelite and impoverished subaltern in order to communicate their political project of racial and economic justice. Political movements for change require such a language to convey the need to remedy stark national inequalities. The decision of Occupy Wall Street activists in 2011 to name themselves "the ninety nine percent" follows the same political imperative. Yet some strategies of political mobilization are impossible to practice in everyday life and I suggest that Bolivia's middling folk confounded MAS' and allied social movements' strategies. The accusations of selfishness and envy in the political discourse in Bolivia reflect deep ambivalence about the inequality created by some people's upward mobility.

In Chapter 2, I showed how newly prosperous people in Sacaba, like Amanda and Edgar, continually articulated multiple, and sometimes conflicting, moral imperatives. They alternated between identifying themselves as poor campesinos and as elite professionals; between asserting that all people ought to be treated equally and asserting that, as professionals, they should be offered more deference. These dilemmas between which path to choose—of egalitarianism or superiority, of rural or urban lifeways understood locally as stark opposites—colored the most intimate of relationships. Such dilemmas spurred anxiety. As during Edgar's deliberations about his daughter's baptism, new Sacaban middle classes expressed equal anxiety about being accused of snobbery and illegitimate aspirants to the middle class.

The conflicting moral imperatives of upward mobility and egalitarianism also deeply shaped politics in Sacaba and, as I have suggested, throughout Bolivia. Some middling Sacabans argued that their legitimate aspirations for upward mobility conflicted with the message of redistribution of wealth and equality promoted by social movements and the MAS party, inclining them to ally themselves with right-wing parties openly dominated by Bolivia's superwealthy. Other middling Sacabans, like Vilma and Don Álvaro, had thrilled to Evo's initial promise of industrialization and an end to state corruption, but expressed concern when their own superior status within the provincial social and political world was threatened. Even prosperous people like Doña Felisa, who in public wholeheartedly embraced every element of the MAS platform of equality and redistribution of wealth, were the targets of other activists' suspicion that their accumulation of wealth meant that there was less to be redistributed to everyone else. Doña Felisa's experience shows the paradox of a politics predicated on power to the poor: once a person attains a leadership position or gains prosperity in a context in which such positions and resources are scarce, he or she must struggle with others' resentment and suspicions.

Several years of MAS government appeared to polarize Deysi and Amanda's political stances beyond their opposition of 2006. In August 2009, Deysi protested that everyone ought to be treated equally (*por igual*), but that Evo was instead giving preference in public sector jobs and legislation to people without professional degrees:

*Deysi:* Evo is favoring the people from the countryside [*campo*].
*Miriam:* Oh, don't you also count as being "from the countryside"?
*Deysi:* No! He wants to push the professionals aside [*poner a un lado*].

As when explaining in 2006 that class distinctions often caused marital arguments, such as in the fight between Norah and Chavo (Chapter 2),

Deysi here was defining class identity rigidly within urban and rural geographies and claiming that Evo's government was marginalizing her.

## Combining Elements of Multiple Political Models in Bolivian Political Culture

Anxiety, ambivalence, and uncertainty surrounding middle-class upward mobility also conditioned Sacaba's political culture. In the face of a succession of different political models—state clientelism, free markets, state decentralization, leftist-indigenism—each of which promoted different models of citizenship, Sacabans wrestled with moral and practical questions about how to conduct themselves. Though almost all Sacaba residents vehemently opposed clientelism in principle, arguing that it was an outmoded and antidemocratic form of political action, most politically active people were at some point accused of clientelism. I have shown in Chapters 4 and 5 how such accusations were inescapable because "clientelism" was a broad umbrella that could include everything from everyday social politeness to the secret giving of illegal favors. Many people posited that the ideal of becoming middle class through a patronage job conflicted directly with the ideal of redistribution of wealth to the poor and the equalization of social life, but they also asserted, in different moments, that they wanted it all. In other words, many Sacabans claimed that individual aspirations for upward mobility nurtured by the coca and cocaine booms conflicted with the collectivist platform of redistribution of wealth and social power, but conveyed that both imperatives were necessary to lead a satisfying and morally upright life.

Mutual accusations of selfishness and envy permeated political life, describing most human conflict as a contest between self-interest versus public interest and making everyday political participation a minefield of conflicting claims and mutual suspicions. The Popular Participation Law reformers' notion of civil society as disinterested, apolitical civic action was grossly inadequate to describe actual political needs and aspirations. Similarly, national MAS leaders' depiction of Sacabans' actions as selfish when their hopes and actions conflicted with party leaders' goals did not recognize the multiplicity of Sacabans' aspirations for redistribution of wealth and for upward mobility. Even within the bosom of its own political base, the coca growers, and in its political heartland of Sacaba Municipality, MAS leaders were unable to address these conflicting desires.

Sacabans used the language of transparency to accuse leaders of reneging on promises of radical distribution of wealth. They used the language of radical democracy to accuse each other of reneging on promises of patron-client reciprocity. They used the language of patron-client relations to assert radical claims to equality. And they used condemnations of clientelism to both reject and affirm the morality of the quest to achieve middle-class status through patronage jobs. Mutual accusations of clientelism emerged as a currency of political life, a necessary step in asserting one's self as a public-minded, morally upright, legitimate political actor.

## Defining Community

Community as an arena of political action also became a battleground shaped by middle-class aspirations and by these intersecting political frameworks. In the Sacaban locality of Choro, many development workers felt compelled to work within definitions of community as geographically bounded, a hybrid between agrarian union syndicalism launched in the 1940s and Territorial Base Organizations promoted by the 1994 Popular Participation Law. In large part because of their institutional positions by which they were charged with facilitating the flow of development resources and constructing public works projects, they were often frustrated when trying to accomplish goals set according to these rigid notions of collectivity. Chapter 6 examined how Choreños' aspirations for upward mobility pulled them back and forth between Choro and other places in Bolivia and beyond. Choreños held many other models of community, from networks of extended family and friends residing throughout the county, whose members came together for occasional celebrations, to a staging ground for family enterprises centered elsewhere, to a vacation locale providing a respite from the heat and insects of the tropics, to a stage set for the drama of middle-class upward mobility. Each of these multiple ideals and practices of community first emerged at different moments in the history of Bolivia and the regional history of Sacaba. Choreños drew on bits and pieces of these models in their own advancement strategies and constructions of collectivity.

## Toward a New Understanding of Political Culture in the Global South

The overarching argument of this book is that striving middle classes are an underacknowledged and critical force in Bolivian politics. The experiences of Sacaba's middle classes suggest important directions for the analysis of politics and class in other countries of the Third World and beyond. Middle classes do not live only in large cities: they live in provincial towns and rural localities. Social imaginaries of rural and urban dichotomies shape their experiences even as they often live on the frenetic boundary between rural and urban geographic spaces. Their political aspirations for grassroots democracy, good governance, and social equality may conflict with their class aspirations of upward mobility and "bettering oneself." Ultimately, middling Sacabans have shown that politics and intimate life, the public and private, are all bound up together. The success or failure of movements for equality and justice in the Third World countries may well hinge on such striving middle classes and their dreams of mobility.

Introduction

1. While debates exist over whether to use the terms First World and Third World, Global North and Global South, or the developed and the "bottom billion," Bolivia's status by most measures falls into the category of a classically dependent economy. And while some measures characterize Bolivia as middle income or medium development (e.g., UNDP 2009), the majority of Bolivians rank as poor or very poor by global standards.

2. Statistical measures of Bolivian incomes and social identities are notoriously inaccurate. While the World Bank (2013), for example, lists 49 percent of Bolivians as living above the national poverty line, such a precise figure should be treated with caution. Nor do income measures reveal how people identify themselves in racial and class terms. I estimate that approximately 20 or 25 percent of Bolivians comprise the group I am terming the "new middle classes," while the older, established urban middle classes and the superelite together comprise approximately 10 percent.

3. I am using the term "subaltern" as used by political theorist Antonio Gramsci to refer generally to nonelite groups in society, defined in racial, class, or ethnic terms, or a combination of all three. Subalternity is defined in different ways in different countries. In Bolivia, an array of terms express subalternity and will be explained more fully throughout the book. These refer to class, race, and culture in varying combinations, including poor/wealthy (*pobre/rico*), campesino/professional (*profesional*), and indigenous/white (*runa/q'ara*).

4. Coca, a leaf that serves as a mild stimulant and appetite suppressant to those who chew it, has been grown for thousands of years in the Andes and has served as an object of spiritual and ceremonial importance. The coca and cocaine boom began in the late 1970s in Bolivia following a steep rise in demand for cocaine in the United States and Europe. As a result, the price of cocaine and coca leaf shot upward in Bolivia. The tropical Chapare region, offering an ideal climate for growing coca, attracted thousands of Bolivians fleeing land scarcity and drought. With the mass firings in mines and factories following Bolivian free-market reforms in 1985, the Chapare became a haven for ex-miners and factory workers and their families searching for work. In the early 1980s, many economists estimated, more than 50 percent of

the Bolivian economy was based on cocaine and coca exports (Flores and Blanes 1984; Painter 1998; Healy 1986). At least 400,000 people (roughly 5 percent of the Bolivian population) were working directly in coca or cocaine production by 1981, and this percentage grew higher in subsequent years (Healy 1986; Flores and Blanes 1984).

5. See, for example, "Aliados del MAS revelan que hay pugnas por pegas," *La Razón*, January 27, 2011; "Evo reconoce que dirigencia sindical sólo busca pegas y candidaturas," *Los Tiempos*, June 8, 2009; "El MAS reconoce que pelea por pegas perjudica a Evo," *Los Tiempos*, November 2, 2007.

6. I conducted a total of thirty-seven months of ethnographic field research in Bolivia. My research trips were May–November 1995, December 1997–December 1998, July–August 2003, July–August 2004, July 2005–June 2006, and August 2009.

7. "Amanda" is a pseudonym. I have used pseudonyms for all people except public figures speaking or acting on the public record. Likewise, the community of Choro is a pseudonym. To preserve the confidentiality of the community and its residents, I have not identified Choro precisely on the map of Sacaba municipality.

8. For exceptions, see work on middle classes in other Third World countries by Dickey 2000; Cahn 2008; Liechty 2002; O'Dougherty 2002; Colloredo-Mansfield [1999] 2004; Rutz and Balkan 2009.

9. For an introduction to the harmful effects of free-market reforms on employment and the Bolivian economy, see Kohl 1999; Postero 2005; Conaghan and Malloy 1994. For an introduction to the effects of free-market reforms more broadly, see Comaroff and Comaroff 2001; Ferguson 2006; Greenhouse 2010; Hale 2005.

10. Bolivian leftist political leaders and many scholars were deeply critical of decentralization reforms like the LPP, arguing that decentralization was part of a larger ideological project to complete the work of reengineering: from a state that promised—someday—to create prosperity and development to a free-market society in which each person must struggle alone (e.g., Kohl 1999; Gill 2000). Along with critics of similar reforms in other countries, they argued that the reforms and the Bolivian government's rhetoric of citizen participation defined participation very narrowly and were merely a screen for attempts by states and development institutions such as the World Bank to shift the responsibility for economic development from the central state to the shoulders of individuals and communities without providing the necessary resources (e.g., Paley 2001; Rose 2000). Bolivian critics (e.g., López and Regalsky 2005) argued that national political leaders and development institutions such as the World Bank promoted the LPP because they believed that it would deflect attention from unpopular economic policies pursued by Bolivian presidents, already the object of protest.

After its inception many former critics became pleasantly surprised by some of the LPP's wildly unintended consequences, however. The law spurred protest because it raised Bolivians' expectations of the state, which the state could not fulfill, while at the same time promoting the language—if not the mechanisms—of direct democracy (e.g., Postero 2007:17). The LPP's new funding and powers for local municipal governments also unexpectedly propelled the national growth of Morales's MAS, which began as a regional party of coca growers not far from Sacaba. Between 2000 and 2005, protesters blocked major highways numerous times and forced the early exit of three presidents, forging the broad-based leftist and indigenous coalition that elected Evo Morales in 2005.

11. My findings contribute to recent scholarship showing that state formation involves a wide array of practices (Joseph and Nugent 1994; Hansen and Stepputat 2001; Corrigan and Sayer 1985; Tsing 2004). Anthropologists in Eastern Europe (Buyandelgeriyn 2008; Verdery 1999; Humphrey 2002), for example, dispel the common assumption that the new free-market rhetoric and policies that followed the fall of state socialism replaced prior frameworks. Verdery (1999) traces how Romanian peasants during the 1990s decollectivization effected a "fuzzy" transition in which they interpreted new private land laws through older frameworks of collectivism and the Marxist labor theory of value. Similarly, Moore's (2005:316) metaphor of "striation," evoking the tangled veins of minerals running through rock, highlights how Zimbabweans created distinct local political practices by interpreting recent state impositions through oppositional frameworks developed during colonialism and wars for independence.

12. Álvaro García Linera, interview by Sara Miller Llana, "Bolivia's Vice President on Indigenous Rights, Coca Crops, and Relations with the U.S.," *Christian Science Monitor*, March 27, 2007.

Chapter 1. The Formation of a New Middle Class

1. Though the Marxist tradition privileged a narrow notion of economic class by defining people as capitalists or as workers, Marxian scholars have, in the past century, shown that people usually hold multiple class identities simultaneously (e.g., see Gibson-Graham 1996:55; Abelmann 1997).

2. The prices of coca leaves, cocaine base paste, and refined cocaine are notoriously volatile. The effects of the drug war on coca and cocaine prices are debated, however (e.g., Farthing and Ledebur 2004; Healy 1986, 1991; Painter 1994; Pinto Ocampo 2004; Sanabria 1993). On the one hand, the drug war reduced supply, thereby increasing the pressure for a price rise. On the other hand, interdiction made possession of coca leaves and cocaine more risky, creating pressure for a decline in prices. In Sacaba Municipality at present, for example, cocaine base paste producers often have to abandon their product midway through the production process when they hear or see the arrival of drug-control officers. This has contributed to lower prices for base paste.

Chapter 2. The Intimate Politics of New Middle Classes in Sacaba

1. I use the title *Doña* in this book based on several considerations, including the women's social status, their level of formality in their relationship with me (how they

referred to themselves when we spoke with each other), and whether other people used *Doña*. Officially, any Bolivian woman who is married merits the term, but professional women sometimes prefer their professional title.

2. Many rural and poor urban Bolivians did not celebrate their weddings until they could afford to pay for an elaborate party, often in middle age and after they had several children. Elite and urban middle-class couples usually married before having children. Edgar clearly feared slipping from an interpretation of his actions as the elite pursuit of an informal sexual affair with a *cholita* to the lower-status recognition of a *cholita* as his common-law wife.

3. *Cholita* is a more affectionate and often more respectful variant of the term *chola*.

4. This difference may reflect both the much higher infant mortality in rural areas and differences between European and indigenous concepts of personhood (see Canessa 2012:120).

5. *Loquita* is the diminutive form of *loca* (crazy), and was meant figuratively rather than literally.

6. *Fregado* in Bolivian Spanish is often used affectionately to describe small children as mischievous. The verb *fregar* can mean "to scrub," as in dishes, or "to screw," in a mild slang term for sex.

7. This increase in overt racism appears to parallel the public raacism of U.S. whites following Barack Obama's election in 2008.

8. *Negrito* and *negrita* were also slang for boyfriend and girlfriend, respectively.

9. Many painful layers shaped the raced, classed, and gendered conflict in the relationship between Norah, her mother, and Chavo. Norah had divulged to me years earlier that Chavo's father had raped Norah's mother as a young woman and this was why Norah's mother initially tried to prohibit her marrying Chavo. Norah claimed that Chavo had eventually won over her mother by his kindness and gentle disposition, before she began belittling him again as a terrible provider. Furthermore, while Chavo's physical violence toward Norah conformed to widespread patterns of gendered domestic abuse in Choro and throughout Bolivia, Chavo broke with such patterns of gendered inequality in the family's daily life. He cared attentively for the couple's two young children nearly full-time during the week while Norah was teaching and commuting to her distant rural elementary school.

10. Their friend Apaza had the same last name as indigenous heroes revered by Bolivia's present-day indigenous movements and the MAS party: Julian and Gregoria Apaza, who together led indigenous rebels in a famous 1781 siege of the city of La Paz. Deysi and Amanda were not active in these social movements, however, and did not connect this episode to the larger political processes then afoot in Bolivia.

11. *Qhawanaku* and *miramiento* literally mean "mutual watching" in Quechua and Spanish, respectively. Many people told me that these terms are synonymous with *envidia*, envy.

12. The expectation that wealthier people ought to share with poorer people resonates with some ideals of social life in the rural Andes, for example the practices of communal land redistribution, work exchanges between families, and community festivals at which wealthier people host lavish meals at which poorer people can eat. As scholars have amply demonstrated, however, the ideal of reciprocity is almost always accompanied by the reality of deep local inequalities (Albó 1975; Lagos 1994; Albro 2000).

13. Even very impoverished people worried that other, even poorer people envied them. A very poor couple was certain that their daughter's fainting fits were caused by the envy-inspired witchcraft (*hechicería*) of the husband's former wife. A family whose infant had just died because they couldn't afford an expensive surgery stopped planting a very visible field next to the highway because they were concerned about some of their neighbors' envy (see similar examples in Taussig 1986:394).

14. Even though the central government funded electrification and water, these new amenities might be credited to the coca and cocaine booms. The Sacaba area benefited from foreign aid, such as USAID funds, intended to try to lure inveterate coca and cocaine producers away from the Chapare with potable water and irrigation canals—one of the rare positive incentives in the war on drugs.

15. Since 2005, Bolivian gross domestic product has grown, but inflation and unemployment have diminished many of the potential gains to middling groups.

16. There were several routes toward acquiring land. Many Choreños and Sacabans procured land through government colonization programs in the Chapare. By the mid-1980s, the land in these colonies was as scarce as was land for sale (Flores and Blanes 1984).

17. Petras (2006a) has made a similar argument that the administration of Evo Morales is "all growl, no claws": that the middle-class aspirations and greater wealth of many coca growers, like Morales, makes their radical platform a sham. I instead emphasize the social and moral dilemmas of this cohort of Bolivians who, like similarly situated groups throughout the world, find themselves longing for multiple goals at once.

Chapter 3. Middling Sacabans Respond to Evo and MAS

1. This was not unlikely in a country of approximately ten million people. Bolivians quite frequently know major political leaders who share their social backgrounds.

2. *Tramitadores* are somewhat similar in function to paralegals in the United States, though this paraprofession is unregulated in Bolivia.

3. A running joke in Bolivia during the previous election campaign in 2002 was that U.S. ambassador Manuel Rocha had inadvertently come close to handing Evo a victory. When he publicly warned Bolivians that the United States would disapprove strongly if Evo were elected, many Bolivians were outraged at this breach of national sovereignty, which added insult to the injury of the long-running drug war. Most

Bolivians saw U.S. foreign aid as a devil's bargain, as it was conditional on drug interdiction, coca plant eradication, and free-market policies. Consequently, many Bolivians looked approvingly at a candidate whom the U.S. diplomats opposed. Evo lost narrowly, by 1.6 percent (20.9 percent of the vote to Sánchez de Lozada's winning 22.5 percent) and most internal and foreign observers argued that he had gained considerable votes as a result of the ambassador's warning (Singer and Morrison 2004). Indeed, after Evo was elected in 2005, President George W. Bush condemned him on several occasions, including in one speech where he claimed that his election represented an "erosion of democracy."

4. Literally, this means "*pegas* seeker." *Pegas* were patronage jobs or the people who received those jobs. The term is most likely drawn from the Spanish verb *pegar*, "to stick to."

5. Some LPP reformers specifically lauded indigenous culture in pastoral, romantic language that echoed Bolivian elite romanticism (*indigenismo*) of the nineteenth and early twentieth centuries. For example, LPP reformer Javier Medina argued that in Bolivia since the Spanish conquest, there had existed two blocs, possessing "opposed . . . cosmovisions." Indigenous culture was based on systems of "participation, representation . . . consensus . . . that correspond to holistic and systematic civilizations" (Medina 1995:9). By contrast, Western civilization was characterized by an exclusive, individualistic, and oppressive modernity. Yet because most LPP reformers repudiated Marxism and protests geared at macroeconomic change (Medina 1995; Molina and Arias 1996; Molina Saucedo 1990:65), or were limited in articulating such desires by the opposition of their institutional superiors, these characterizations of a dual Bolivian society did not inspire radical dreams of transformation, as in the MAS platform.

6. For example, Román Loayza, a veteran agrarian union leader and MAS leader in 2006, similarly to LPP reformers set up a binary contrast between indigenous culture, characterized by "solidarity, consensus, reciprocity, redistribution, and complementarity" and Western civilization characterized by "destruction, trickery, usurpation, pillaging" (CSTUCB 2006:5). Like the LPP reformers, MAS leaders argued that Bolivian society was divided into two, that that majority was defined as indigenous as well as poor and campesino, and that indigenous culture was characterized by communal harmony and harmony with the natural world.

7. See Hale 2002 for similar perspectives in Guatemala.

8. This call to "others" clearly referred to right-wing ultra-elites in eastern Bolivia, who opposed MAS most vehemently.

9. Some of this support waned during the next few years as many people became disillusioned when the MAS party was unable to bring about the sea change in political practice and economic prosperity they had heralded.

10. By 2009, this hope had also dimmed. While few people suspected Evo himself of stealing public funds, widespread accusations of graft targeted his close associates.

11. While Remigio and Vilma weren't certain about the causes of this shift, in all likelihood this "empowerment" stemmed from a combination of the Law of Popular

Participation's new opportunities for local planning and funding, the explosion of political party activity in rural areas following the onset of provincial elections in the 1990s, and the rise of indigenist and popular movements allied with the MAS party during much of the 2000s.

12. Remigio and Vilma did not remark on the paradox of Vilma's hope to establish a relationship of clientelist reciprocity with municipal residents in rural communities by giving away baseball caps while also hoping that MAS would create a nonclientelistic party politics.

13. I am grateful to Bret Gustafson for his insights on this question.

14. Many Sacabans on both sides of the conflict explained that El Chino's favoring rural areas had led to his forced resignation after ten months in office. El Chino, for his part, assured me vigorously that he had, in fact, favored urban districts.

15. Though the majority of Sacaba residents were classified as poor by the Bolivian census, Sacaba municipality was wealthier overall than many other provincial Bolivian municipalities. 26 percent of Sacabans were classified as extremely poor by the National Statistical Institute, based on the 2001 census, as compared to 37 percent of all Bolivians (Interamerican Development Bank 2008).

16. Low-level cocaine producers were, in fact, often impoverished. Particularly after the mass eradication of coca in 1998, only higher-level traffickers who controlled others' labor were able to amass wealth in the industry.

17. Occasionally, poor families baptized younger infants if they became very sick.

18. It also made sense that individuals' hopes for upward mobility would spur them to see clientelist favors, such as jobs in the municipal MAS government, as their due, because they interpreted such favors to them as subalterns as in keeping with the MAS promise to lift all boats.

19. The antagonism between Quechuas and Aymaras has waxed and waned historically. Elite nationalist narratives of the nineteenth and twentieth centuries portrayed Aymaras as more culturally pure but also more politically insular and more "backward" than Quechuas. During the drug war of the 1980s and 1990s, military commanders routinely exploited this social cleavage by setting Aymara-speaking conscripts against Quechua-speaking coca growers, and vice versa.

Chapter 4. Condemning Clientelism

1. Clientelism was called *prebendalismo* and *peguismo* as well as *clientelismo* in Bolivian Spanish. Clientelism has many colonial antecedents—from colonial practices of indirect rule to postcolonial inequalities that forced subordinates into relations of patronage with elites. Many Bolivians, both elite and subaltern, participated in patron-client patterns in situations that are not overtly about vote buying, such as godparenthood between socially or economically unequal families, or when wealthy merchants bought peasants' crops at a reduced price in exchange for small gifts (see Lagos 1994; Platt 1993). For helpful definitions of clientelism and comparative examples, see Gellner and Waterbury 1977; Lande 1983; Scott 1983; Auyero 2001.

2. For other examples of hybrid frameworks of citizenship and identity within and beyond Bolivia, see Goldstein 2012; Lazar 2008; Gustafson 2009; Hall 1986:53; and Tsing 2004.

3. The military dictatorship's 1974 massacre of campesinos in Tolata was an important turning point in agrarian unions' shift from loyalty as patrons to active critics of the Bolivian state.

4. Civil society was an idea originally coined by Scottish intellectuals of the eighteenth century and resurrected by democratization policy makers since the fall of the Berlin Wall. Adam Smith, for example, proposed civil society as a "realm of solidarity held together by the force of moral sentiments and natural affections" that are separate from self-interest (Seligman 1992:33). Bolivian LPP reformers' emphasis on civil society aligned with the emphasis on "democratic values" (usually specified as tolerance of differing opinions, commitment to electoral institutions rather than violent protest, and everyday civility) as essential to democracy within transnational development institutions, such as USAID and the World Bank (e.g., USAID 2005; Medina 1995; Reilly et al. 1999; World Bank 2007; Finkel et al 2007; Seligson 1998:12).

Many anthropologists have rightly criticized the concept of civil society as an analytical term, focusing on six principal arguments: (1) The contradictory definition as actually existing society and of an ideal future society (Hann and Dunn 1996:4); (2) the artificiality of its definition of the state as separate from society; (3) the privileging of formal associations of individuals and blindness to informal social networks; (4) the erasure of class, race, gender, and ethnic inequalities; (5) the flawed assumption that free markets are compatible with meaningful democracy; (6) the separation of macroeconomic policy from the realm of public deliberation (cf. Schaffer 1996; Schmit 1996; Sampson 1996; Comaroff and Comaroff 1999:vii; Hann and Dunn 1996; Coombe 1997:3; Seligman 1992; Paley 2001b; Rose 1999; Cooke and Kothari 2001). Furthermore, as F. G. Bailey notes, political scientists and democratization policy makers tend to assume that political leaders' desires to rule—their self-interest—can be excised from politics, rather than constituting an inevitable, perennial part of leader's motivations (Bailey 2001:1–30; see also Albro 2010). Finally, as social scientists inspired by Foucault have noted, the concept of civil society can be an elite imposition on subalterns and an instance of governmentality, intended to reform citizens' values to take responsibility for social services and economic development to allow states to wash their hands of human well-being (Foucault 1991; Ferguson 1994; Blom Hansen and Stepputat 2001:4; West 2005; Kohl 2003; Li 2007; Postero 2007).

Bolivian LPP reformers' notions of civil society *were* flawed in their assumptions that an altruistic "society" can exist separately from corrupt "politics" and that rural folk naturally create harmonious and bounded communities (e.g., Molina and Arias 1996; Medina 1995). Bolivian notions of civil society differed somewhat from individualist notions of civil society promoted in Eastern Europe by emphasizing (a narrow form of) collective action and the valuable contribution of indigenous culture to civility, collective management of public works, and anti-corruption (e.g., Hann and

Dunn 1996; Sampson 1996; Comaroff 1999; Steven Caton, personal communication; Rose 1999). Furthermore, while models of civil society in recent times have often blamed the rank and file's deficit of civic virtue (cf. Comaroff and Comaroff 1999; Englund 2006; West 2005), in Sacaba, leaders and blamed both leaders and the rank and file for envy, self-interest, and clientelism.

5. The International Monetary Fund defines good governance as "ensuring the rule of law, improving the efficiency and accountability of the public sector, and tackling corruption" (IMF 1997).

6. New municipal organizations included Territorial Base Organizations (Organizaciones Territoriales de Base, OTBs), consisting of all registered residents of rural communities and urban neighborhoods. In 2002, Citizen Groups (Agrupaciones Ciudadanas) were created as alternative electoral organizations to circumvent political parties' authoritarianism and corruption. Many Bolivians quickly became disenchanted when they saw that political party leaders were simply joining the new groups.

7. Many municipalities were conflictive like Sacaba. See, for example, "Opositores liberan a concejala de municipio de Villa Rivero," *Los Tiempos*, April 22, 2007, and "La FAM denuncia intereses que sacuden a las comunas," *La Prensa* (La Paz), March 9, 2007. By contrast, in other municipalities, agrarian unions successfully won municipal governments and administered those governments to the majority of residents' satisfaction; in still other municipalities, old-guard wealthy elites quashed peasant and indigenous organizations (see Medeiros 2001; Antezana 2003; de la Fuente 2001; Postero 2007).

8. While LPP reformers and MAS leaders both condemned clientelism, they did so on opposite grounds. LPP reformers specifically sought to root out clientelism in order to promote liberal individual autonomy, while MAS leaders such as Salazar condemned clientelism as an immoral individualism.

9. The Bolivian political environment is similar to that found by political scientist Narendra Subramanian in south India, in which political clients were highly mobilized in unions, political parties, and neighborhood associations (Subramanian 1999:70). Some South Indian Tamils, like Bolivians, have used this organizational prowess to successfully pressure elected leaders to deliver substantial benefits to broad constituencies in exchange for the promise of votes (see also A. Subramanian 2009:70; Shakow 2011). Similarly, Bolivian anthropologist Jorge Dandler has argued that during the heyday of agrarian organizing in the 1940s and 1950s, Bolivian peasant movements combined clientelistic practices with class- and race-based solidarity (Dandler 1975). Rank-and-file members of Cochabamba valley agrarian unions supported regional agrarian leaders based on shared self-identification peasants and as fellow protagonists in the revolutionary movement, as well as in direct exchange for immediate benefits such as land parcels and food aid. Sociologist Adolfo Mendoza has made similar arguments (personal communication with author, 2006).

10. The phrase *mandar obedeciendo* was also favored by Subcomandante Marcos, Mexican Zapatista leader (Callahan 2004b).

11. UCS and CONDEPA, like MAS in Sacaba, had in fact pledged to promote equality and indigenous rights. Unlike MAS, however, neither party formally condemned clientelism; their leaders explicitly framed their role as that of a *padrino*, or godfather (see Albro 2001, 2007, 2010; and Mayorga 2002).

12. Unlike Rob Albro in the nearby municipality of Quillacollo, I rarely heard politically active men refer to themselves as *cholos* to identify themselves as either middle class or subaltern. For the most part, furthermore, *chola* and *cholita* in Sacaba appeared to be used as a synonym with *mujer campesina*, "peasant woman" (see Albro 2000 and 2001). Occasionally I heard someone imply that *chola* meant a wealthy campesina when explicitly remarking about the elaborateness of her *polleras*, earrings, or other jewelry.

13. Albro (1997; 2001) suggests that Bolivian provincial leaders may strategically blur their public identities so as to appeal to as many constituents as possible, attempting to simultaneously embody ethics of middle-class upward mobility and of social equality. Here I wish to point out that this strategy contributed to political crises and a climate of suspicion as well as to potential political opportunities.

14. "Quieren posesión oficial: Campesinos de Sacaba aguardan subprefecto," *Los Tiempos*, March 22, 2006.

15. A similar controversy over motivations and classification of actions occurred after each of Sacaba's many public protests in 2005 and 2006. Each protesting group argued that mayors were failing the Popular Participation Law's norms of good governance and failing the left-indigenist promise of redistribution of wealth and power within the municipality. And each time, protesters were denounced by other groups as fomenting conflict simply to gain office for themselves and their political patrons. Yet still other people expressed confusion as to whether any given municipal protest represented the citizens' struggle for good governance or redistribution of wealth, or clientelistic desires to take over city hall. They debated whether protest leaders were elite or subaltern. Most Sacabans, however, agreed that the sheer quantity of protests and the repeated turnover of municipal government officials sapped the energy of leaders and rank and file alike and obstructed municipal development.

16. *Inti* means "sun" in Quechua.

17. The organization's formal title was the Confederación Nacional de Mujeres Indígenas Originarias "Bartolina Sisa."

18. In other moments, Don Carlos acknowledged the necessity of supporting particular political leaders whom he mistrusted, through marches and public statements, in exchange for significant community infrastructure projects (see Chapter 6).

19. As Foster (1972:167) points out, the etymology of the Latin *invidia* meant competition and rivalry, as well as to covet something held by another person. It seems likely that this broader meaning remains in Bolivian concepts of *envidia*, *qhawanaku*, and *miramiento* even as, in English, *envy* focuses more on covetousness.

20. In the 1960s, George Foster (1965) argued, based on village studies in rural southern Mexico, that envy and the wish to avoid being the target of envy were holdovers of a peasant, premodern understanding of the world. He held that villagers

subscribed to a false worldview of "limited good": that all good things in life existed in finite amounts. Anyone who was wealthier, more fortunate, more beloved, or more talented than his or her neighbors feared being the object of envy. Lamenting that the fear of envy inspired villagers to hide their wealth and to avoid cooperating with each other on development projects, Foster saw envy as a chief obstacle to development in rural Mexico, and by extension, throughout the Third World. Basing his argument on the questionable assumption that economic opportunities were expanding for poor people in the Third World, he maintained that envy was the principal impediment to both communal cooperation and the desire for wealth that drove progress. Many anthropologists directly challenged Foster's thesis, however, rightly arguing that most resources are, in fact, limited for the poor in the Third World and that resentment is a natural response to inequality (e.g., Gregory 1975; du Boulay and Williams 1987;Taussig 1980: 7, 1986; West 2005; see also Comaroff and Comaroff 1993; Ferguson 1999; Geschiere 1997). Foster later acknowledged that envy pervaded the world and all social classes, rather than only poor people (e.g., Foster 1972).

21. Sacaba politics shared some commonalities with the dynamics of witchcraft accusation and counter-accusation in east Africa (see West 2005; Geschiere 1997; Ferguson 1999). While witchcraft (*hechicería*) was certainly a concern for some people in Sacaba in their personal lives, political leaders and activists did not openly complain of being the victims of witchcraft as a result of envy in politics. The common denominator in envious clientelism and envious witchcraft, however, is the concern about the secrecy of harmful acts.

22. See, for example, "¿Cuál es la principal característica del cochabambino?" *Los Tiempos*, September 12, 2010.

23. This is a common joke expressing self-criticism found throughout the Americas in areas colonized by the Spanish.

24. West (2005:244) expresses a similar concern that envy served as a downward leveling force in rural Mozambique following the civil war. A few dissenters in Cochabamba painted envy in a constructive light. Several sociologists in Cochabamba development agencies whom I interviewed professed the view that envy served a functional good of "social control" (*control social*), laudably inspiring wealthier people in rural communities to share their wealth with poorer people. This idea paralleled Gregory's (1975) definition of envy as the "expectation of reciprocity." Alternatively, some development workers told me they believed that envy helpfully sparked poorer people's ambitions to enter the middle class through hard work and developing their entrepreneurial skills. These positive evaluations of envy were in the minority, however.

25. In some moments, national MAS leaders have emphasized indigenous collectivism through village institutions at the level of discourse, though little at the level of policy (e.g., MAS-IPSP 2006:154).

26. Ernesto Laclau's discussion of elites' attempts to convince others that their particular interests are universal speaks to a similar issue (Laclau 1992:9).

Chapter 5. Laments of Betrayal

1. Doña Patricia had helped launch H. Obras as a rival Sacaba municipal political party while adamantly insisting that she had done so because the Sacaba MAS leaders had strayed from their platform, and that she remained loyal to the national MAS party and its leaders.

2. See Needham 1972 and Herzfeld 2008 for further reflections on the unknowability of others' beliefs and feelings.

3. Several Sacabans made similar complaints about Doña Felisa and other Sacaba leaders elected or appointed to national office.

Chapter 6. Middle Classes and Debates over the Definition of Community

1. MAS government leaders also occasionally used the term "civil society" (*sociedad civil*) (e.g., Álvaro García Linera, interview by Sara Miller Llana, "Bolivia's Vice President on Indigenous Rights, Coca Crops, and Relations with the U.S.," *Christian Science Monitor*, March 27, 2007), alongside other broadly inclusive subaltern terms such as *popular* (plebeian) and *pueblo* (nation, community, the people) to highlight their analysis that the interests of the majority of Bolivians diverged from those of the superelite (Stefanoni and do Alto 2006:68; Postero 2005; Canessa 2007; Albro 2007; Hylton and Thomson 2007; Lazar 2008:259). MAS leaders' (rare) use of the term "civil society" has promoted agrarian unions that articulate multiple scales—community, regional, and national—and engage in national decision making, in contrast to the local focus, territorial boundedness, and apolitical framing of the civil society concept used by LPP policy makers and their counterparts in other countries (see Postero 2007). For example, Article 24.1 of the new Bolivian Constitution of 2009, championed by the MAS party, asserts, "The sovereign people [*pueblo*], through organized civil society, will participate in the design of public policy. Organized civil society will exercise social control over public planning [*gestión pública*] on all levels of the State, and over all private companies." Bolivian political scientist Moira Zuazo characterizes MAS leaders' definition of legitimate leaders as emerging from union organizations (*organización sindical*), which she defines as synonymous with "organized society" (*sociedad organizada*) and with "civil society" (*sociedad civil*) (Zuazo 2009:50).

2. I am using the term "state-sponsored" for the purposes of clarity, recognizing that this term glosses over the diversity of state actors and the hybridity of their rhetorical definitions of community. See Abrams's "Notes on the Difficulty of Studying the State" (1977) and Corrigan and Sayer's *The Great Arch* (1985) on the hybridity and multifaceted nature of actions and rhetoric in the name of state.

3. See Joseph and Nugent 1994; Gupta and Ferguson 1997; Subramanian 2009; Eric Wolf 1986. For an exploration of these themes in Bolivian history, see Gotkowitz 2007; Larson 1998; Gordillo 2000; Jackson 1994.

4. She emphasized, as did all Choreños, that this period was no idyll given that *colonos* lived under the domination of large landowners. Landowners also terrorized freeholding *piqueros* with violence, at times, and often blocked *piqueros* and *colonos*

alike from accessing vital resources like water and firewood. What is significant in her narrative for the current discussion is that landowners' authority formed a geographic patchwork that comprised different geographic boundaries than the "community" as defined in the *sindicato* and LPP models that came later.

5. Furthermore, the diversity of class and racial identities within the Cochabamba valleys—and active movement between urban and rural spaces—also facilitated the formation of *sindicatos* as campesino communities during this time. Historians Jorge Dandler (1975) and José Gordillo (2000), among others, have shown how the low social barriers between Cochabamba elite, middling, and subaltern groups, relative to other regions of Bolivia, allowed valley residents to form alliances with people of other classes, to learn techniques of union organizing, to expel large landowners, and to pressure the central government to sign the Agrarian Reform in 1953. *Colonos* gathered the support of *piqueros* and of provincial middle classes, such as schoolteachers and midranking military officers.

6. They described indigenous community practices and commitment to local development as, for example, "saved in the hard drive of the unconscious of society" (Medina 1995:11). This subset of LPP reformers argued that rural and poor communities served as Bolivia's eternal "organized civil society" because of their indigenous culture (Medina 1995; Molina and Arias 1996; see also Molina Monasterios 1997:212). Such arguments drew on Robert Putnam's influential idea that "social capital" was the necessary basis for economic development. They also dovetailed with the assertion by the World Bank and other international development institutions that communities, defined as civil society, could enact development where centralized states had failed in the Third World (Putnam 1993; World Bank 2007; for critiques see Rose 1999; Rose 2000; Cooke and Kothari 2001; Paley 2001; Mosse 1999; Fine 1999).

7. For example, Vice President Álvaro García Linera asserted that the Morales administration's vision of indigeneity was pragmatic and nuanced. He declared: "I don't have a romanticized idea of the indigenous world: in the indigenous world there are social classes, personal appetites, personal interests, divisions and injustices, but deep down there is also a small, communal nucleus that could be strengthened" (Miller Llana and García Linera 2007).

8. See, for example, Morales's proclamation, while inaugurating the new Bolivian constitution, of the beginning of a new era of "communitarian socialism" ("Evo Morales lanzó el 'socialismo comunitario,'" *La Nación*, February 8, 2009).

9. Choro residents' nostalgic narratives of 1950s unity also glossed over deep political divides. As some elderly people occasionally noted, violence ensued when some Choro residents in the 1950s "took the large landowners' part" and opposed land reform even though they were not landowners themselves. Enmity between neighbors divided by these ideological camps—pro-landowner and pro-revolution— made daily life tense. Another deep and bitter ideological split opened within Choro, as within the Cochabamba regional agrarian unions and the ruling MNR party, over whether to push for "agrarian reform" or "agrarian revolution." A reform would end

peasant serfdom to large landowners (*pongueaje*), but not radically redistribute land, while a revolution would confiscate lands from all but the smallest estates and redistribute them to campesino cooperatives. In Choro and surrounding areas, the late 1950s and early 1960s was a time of assassinations and battles with dynamite over these ideological differences as well as personal power struggles between agrarian leaders and their respective followers (Dandler 1975; Gordillo 2000).

10. Some of the despairing complaints of disunity reflected locals' concerns about organization changes in community governance since the advent of the LPP. First, *sindicato* leaders had divided what had once been only one Choro *sindicato* into four separate Territorial Base Organizations (OTBs). While the leaders who supported this political semipartition explained that this would help attract more Popular Participation funds than if the *sindicato* of Choro formed a single OTB, other people lamented this partition as exacerbating political division and complained that leaders were doing so to try to gain power at the expense of other OTBs. A second phenomenon, also sparked by the LPP, saw outlying hamlet residents who had formerly belonged to the Choro *sindicato* convinced by leaders from surrounding hamlets to join those OTBs. Under the LPP, the per capita allocation of funding within Sacaba municipality meant that residents brought funding to OTBs. Political struggles were then occurring throughout Bolivia over jurisdiction boundary lines—between OTBs, "communities," counties, districts, and municipalities—in the competition for residents.

11. The Bolivian government began an eastern tropics colonization program for small farmers in the early 1960s, offering land and a few basic farming implements to campesino colonist organizations as an escape valve for the discontent of rural folk, as the land distributed under the 1953 Agrarian Reform became insufficient to support the next generation.

12. While most rank-and-file residents, like NGO workers and elected community officials, lamented "lack of unity," described Choro's *sindicato* as a failure, and compared the present unfavorably to the revolutionary-era *sindicato*, several notable infrastructure projects had, in fact, been built since the late 1960s. Most of these had been gotten through a combination of communal labor, dogged persistence of particular leaders, and clientelism. The half-dozen plaques affixed next to the sluice gate on Choro's largest irrigation water reservoir commemorated the patronage of several Bolivian presidents, from 1960s dictator René Barrientos to 1980s dictator Luis García Meza. Several kilometers of concrete canals, like the plaques, attested to dozens of leaders' trips to La Paz since the 1960s to plead with ministers and their lackeys to fund the project in its various stages of construction.

13. I did not hear any of the Choro rank and file explicitly agreeing or disagreeing with Don Carlos and other elected leaders that "communal unity" had increased.

Conclusion

1. "El Gobierno confirma que cocaleros son su fuerza de movilización," *Los Tiempos*, May 9, 2012.

2. "Evo culpa a dirigentes de la división y conflictos," *Los Tiempos*, July 23, 2012.

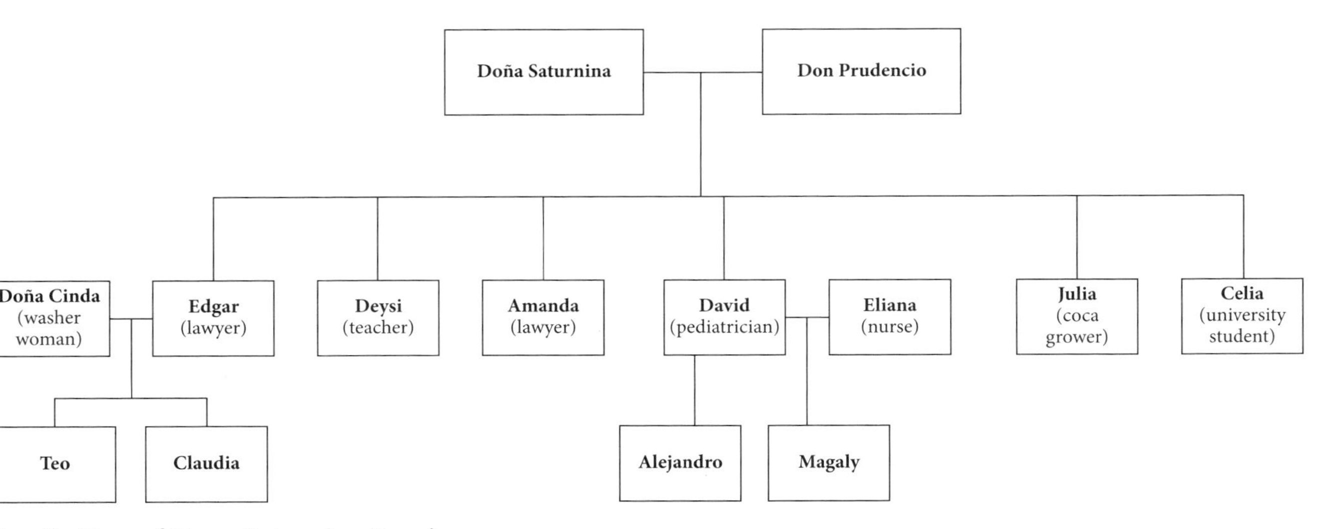


Family Tree of Dona Saturnina Ramírez

# Glossary

*alcaldía*—City hall, the seat of county government. In Sacaba Municipality, located in the municipal (county) seat of the town of Sacaba.

*ayllu*—Rural Andean indigenous peasant community with rotating leadership positions and collectively owned land.

Aymara—Indigenous language spoken in Bolivian highlands.

Bartolinas Federation—Confederación Nacional de Mujeres Campesinas Indígenas Originarias de Bolivia "Bartolina Sisa," the women's arm of the CSUTCB national agrarian union.

*busca pega*—Person seeking a *pega* (patronage job).

*campesino* – Peasant, small-scale farmer (Sp.). In Bolivia, this term often also connotes indigenous race or culture.

*chicha*—Corn beer drunk throughout the Cochabamba region, often brewed in home-based taverns on a small scale.

*chola*—Woman who wears a full *pollera* skirt and her hair in two braids; associated with peasant, indigenous, merchant, and working-class identity.

*cholita*—Polite term for *chola.*

*clientelismo*—Clientelism, political patronage.

*cocalero*—Coca grower, usually a member of one of Bolivia's coca growers' unions.

*colono*—A serf on an agricultural estate prior to the 1953 Agrarian Reform.

CSUTCB—Confederación Sindical Única de Trabajadores Campesinos de Bolivia, Bolivia's central peasant union federation.

*de pollera*—Polite term for *cholita* (Sp.).

*dirigente*—Elected union leader.

*envidia*—Envy (Sp.).

*gringo/gringa*—North American or European foreigner or a Bolivian who has very pale skin and hair (Sp.).

H. Obras—Honestidad y Obras, local political party existing only in Sacaba Municipality.

*indio*—Indian, pejorative term (Sp.).

*interés*—Self-interest (Sp.).

Inti—NGO based in Sacaba focused on women's employment, health, and education. *Inti* means "sun" in Quechua.

IPSP—Instrumento Político para la Soberanía de los Pueblos. The social movement that became the MAS party of Evo Morales.

*lari*—Highland indian, pejorative term.

LPP—Ley de Participación Popular (Law of Popular Participation), Bolivia's state decentralization reform, passed in 1994.

MAS—Movimiento al Socialismo (Movement Toward Socialism), the political party of Evo Morales.

MIR—Movimiento de la Izquierda Revolucionaria. Political party founded in 1971 that MAS leaders condemned as clientelistic. Began as a leftist opposition to the MNR, but moved to the center and leaders eventually embraced free market neoliberal reforms.

*miramiento*—Spanish word that in Bolivia is synonymous with English *envy* and Quechua *qhawanaku*. Literally means "watching."

MNR—Movimiento Nacional Revolucionario. Political party that emerged victorious in Bolivia's 1952 Revolution.

*obras* – Public works, infrastructure projects such as schools and roads (Sp.).

*originario* – Indigenous person, polite term (Sp.).

*pega*—Patronage job or a person who has received a patronage job.

*pijchicata*—Cocaine, cocaine base paste, or cocaine trafficking (Quechua).

*piquero*—A farmer during the late nineteenth and early twentieth centuries in Cochabamba who achieved freedom from serfdom on agricultural estates by buying his or her own plots of agricultural land.

*pollera* – A full, pleated skirt that some women in Andean countries wear to signify peasant or indigenous origins. Polleras are modern reappropriations of colonial Spanish women's attire.

*profesional*—University educated (Sp.).

*q'ara*—Derogatory Quechua and Aymara term meaning "white, elite, city dweller."

*qhawanaku*—Quechua word for envy, literally means "mutual watching."

Quechua—Indigenous language spoken widely in Peru and Bolivia, including Cochabamba valleys such as Sacaba.

*sindicato*—Local union, often used to refer specifically to a community-based peasant agrarian union.

UCS—Union Cívica Solidaridad. Populist political party that emerged in Bolivia in 1989 and which MAS leaders condemned as clientelistic.

*vecino*—Spanish term for city or town dwellers. *Vecinos* held citizenship rights under Spanish colonial rule, in contrast to indigenous people who lived in rural areas and were noncitizens. In postcolonial Bolivia, *vecinos* have often enjoyed higher social status than rural residents.

# Bibliography


Abelmann, Nancy. 1997. "Women's Class Mobility and Identities in South Korea: A Gendered, Transnational, Narrative Approach." *Journal of Asian Studies* 56 (2): 398–420.

Abrams, Philip. 1988. "Notes on the Difficulty of Studying the State." *Journal of Historical Sociology* 1 (1): 58–89.

Agrawal, Arun, and Clark C. Gibson, eds. 2001. *Communities and the Environment: Ethnicity, Gender, and the State in Community-Based Conservation.* New Brunswick, N.J.: Rutgers University Press.

Alanoca, Elio. 2009. Interview of Valerio Torihuano, 94. In Moira Zuazo, ed., *¿Cómo nació el MAS? La ruralización de la política en Bolivia: Entrevistas a 85 parlamentarios del partido.* La Paz, Bolivia: FES-ILDIS.

Albó, Xavier. 1975. *La paradoja Aymara: Solidaridad y faccionalismo.* Cuadernos de Investigación, No. 8. La Paz, Bolivia: Centro de Investigación y Promoción del Campesinado.

Albro, Robert. 1997. "Virtual Patriliny: Image Mutability and Populist Politics in Quillacollo, Bolivia." *PoLAR: Political and Legal Anthropology Review* 20 (1): 73–92.

———. 2000. "The Populist Chola: Cultural Mediation and the Political Imagination in Quillacollo, Bolivia." *Journal of Latin American Anthropology* 5 (2): 30–88.

———. 2001. "Reciprocity and Realpolitik: Image, Career, and Factional Genealogies in Provincial Bolivia." *American Ethnologist* 28 (1): 56–93.

———. 2006. "The Culture of Democracy and Bolivia's Indigenous Movements." *Critique of Anthropology* 26: 387–410.

———. 2007. "Indigenous Politics in Bolivia's Evo Era: Clientelism, Llunkerío, and the Problem of Stigma." *Urban Anthropology and Studies of Cultural Systems and World Economic Development* 36 (3): 281–320.

Andersen, Lykke, and José Luís Evia. 2003. "The Effectiveness of Foreign Aid in Bolivia." Documento de Trabajo. La Paz, Bolivia: Instituto de Investigaciones Socio-Económicas (IISEC).

Antezana, Fernando, ed. 2003. *Participación popular: vivencias y perspectivas.* Cochabamba, Bolivia: CEPLAG.

Asistiri Calle, Agustina. 2009. Interview of Sipriano Bautista, 144. In Moira Zuazo, ed., 2009. *¿Cómo nació el MAS? La ruralización de la política en Bolivia: Entrevistas a 85 parlamentarios del partido*. La Paz, Bolivia: FES-ILDIS.

Auyero, Javier. 2001. *Poor People's Politics: Peronist Survival Networks and the Legacy of Evita*. Durham, N.C.: Duke University Press.

Ayo, Diego. 2004. *Voces críticas de la descentralización: Una década de Participación Popular*. La Paz, Bolivia: Plural Editores, FES-ILDIS.

Bailey, F. G. 2001. *Treasons, Stratagems, and Spoils: How Leaders Make Practical Use of Values and Beliefs*. Boulder, Colo.: Westview Press.

Bledstein, Burton J., and Robert D. Johnston, eds. 2001. *The Middling Sorts: Explorations in the History of the American Middle Class*. New York: Routledge.

Botelho Gosalvez, Raúl. 1982 [1945]. *Altiplano: Novela india*. La Paz, Bolivia: Editorial Juventud.

Bourdieu, Pierre. 1984. *Distinction: A Social Critique of the Judgment of Taste*. Cambridge, Mass.: Harvard University Press.

Brinkerhoff, Derick W. and Arthur A. Goldsmith. 2002. "Clientelism, Patrimonialism and Democratic Governance: An Overview and Framework for Assessment and Programming." Working paper prepared for the USAID Office of Democracy and Governance, IQC#AEP-I-00–00–00005–00. http://pdf.usaid.gov/pdf_docs/PNACR426.pdf

Burdick, John. 1998. *Blessed Anastácia: Women, Race, and Popular Christianity in Brazil*. New York: Routledge.

Buyandelgeriyn, Manduhai. 2008. "Post-Post Transition Theories: Walking on Multiple Paths." *Annual Review of Anthropology* 37: 235–250.

Cahn, Peter. 2008. "Consuming Class: Multilevel Marketers in Neoliberal Mexico." *Cultural Anthropology* 23 (3): 429–452.

Calderón, Fernando, and Jorge Dandler. 1984. *Bolivia, la fuerza histórica del campesinado: Movimientos campesinos y etnicidad*. Cochabamba, Bolivia: Centro de Estudios de la Realidad Económica y Social; UNRISD.

Callahan, Manuel. 2004b. "Zapatismo Beyond Chiapas." In *Globalize Liberation: How to Uproot the System and Build a Better World*, David Solnit, ed. San Francisco: City Lights Books.

Canessa, Andrew, ed. 2005. *Natives Making Nation: Gender, Indigeneity, and the State in the Andes*. Tucson: University of Arizona Press.

———. 2007. "Who Is Indigenous? Self-Identification, Indigeneity, and Claims to Justice in Contemporary Bolivia." *Urban Anthropology* 36 (3): 195–237.

———. 2012. *Intimate Indigeneities: Race, Sex, and History in the Small Spaces of Andean Life*. Durham, N.C.: Duke University Press.

Carter, William and Xavier Albó. 1988. "La comunidad Aymara: un mini-estado en conflicto," 451–493. In *Raices de América: El mundo Aymara*. Xavier Albo, ed. Madrid: Alianza.

Colloredo-Mansfield, Rudi. (1999) 2004. The Native Leisure Class: Consumption and Cultural Creativity in the Andes. Chicago: University of Chicago Press.

———. 2009. *Fighting Like a Community: Andean Civil Society in an Era of Indian Uprisings.* Chicago: University of Chicago Press.

Comaroff, Jean, and John L. Comaroff, eds. 1993. *Modernity and Its Malcontents: Ritual and Power in Postcolonial Africa.* Chicago: University of Chicago Press.

———. 2001. *Millennial Capitalism and the Culture of Neoliberalism.* Durham, N.C.: Duke University Press.

Comaroff, John L., and Jean Comaroff, eds. 1999. *Civil Society and the Political Imagination in Africa: Critical Perspectives.* Chicago: University of Chicago Press.

Conaghan, Catherine, and James Malloy. 1994. *Unsettling Statecraft: Democracy and Neoliberalism in the Central Andes.* Pittsburgh: University of Pittsburgh Press

Cooke, Bill, and Uma Kothari, eds. 2001. *Participation, the New Tyranny?* London: Zed Books.

Coombe, Rosemary J. 1997. "Identifying and Engendering the Forms of Emergent Civil Societies: New Directions in Political Anthropology." *PoLAR: Political and Legal Anthropology Review* 20 (1): 1–12.

Corrigan, Philip, and Derek Sayer. 1985. *The Great Arch: English State Formation as Cultural Revolution.* Oxford: Basil Blackwell.

Corte Nacional Electoral de Bolivia. 2005. "Consulta Geográfica." http://www.cne .org.bo/sirenacomp/index.aspx. Accessed December 26, 2010.

(CSUTCB). Confederación Sindical Única de Trabajadores Campesinos de Bolivia. 1987. *III Congreso Ordinario de la CSUTCB: Un Congreso Inconcluso.* Cochabamba, Bolivia: Centro de Documentación e Información (CEDOIN).

———.1994. *VI Congreso Ordinario de la Confederación Sindical Única de Trabajadores Campesinos de Bolivia.* La Paz, Bolivia: CEDOIN.

———. 2006. *Nueva Constitución Plurinacional: Propuesta política desde la vision de campesinos, indígenas y originarios. Hacia la reconstrucción del sueño suma qamana, sumaj kausay, nandereko.* La Paz, Bolivia: Apostamos Por Bolivia: Asociación para la ciudadanía. Centro Gregoria Apaza, Centro de Investigación y Promoción del Campesinado, Fundación Tierra.

Dandler, Jorge. 1975. *Campesinado y reforma agraria en Cochabamba, 1952–1953: Dinámica de un movimiento campesino en Bolivia.* Cuadernos de Investigación. La Paz, Bolivia: Centro de Investigación y Promoción del Campesinado.

de la Cadena, Marisol. 2000. *Indigenous Mestizos: The Politics of Race and Culture in Cuzco, Peru, 1919–1991.* Durham, N.C.: Duke University Press.

de la Fuente, Manuel. 2001. Participación Popular y desarrollo local: La situación de los municipios rurales de Cochabamba y Chuquisaca. Cochabamba, Bolivia: PROMEC-CEPLAG-CESU.

Dickey, Sara. 2000. "Permeable Homes: Domestic Service, Household Space, and the Vulnerability of Class Boundaries in Urban India." *American Ethnologist* 27 (2): 462–489.

Diez de Medina, Fernando. 1950. *Nayjama: Introducción a la mitología andina.* Madrid: Paraninfo.

Du Boulay, Juliet, and Rory Williams. 1987. "Amoral Familism and the Image of Limited Good: A Critique from a European Perspective." *Anthropological Quarterly* 60 (1): 12–24.

Dunkerley, James. 2007. "Evo Morales, the 'Two Bolivias' and the Third Bolivian Revolution." *Journal of Latin American Studies* 39 (1): 113–166.

Edelman, Marc. 2001. "Social Movements: Changing Paradigms and Forms of Politics." *Annual Review of Anthropology* 30: 285–317.

Ehrenreich, Barbara. 1989. *Fear of Falling: The Inner Life of the Middle Class.* New York: Pantheon.

Englund, Harri. 2006. *Prisoners of Freedom: Human Rights and the African Poor.* Berkeley: University of California Press.

Fabricant, Nicole. 2012. *Mobilizing Bolivia's Displaced: Indigenous Politics and the Struggle over Land.* Chapel Hill: University of North Carolina Press.

Farthing, Linda, and Kathryn Ledebur. 2004. "The Beat Goes On: The U.S. War on Coca." *NACLA Report on the Americas* 38 (3).

Ferguson, James. 1994. *The Anti-Politics Machine: "Development," Depoliticization, and Bureaucratic Power in Lesotho.* Minneapolis: University of Minnesota Press.

———. 1999. *Expectations of Modernity: Myths and Meanings of Urban Life on the Zambian Copperbelt.* Berkeley: University of California Press.

———. 2006. *Global Shadows: Africa in the Neoliberal World Order.* Durham, N.C.: Duke University Press.

Ferme, Mariane. 1999. "Staging Politisi: The Dialogics of Publicity and Secrecy in Sierra Leone." In *Civil Society and the Political Imagination in Africa: Critical Perspectives.* Jean Comaroff and John Comaroff, eds. Chicago: University of Chicago Press.

Fernandes, Sujatha. 2010. *Who Can Stop the Drums? Urban Social Movements in Chávez's Venezuela.* Durham, N.C.: Duke University Press.

Fine, Ben. 1999. "The Developmental State Is Dead—Long Live Social Capital?" *Development and Change* 30 (1): 1–19.

Finkel, Steven E, Aníbal Pérez-Liñán, and Mitchell A. Seligson. 2007. "The Effects of U.S. Foreign Assistance on Democracy Building, 1990–2003." *World Politics* 59: 404–439.

Finot, Iván 1990. *Democratización del estado y descentralización.* La Paz, Bolivia: Instituto Latinoamericano de Investigaciones Sociales.

Flores, Gonzalo, and José Blanes. 1984. *¿Dónde va el Chapare?* La Paz, Bolivia: Centro de Estudios de la Realidad Económica y Social.

Foster, George M. 1965. "Peasant Society and the Image of Limited Good." *American Anthropologist* 67 (2): 293–315.

———. 1972. "A Second Look at Limited Good." *Anthropological Quarterly* 45 (2): 57–64.

Foucault, Michel. 1991. *Governmentality*. Chicago: University of Chicago Press.

Frykman, Jonas, and Orvar Löfgren. (1979) 1987. *Culture Builders: A Historical Anthropology of Middle-Class Life*. Translated by Alan Crozier. New Brunswick: Rutgers University Press.

Gamarra, Eduardo. 2003. "The Construction of Bolivia's Multiparty System." In *Proclaiming Revolution: Bolivia in Comparative Perspective*, edited by Merilee Grindle and Pilar Domingo Cambridge, Mass.: David Rockefeller Center for Latin American Studies; Harvard University Press.

García, María Elena. 2005. *Making Indigenous Citizens: Identities, Education, and Multicultural Development in Peru*. Stanford, Calif.: Stanford University Press.

Gellner, Ernest, and John Waterbury, eds. 1977. *Patrons and Clients in Mediterranean Societies*. London: Duckworth; Hanover, N.H.: Center for Mediterranean Studies of the American Universities Field Staff.

Geschiere, Peter. 1997. *The Modernity of Witchcraft: Politics and the Occult in Postcolonial Africa*. Charlottesville: University of Virginia Press.

Ghosh, Amitav. 1994. *In an Antique Land*. New York: Vintage Books.

Gibson-Graham, J. K. 1996. "Class and the Politics of 'Identity.'" In *The End of Capitalism (As We Knew It): A Feminist Critique of Political Economy*, 46–71. Malden, Mass.: Blackwell.

Gill, Lesley. 1987. *Peasants, Entrepreneurs, and Social Change: Frontier Development in Lowland Bolivia*. Boulder, Colo.: Westview Press.

———. 2000. *Teetering on the Rim: Global Restructuring, Daily Life, and the Armed Retreat of the Bolivian State*. New York: Columbia University Press.

Gilroy, Paul. 2000. *Against Race: Imagining Political Culture Beyond the Color Line*. Cambridge, Mass.: Belknap Press of Harvard University Press.

Glick Schiller, Nina. 2003. "Same Old, Same Old? . . . Resurrecting Political Culture or Conducting Ethnographies of Human Possibilities?" *American Ethnologist* 30 (4): 497–499.

Goldstein, Daniel M. 2012. *Outlawed: Between Security and Rights in a Bolivian City*. Durham, N.C.: Duke University Press.

Goodale, Mark. 2009. *Dilemmas of Modernity: Bolivian Encounters with Law and Liberalism*. Stanford, Calif.: Stanford University Press.

Goodale, Mark and Nancy Postero, eds. 2013. *Neoliberalism, Interrupted: Social Change and Contested Governance in Contemporary Latin America*. Stanford, Calif.: Stanford University Press.

Gordillo, José M. 2000. *Campesinos revolucionarios en Bolivia: Identidad, territorio y sexualidad en el Valle Alto de Cochabamba, 1952–1964*. La Paz, Bolivia: Plural Editores.

Gotkowitz, Laura. 2003. "Trading Insults: Honor, Violence, and the Gendered Culture of Commerce in Cochabamba, Bolivia, 1870s–1950s." *Hispanic American Historical Review* 83 (1): 83–118.

————. 2007. *A Revolution for Our Rights: Indigenous Struggles for Land and Justice in Bolivia, 1880–1952.* Durham, N.C.: Duke University Press.

Gramsci, Antonio. 1971. *Selections from the Prison Notebooks of Antonio Gramsci.* Edited and translated by Quintin Hoare and Geoffrey Nowell Smith. New York: International Publishers.

Greenhouse, Carol J., ed. 2010. *Ethnographies of Neoliberalism.* Philadelphia: University of Pennsylvania Press.

Gregory, James R. 1975. "Image of Limited Good or Expectation of Reciprocity?" *Current Anthropology* 16 (1): 73–92.

Gupta, Akhil, and James Ferguson, eds. 1997. *Culture, Power, Place: Explorations in Critical Anthropology.* Durham, N.C.: Duke University Press.

Gustafson, Bret. 2009. *New Languages of the State: Indigenous Resurgence and the Politics of Knowledge in Bolivia.* Durham, N.C.: Duke University Press.

Hahn, Dwight. 1991. *The Divided World of the Bolivian Andes: A Structural View of Domination and Resistance.* New York: Taylor and Francis.

Hale, Charles. 2002. "Does Multiculturalism Menace? Governance, Cultural Rights and the Politics of Identity in Guatemala." *Journal of Latin American Studies* 34 (3): 485–524.

————. 2005. "Neoliberal Multiculturalism: The Remaking of Cultural Rights and Racial Dominance in Central America." *PoLAR: Political and Legal Anthropology Review* 28 (1): 10–28.

Hall, Stuart and Lawrence Grossberg. 1986. "On Postmodernism and Articulation: An Interview with Stuart Hall." *Journal of Communication Inquiry* 10 (2): 45–60.

Hann, Chris, and Elizabeth Dunn, eds. 1996. *Civil Society: Challenging Western Models.* London: Routledge.

Hansen, Thomas Blom, and Finn Stepputat, eds. 2001. *States of Imagination: Ethnographic Explorations of the Postcolonial State.* Durham, N.C.: Duke University Press.

Haugerud, Angelique. 1995. *The Culture of Politics in Modern Kenya.* Cambridge: Cambridge University Press.

Healy, Kevin. 1986. "The Boom Within the Crisis: Some Recent Effects of Foreign Cocaine Markets on Bolivian Rural Society and Economy." In *Coca and Cocaine, Effects on People and Policy in Latin America,* ,edited by Deobrah Pacini and Christine Franquemont. Cultural Survival Report 23. Cambridge, Mass.: Cultural Survival; Ithaca, N.Y.: Latin American Studies Program, Cornell University.

————. 1991. "Structural Adjustment, Peasant Agriculture and Coca in Bolivia." Paper Presented at the XVI International Congress of the Latin American Studies Association, April 4–6, Washington, D.C.

Herzfeld, Michael. 1981. "Meaning and Morality: A Semiotic Approach to Evil Eye Accusations in a Greek Village." *American Ethnologist* 8 (3): 560–574.

————. 2008. *Evicted From Eternity: The Restructuring of Modern Rome.* Chicago: University of Chicago Press.

Hess, David J. 2007. "Crosscurrents: Social Movements and the Anthropology of Science and Technology." *American Anthropologist* 109 (3): 463–472.

Hetherington, Kregg. 2011. *Guerrilla Auditors: The Politics of Transparency in Neoliberal Paraguay*. Durham, N.C.: Duke University Press.

Humphrey, Caroline. 2002. *The Unmaking of Soviet Life: Everyday Economies After Socialism*. Ithaca, N.Y.: Cornell University Press.

Hylton, Forrest, and Sinclair Thomson. 2007. *Revolutionary Horizons: Past and Present in Bolivian Politics*. New York: Verso.

Interamerican Development Bank. 2008. "The Bank's Country Strategy with Bolivia: 2008–2010." Washington, D.C.

International Monetary Fund. 1997. "Good Governance: The IMF's Role." Washington, D.C. http://www.imf.org/external/pubs/ft/exrp/govern/govindex.htm.

Jackson, Jean E., and Kay B. Warren. 2005. "Indigenous Movements in Latin America, 1992–2004: Controversies, Ironies, New Directions." *Annual Review of Anthropology* 34: 549–573.

Jackson, Robert H. 1994. *Regional Markets and Agrarian Transformation in Bolivia: Cochabamba, 1539–1960*. Albuquerque: University of New Mexico Press.

Jacobsen, Nils and Cristóbal Aljovín de Losada. 2005. *Political Cultures in the Andes: 1750–1950*. Durham, N.C.: Duke University Press.

Joseph, Gilbert M., and Daniel Nugent, eds. 1994. *Everyday Forms of State Formation: Revolution and the Negotiation of Rule in Modern Mexico*. Durham, N.C.: Duke University Press.

Jung, Courtney. 2003. "The Politics of Indigenous Identity: Neoliberalism, Cultural Rights, and the Mexican Zapatistas." *Social Research* 70 (2): 433–462.

Kearney, Michael. 1996. *Reconceptualizing the Peasantry: Anthropology in Global Perspective*. Boulder, Colo.: Westview Press.

Klein, Herbert. 2003. "Social Change in Bolivia Since 1952." In *Proclaiming Revolution: Bolivia in Comparative Perspective*, edited by Merilee Grindle and Pilar Domingo, 232–258. Cambridge, Mass.: Harvard University Press.

Kohl, Benjamin. 1999. "Economic and Political Restructuring in Bolivia: Tools for a Neoliberal Agenda?" Ph.D. diss., Cornell University.

———. 2003. "Restructuring Citizenship in Bolivia: El Plan de Todos. *International Journal of Urban and Regional Research* 27 (2): 337–351.

Laclau, Ernesto. 1992. "Universalism, Particularism, and the Question of Identity." *October* 61: 83–90.

Lagos, Maria L. 1994. *Autonomy and Power: The Dynamics of Class and Culture in Rural Bolivia*. Philadelphia: University of Pennsylvania Press.

Landé, Carl H. 1983. "Political Clientelism in Political Studies: Retrospect and Prospects." *International Political Science Review* 4 (4): 435–454.

Larson, Brooke. 1998. *Cochabamba, 1550–1900: Colonialism and Agrarian Transformation in Bolivia*. Expanded ed. Durham, N.C.: Duke University Press.

———. 2005. "Capturing Indian Bodies, Hearths, and Minds: The Gendered Politics of Rural School Reform in Bolivia, 1920s-1940s." In Andrew Canessa, ed., *Natives Making Nation: Gender, Indigeneity, and the State in the Andes,* 32–59. Tucson: University of Arizona Press.

Lazar, Sian. 2008. *El Alto, Rebel City: Self and Citizenship in Andean Bolivia.* Durham, N.C.: Duke University Press.

Leidel, Steffen. 2006. "El Texas boliviano." Deutche-Welle.com, posted November 27. Accessed October 24, 2011. http://dw.de/p/9RAZ

Li, Tania Murray. 1996. "Images of Community: Discourse and Strategy in Property Relations." *Development and Change* 27 (3): 501–528.

———. 2007. *The Will to Improve: Governmentality, Development, and the Practice of Politics.* Durham, N.C.: Duke University Press.

Liechty, Mark. 2002. *Suitably Modern: Making Middle-Class Culture in a New Consumer Society.* Princeton, N.J.: Princeton University Press.

López, Luís Enrique, and Pablo Regalsky, eds. 2005. *Movimientos indígenas y Estado en Bolivia.* Cochabamba, Bolivia: Plural Editores.

Luhrmann, Tania M. 2006. "Subjectivity." *Anthropological Theory* 6 (3): 345–361.

Luykx, Aurolyn. 1999. *The Citizen Factory: Schooling and Cultural Production in Bolivia.* Albany, N.Y.: State University of New York Press

(MAS-IPSP) Movimiento al Socialismo–Instrumento Político Para la Soberanía de los Pueblos. 2005. *Programa de Gobierno 2006–2010: "Bolivia digna soberana y productiva para vivir bien."* La Paz, Bolivia.

———. 2006. *La revolución democrática y cultural: Diez discursos de Evo Morales.* La Paz, Bolivia: Editorial Malatesta.

———. 2010. *MAS-IPSP 2010–2015 Programa de Gobierno: Bolivia: País Líder.* La Paz, Bolivia.

Mayorga, Fernando. 2002. *Neopopulismo y democracia: Compadres y padrinos en la política boliviana, 1988–1999.* La Paz, Bolivia: Plural Editores.

Medina, Javier. 1995. *La participación popular como fruto de las luchas sociales en Bolivia.* La Paz, Bolivia: Ministerio de Desarrollo Humano, Secretaría Nacional de Participación Popular.

Miller Llana, Sara. 2007. Interview of Álvaro García Linera: "Bolivia's Vice President on Indigenous Rights, Coca Crops, and Relations with the U.S." *Christian Science Monitor,* March 27.

Molina, Sergio, and Iván Arias. 1996. *De la nación clandestina a la participación popular.* Informes especiales 2. La Paz, Bolivia: Centro de Documentación e Información.

Molina Monasterios, Fernando. 1997. *Historia de la Participación Popular.* La Paz, Bolivia: Ministerio de Desarrollo Humano, Secretaría Nacional de Participación Popular.

Molina Saucedo, Carlos Hugo. 1990. *La descentralización imposible y la alternativa municipal.* Santa Cruz, Bolivia: Editorial Cabildo.

Moore, Donald S. 2005. *Suffering for Territory: Race, Place, and Power in Zimbabwe.* Durham, N.C.: Duke University Press.

Moore, Sally Falk, ed. 1993. *Moralizing States and the Ethnography of the Present.* American Ethnological Society Monograph Series 5. Arlingon, Va.: American Anthropological Association.

Mosse, David. 1999. "Colonial and Contemporary Ideologies of 'Community Management': The Case of Tank Irrigation and Development in South India." *Modern Asian Studies* 33 (2): 303–338.

Needham, Rodney. 1972. *Belief, Language, and Experience.* Oxford: Oxford University Press.

O'Dougherty, Maureen. 2002. *Consumption Intensified: The Politics of Middle-Class Daily Life in Brazil.* Durham, N.C.: Duke University Press.

Ortner, Sherry B. 2005. "Subjectivity and Cultural Critique." *Anthropological Theory* 5 (1): 31–52.

Painter, James. 1994. *Bolivia and Coca: A Study in Dependency.* Tokyo: United Nations University Press.

———. 1998. *Economic Development and the Origins of the Bolivian Cocaine Industry.* Wilmington, Del.: Scholarly Resources, Jaguar Books on Latin America.

Paley, Julia. 2001. *Marketing Democracy: Power and Social Movements in Post-dictatorship Chile.* Berkeley: University of California Press.

Parry, Jonathan and Maurice Bloch, eds. 1989. *Money and the Morality of Exchange.* Cambridge: Cambridge University Press.

Paulson, Susan. 1996. "Familias que no 'conyugan' e identidades que no conjugan: la vida en Mizque desafía nuestras categorías." In *Ser mujer indígena, chola o birlocha en la Bolivia postcolonial de los 90*, Silvia Rivera, ed. 85–154. La Paz, Bolivia: Ministerio de Desarrollo Humano.

Paulson, Susan, and Pamela Calla. 2000. "Gender and Ethnicity in Bolivian Politics: Transformation or Paternalism?" *Journal of Latin American Anthropology* 5 (2): 112–149.

Peters, Pauline. 2004. "Inequality and Social Conflict over Land in Africa." *Journal of Agrarian Change* 4 (3): 269–314.

Petras, James. 2006a. "The Bankers Can Rest Easy: Evo Morales: All Growl, No Claws?" *Counterpunch*, January 4.

Phillips, Lynne, ed. 1997. *The Third Wave of Modernization in Latin America: Critical Perspectives on Neoliberalism.* Wilmington, Del.: Scholarly Resources, Jaguar Books on Latin America Number 16.

Pigg, Stacey Leigh. 1992. "Inventing Social Category Through Place: Social Representations and Development in Nepal." *Comparative Studies in Society and History* 34 (3): 491–513.

Pinto Ocampo, Maria Teresa. 2004. "Entre la represión y la concertación: Los cocaleros en el Chapare y en el Putumayu. Informe final del concurso: Movimientos sociales y nuevos conflictos en America Latina y el Caribe. Programa Regional de Becas. Buenos Aires: CLACSO.

Platt, Tristan. 1993. "Simon Bolívar, the Sun of Justice and the Amerindian Virgin: Andean Conceptions of the Patria in Nineteenth-Century Potosí." *Journal of Latin American Studies* 25 (1): 159–185.

Poole, Deborah. 1997. *Vision, Race, and Modernity: A Visual Economy of the Andean Image World.* Princeton, N.J.: Princeton University Press.

Postero, Nancy. 2005. "Indigenous Responses to Neoliberalism: A Look at the Bolivian Uprising of 2003." *PoLAR: Political and Legal Anthropology Review* 28 (1): 73–92.

———. 2007. *Now We Are Citizens: Indigenous Politics in Postmulticultural Bolivia.* Stanford, Calif.: Stanford University Press.

———. 2010. "The Struggle to Create a Radical Democracy in Bolivia." *Latin American Research Review* 45 (4): 59–78.

Prudencio Böhrt, Julio. 1991. *Políticas agrarias y seguridad alimentaria en Bolivia, 1970–1990.* La Paz, Bolivia: Estudios y Proyectos; UNITAS.

Putnam, Robert D., with Robert Leonardi and Raffaella Y. Nanetti. 1993. *Making Democracy Work: Civic Traditions in Modern Italy.* Princeton, N.J.: Princeton University Press.

Quispe Canaviri, Juan José. 2009. Interview of Hilario Callisaya Quispe, 101. In Moira Zuazo, ed., ¿*Cómo nació el MAS? La ruralización de la política en Bolivia: Entrevistas a 85 parlamentarios del partido.* La Paz, Bolivia: FES-ILDIS.

Regalsky, Pablo. 2010. "Political Processes and the Reconfiguration of the State in Bolivia." *Latin American Perspectives* 37 (35): 35–50.

Reilly, Thomas K., Ruben Ardaya, and Carlos Laserna. 1999. *Ciudadanía en la Participación Popular: Guía para facilitadores.* La Paz, Bolivia: Ministerio de Desarrollo Sostenible y Planificación, Viceministerio de Planificación Estratégica y Participación Popular, Dirección de Participación Popular, Unidad Nacional de Fortalecimiento Comunitario.

Ribot, Jesse. 1999. "Decentralisation, Participation, and Accountability in Sahelian Forestry: Legal Instruments of Political-Administrative Control." *Africa* 69 (1): 23–65.

Rivera Cusicanqui, Silvia. 1986. *Oprimidos pero no vencidos: luchas del campesinado aymara y qhechwa de Bolivia, 1900–1980.* Geneva: United Nations Research Institute for Social Development.

———. 1990. "Liberal Democracy and *Ayllu* Democracy in Bolivia: The Case of Northern Potosí." *Journal of Development Studies* 26 (4): 97–121.

Rose, Nikolas. 1999. *Powers of Freedom: Reframing Political Thought.* Cambridge: Cambridge University Press.

———. 2000. "Community, Citizenship, and the Third Way." *American Behavioral Scientist* 43 (9): 1395–1411.

Rutz, Henry J., and Erol M. Balkan. 2009. *Reproducing Class: Education, Neoliberalism, and the Rise of the New Middle Class in Istanbul.* New York: Berghahn Books.

Sanabria, Harry. 1993. *The Coca Boom and Rural Social Change in Bolivia*. Ann Arbor: University of Michigan Press.

Sandbrook, Richard. 1972. "Patrons, Clients, and Factions: New Dimensions of Conflict Analysis in Africa." *Canadian Journal of Political Science* 5 (1): 104–119.

Schultz, Jim, Aldo Orellana and Yi-Ching Hwang. 2008. "Racism Runs Amok in Sucre." May 26. http://democracyctr.org/blogfrombolivia/bolivian-racism-runs-amok-in-sucre/. Accessed October 27, 2013.

Scott, James C. 1983. "Everyday Forms of Class Struggle between Ex-Patrons and Ex-Clients: The Green Revolution in Kedah, Malaysia." *International Political Science Review* 4 (4): 547–556.

Seligman, Adam B. 1992. *The Idea of Civil Society*. New York: Free Press.

Seligmann, Linda. 1989. "To Be in Between: The Cholas as Market Women." *Comparative Studies in Society and History* 31 (4): 694–721.

Seligson, Mitchell. 1998. *The Political Culture of Democracy in Bolivia: 1998*. Nashville: Vanderbilt University, Latin American Public Opinion Project and USAID.

Shakow, Miriam. 2011. "The Peril and Promise of Noodles and Beer: Condemnation of Patronage and Hybrid Political Frameworks in 'Post-neoliberal' Cochabamba, Bolivia." *PoLAR: Political and Legal Anthropology Review* 34 (2): 315–336.

Shipton, Parker. 1989. *Bitter Money: Cultural Economy and Some African Meanings of Forbidden Economies*. American Ethnological Society Monograph Series, 1. Washington, D.C.: American Anthropological Association.

Singer, Matthew M., and Kevin M. Morrison. 2004. "The 2002 Presidential and Parliamentary Elections in Bolivia." *Electoral Studies* 23: 172–192.

Sivak, Martín. 2008. *Jefazo: Retrato Íntimo de Evo Morales*. La Paz, Bolivia: Editorial Literatura.

Starn, Orin. 1991. "Missing the Revolution: Anthropologists and the War in Peru." *Cultural Anthropology* 6 (1): 63–91.

Stefanani, Pablo, and Hervé do Alto. 2006. *Evo Morales, de la coca al palacio: Una oportunidad para la izquierda indígena*. La Paz, Bolivia: Editorial Malatesta.

Subramanian, Ajantha. 2009. *Shorelines: Space and Rights in South India*. Stanford, Calif.: Stanford University Press.

Subramanian, Narendra. 1999. *Ethnicity and Populist Mobilization: Political Parties, Citizens, and Democracy in South India*. Delhi: Oxford University Press.

Tarrow, Sidney. 1998. *Power in Movement: Social Movements and Contentious Politics*. Cambridge, U.K.: Cambridge University Press.

Taussig, Michael T. 1980. *The Devil and Commodity Fetishism in South America*. Chapel Hill: University of North Carolina Press.

———. 1986. *Shamanism, Colonialism, and the Wild Man: A Study in Terror and Healing*. Chicago: University of Chicago Press.

Tsing, Anna Lowenhaupt. 2004. *Friction: An Ethnography of Global Connection*. Princeton, N.J.: Princeton University Press.

UNDP (United Nations Development Programme). 2009. *Human Development Report 2009: Overcoming Barriers; Human Mobility and Development.* New York: UNDP.

USAID. 2005. "Democracy Assistance Project." Nashville: Vanderbilt University, USAID. Latin America Public Opinion Project (LAPOP).

Van Cott, Donna Lee. 2005. *From Movements to Parties in Latin America: The Evolution of Ethnic Politics.* Cambridge: Cambridge University Press.

Verdery, Katherine. 1999. "Fuzzy Property: Rights, Power, and Identity in Transylvania's Decollectivization." In *Uncertain Transition: Ethnographies of Change in the Postsocialist World,* edited by Michael Burawoy and Katherine Verdery, 102–117. Lanham, Md.: Rowman and Littlefield Publishers.

Villarroel, Gratzia. 2008. "In the Footsteps of Bartolina Sisa: Bolivian Indigenous Women, Evo Morales and the Bolivian Indigenous Revolution." David Rockefeller Center for Latin American Studies Research Colloquium, Harvard University March 27, 2008.

Warren, Kay B. 1998. *Indigenous Movements and Their Critics: Pan-Maya Activism in Guatemala.* Princeton, N.J.: Princeton University Press.

Warren, Kay B., and Jean E. Jackson, eds. 2002. *Indigenous Movements, Self-Representation, and the State in Latin America.* Austin: University of Texas Press.

Water and Sanitation Program (WSP). 2006. "Bolivia at a Glance." http://www .wsp.org/filez/country/2142007122644_Bolivia.pdf.

Weisbrot, Mark, and Luis Sandoval. 2008. "The Distribution of Bolivia's Most Important Natural Resources and the Autonomy Conflicts." *Issue Brief* July. Washington, D.C.: Center for Economic and Policy Research.

Weismantel, Mary. 2001. *Cholas and Pishtacos: Stories of Race and Sex in the Andes.* Chicago: University of Chicago Press.

West, Harry G. 2005. *Kupilikula: Governance and the Invisible Realm in Mozambique.* Chicago: University of Chicago Press.

West, Harry G., and Todd Sanders. 2003. *Transparency and Conspiracy: Ethnographies of Suspicion in the New World Order.* Durham, N.C.: Duke University Press.

Williams, Raymond. 1977. *Marxism and Literature.* Oxford: Oxford University Press.

Wolf, Eric. 1986. "The Vicissitudes of the Closed Corporate Peasant Community." *American Ethnologist* 13 (2): 325–329.

World Bank. 2000. *Bolivia: From Patronage to a Professional State: Bolivia Institutional and Governance Review.* Report No. 20115-BO. August 25. Washington, D.C.: World Bank, Poverty Reduction and Economic Management, Latin America and the Caribbean Region.

———. 2002. *Bolivia: Poverty Diagnostic 2000.* Report No. 20530–80, June 28. Washington, D.C.: World Bank, Poverty Reduction and Economic Management, Latin America and the Caribbean Region.

———. 2013. "Bolivia at a Glance." Accessed October 27, 2013. http://devdata.world-bank.org/aag/bol_aag.pdf.

———. 2007. "World Bank and Civil Society." http://web.worldbank.org/WBSITE/
EXTERNAL/TOPICS/CSO/0,,contentMDK:20101499~menuPK:244752~page
PK:220503~piPK:220476~theSitePK:228717,00. html.

Yashar, Deborah J. 2005. *Contesting Citizenship in Latin America: The Rise of Indigenous Movements and the Postliberal Challenge*. Cambridge: Cambridge University Press.

Young, Tom. 1993. "Elections and Electoral Politics in Africa." *Africa* 63 (3): 299–312.

Zuazo, Moira, ed. 2009. *¿Cómo nació el MAS? La ruralización de la política en Bolivia: Entrevistas a 85 parlamentarios del partido*. La Paz, Bolivia: FES-ILDIS.

*Acknowledgments*

On the long road that has led to this book, I have been lucky to have wonderful guides and traveling companions. My first thanks go to Brunilda Sánchez, Cristóbal Díaz, and Armando, Efraín, Emiliano, Felicidad, Herminia, and Ladislao Díaz Sánchez, as well as Luís Alberto Díaz Hinojosa. I am also greatly indebted to Sonia Hidalgo, Víctor Hugo Sánchez, and Rosa Sánchez for research assistance. Nélida Sánchez, Norah Hidalgo, Feliza Sánchez, Norah Mérida Balderrama, Antonio García, Marga Mair, Deysi Ramírez, Blanca Vargas, and Orlando Orellana, among many others in Sacaba, offered their warm friendship and important insights.

I extend my deepest appreciation to Michael Herzfeld, Kay Warren, Ajantha Subramanian, Kimberly Theidon, Lesley Gill, and Beth Conklin for their generous support and encouragement. Their synthesis of activism and impeccable scholarship has been an inspiration for me. I am also extremely grateful to Gary Urton, Smita Lahiri, Rosemary Coombe, Pauline Peters, Miguel Díaz Barriga, Ken Sharpe, and Aurora Camacho de Schmidt.

I would like to express my thanks to the institutions that have provided me with financial support for this research. The bulk of the writing and research were funded by a Wenner-Gren Hunt Postdoctoral Fellowship and a Fulbright-Hays Research Award. I received generous preliminary research support from the Fulbright IIE, the Harvard University Weatherhead Center for International Affairs Program in Justice, Welfare and Economics, and the David Rockefeller Center for Latin American Studies. A Foreign Language and Area Studies summer grant through Cornell University provided support for Quechua language study. The Harvard University Graduate School of Arts and Sciences, Vanderbilt University, and the College of New Jersey provided generous support for research and writing.

Thanks are due, as well, to the members of the Harvard Latin America Working Group and the Harvard Political Ecology Working Group. I am also grateful to the students of the Harvard Junior Tutorial in Politics and the State in Latin America, and students at Vanderbilt University and the College of New Jersey for their editorial suggestions. In particular, Jack Meyers at the College of New Jersey provided incisive and thoughtful comments at a crucial juncture.

Tom Kruse and Pamela Calla provided a superb introduction to Bolivia, as did Susan Paulson. In Cochabamba, I was aided immensely by the institutional support and kindness of the directors and staff of the Centro de Estudios de la Realidad Económica y Social (CERES), including Pablo Cuba, Rosario León, and Blanca León. Susan Southerwood, Abraham Aruquipa, Deysi Vargas Salvatierra, Heidi Baer-Postigo, Theodoro Claros, Steve Vanek, and Leia Raphaelidis were extremely hospitable and encouraging. Many thanks to Bret Gustafson, Andrew Canessa, Isabel Scarborough, Carrie Furman, Christine Hippert, Amber Wutich, Maria Tapias, Krista van Vleet, Rob Albro, Daniel Goldstein, David Guss, Andy Orta, Nancy Postero, and Jill Wightman for their generosity in welcoming me to the community of *bolivianistas*. Esperanza Angelo and Micaela Calvetti gave me a home away from home, as did Nila Pinto, Eddy Mancilla, and their children.

Many thanks to Analucy Choquechambi, Fernando Rea Campos, Deysi Vargas, and Gilka Gordillo Bazán for providing crucial help with transcription. Luís Morató Peña, Daniel Cotari, and Viviana Flores were wonderful Quechua teachers and perceptive analysts of Bolivian social and political life. The directors and staff of the Centro de Estudio y Trabajo de la Mujer (CETM) and of Yachay Chhalaku very generously allowed me to accompany them on their work in Sacaba. Andrés Uzeda at the Universidad Mayor de San Simon was exceedingly hospitable. I am especially indebted to Rosario Mérida Balderrama and Esperanza Angelo for taking such wonderful care of my son.

I am very grateful to my editors. At the University of Pennsylvania Press, Peter Agree has been an editor sent from heaven: patient, kind, supportive, and a sharp reader. Alma Gottlieb, Noreen O'Connor, Sara Lickey, and Claudia Castañeda offered skillful editing. I also benefitted enormously from the perceptive comments of Bret Gustafson and an anonymous reviewer.

I extend my gratitude to Rusaslina Idrus, Lilith Mahmud, Lindsay Smith, Maria Stalford, and Anne Pollock for their companionship on this project from start to finish. Words fail me in describing my debt to them for their optimism, empathy, and lavish meals. Amanda Vogel, Tara Schubert, Kate Atkins, Catherine Chu, Jesse Shore, and Rhondee Benjamin-Johnson offered their friendship and encouragement. The love and confidence of Carol Shakow, Mel Leiman, and Dianne and Jack McGreevey have sustained me in this project, while Aaron Shakow and Rob McGreevey have been essential fellow travelers, patient editors, and hand-holders. Theo Don McGreevey was a delightful companion during fieldwork and Jacob Owen McGreevey arrived as a delightful companion during the very last stages of writing. My final thanks go to my father, Don Shakow, who ended every conversation by remarking, ever so wisely, that people are a bundle of contradictions.